MOOD

MOOD

The Key to Understanding
Ourselves and Others

Patrick M. Burke

 Prometheus Books

59 John Glenn Drive
Amherst, New York 14228–2119

Published 2014 by Prometheus Books

Cover design by Nicole Sommer-Lecht

Inquiries should be addressed to
Prometheus Books
59 John Glenn Drive
Amherst, New York 14228-2119
VOICE: 716-691-0133
FAX: 716-691-0137
WWW.PROMETHEUSBOOKS.COM

18 17 16 15 14   5 4 3 2 1

Library of Congress Cataloging-in-Publication Data

Burke, Patrick M., 1946-
    Mood : the key to understanding ourselves and others / by Patrick M. Burke.
        pages cm
    Includes bibliographical references and index.
    ISBN 978-1-61614-833-1 (pbk.)
    ISBN 978-1-61614-834-8 (ebook)
    1. Affective disorders. 2. Affective disorders—Treatment. 3. Emotions—Psychological aspects. 4. Resilience (Personality trait) I. Title.

RC537.B8684 2013
616.85'27—dc23

2013024868

Printed in the United States of America

This book is dedicated to my late wife, Velma Dobson, PhD,
the single greatest and enduring influence in my life,
for showing us how to live a life of integrity
and in the end how to die with grace and dignity;
and to our children, Meg and Andrew,
and to the newest additions to our family, Tiffany Gromlich and little Oliver.
I am forever grateful for their willingness to help; their expertise;
and their unquestioning love, support, and encouragement.

CONTENTS

ACKNOWLEDGMENTS

This book is the fulfillment of a promise made to my wife, Velma Dobson, before she passed away from complications of Amyotrophic Lateral Sclerosis (ALS, or Lou Gehrig's disease) in April 2010. I had started out to write a book about psychiatric disorders in youth for the nonexpert, but a radically different book emerged as we grappled with her disease, and I began to better understand the role mood plays in our lives and how the forces that act on mood could serve as a unifying theme for the book and help us surmount the challenges of ALS.

The original impetus for a book grew out of the frustration I experienced as a child psychiatrist as changes in healthcare delivery increasingly limited my time with children and families to brief assessments and medication management with little room for any but the most formulaic explanations and answers to questions. There was in addition an underlying dissatisfaction with the standard approach of discrete disorders with overlapping risk factors and treatments that put the disorder and not the person at the center.

The solution came when, stimulated by a lectures series by Richard Solomon,[1] I realized that Martin Heidegger's ideas on mood could provide the needed theme. The approach and ideas for this book were initially developed and tried out at La Frontera, Inc., in Tucson, Arizona, and I am especially thankful to the staff and patients of the center. When my wife became homebound, I stayed home to help. We worked in parallel—she continuing to work with her research colleagues in an incredible display of courage and perseverance, while I researched background material and worked on a book proposal. The book was written after she died, informed by a now-deeper understanding of the role of mood and the connections between mood, relationships, commitment, and action.

Many people have helped me along the way to writing this book. I most gratefully acknowledge two individuals who played seminal roles in my career. The late Sean Lavelle, MD, a professor in my medical school in Galway, Ireland, saw something in a bored medical student who told him he really wanted to study developmental psychology. He started me on a path that led to Lewis P. Lipsitt, PhD, who graciously took me on and persevered with me as his graduate student at Brown University. This was one of the great adventures of my life, an exciting time when I was exposed to investigators and graduate students, among them my future wife, full of ideas and doing cutting-edge research.

My psychiatric education followed at the University of Washington under the tutelage especially of David Raskin, MD, and David Rowlette, MD, and where Charles Nagel, MD, advised me that the key to difficult psychiatric problems was to "find the affect," an adage that has been with me since. And where Eric Trupin, PhD, and Robert Reichler, MD, taught me the value and necessity of an empirical and multidisciplinary approach to child psychiatry.

Throughout the process of writing this book many friends and colleagues listened patiently to my musings, helping me think out ideas, providing insights, confirming the value of my approach, and in many cases providing helpful comments on various drafts of proposals and chapters. I particularly want to thank Anne Libecap; Linda Karl, MD; Helen Herziger; Clara Billotte; Kelly Vogiatis; Caroline Duffield; and Richard Hinton, PhD. I am also grateful to the child psychiatry fellows (especially Adolfo Martinez, MD, and Anna Shier, DO), residents, and students in the Child and Adolescent Psychiatry program at the University of Arizona for their patience with my lectures and supervision, insightful comments, and encouragement.

Victoria Blake helped with my initial efforts at writing a proposal and gave me spot-on advice on getting an agent. I am forever indebted to my agent Nancy Rosenfeld, AAA Books Unlimited, for her unfailing support, encouragement, persistence, and editorial advice. My editors Steven L. Mitchell and Julia DeGraf and the staff at Prometheus Books have been unfailingly supportive, professional, and expert in shaping the book. Pat Broyles in her inimitable calm and proficient way helped in formatting and typing notes, as well as being an important link to my wife for whom she was an administrative assistant for many years. Finally, thanks to Dave Cantrell for creating the figures that appear in chapters 4 and 6.

CHAPTER 1

OVERVIEW

We are told that nothing in the world is certain except death and taxes. But we can add a third certainty. We are always in a mood. What is more, we are constantly faced with references to mood: popular tunes of happiness or sadness; pundits opining that the economic mood of the country will determine the outcome of an election or that the mood in the locker room will determine which team wins the game; advertisements telling us a product will change our mood and our lives. Mood is everywhere and somehow is linked to what we find important and meaningful. Emerson described life as a train of moods strung like beads, which, as we pass through them, prescribe what we see.[1] For the poet W. B. Yeats, literature is wrought about a mood or a community of moods.[2]

But our moods change, and we seem to have little control over when and how the change occurs. It seems we can neither command nor will our mood to change. Rather, our mood changes, and it is only after the change that we realize we are in a different mood. Most of the time, we pay little attention to changes in our mood or how the changes occur. But the change can be disturbing. We find we are sad, anxious, uneasy, or feel threatened. If the new mood interferes with our ability to function, the change may amount to a mood disorder. For many, these disorders can be destructive to their lives and can warrant professional attention. How does this happen?

We have good reason to suspect that difficulties with mood originate in developmental events. Changeable moods are accepted as part of childhood and adolescence. Take, for example, the irritable colicky infant, the temper-prone toddler and preschooler, or the moody adolescent. There is abundant evidence that most psychiatric disorders among adults that involve significant changes in mood first become evident in youth. At a clinical level, the annual rate of depression in adolescents is estimated to be 5–9 percent, and in prepubertal children the rate is estimated to be 1–2.5 percent.[3] Between 2–5 percent of youth are diagnosed with an anxiety disorder.[4]

How do these disorders come about? And what can be done about them? Perhaps the most common view is that dysfunction in brain chemicals is the underlying issue. Stress is implicated, whether due to conflicts or loss in relationships, or other life events. Genetic influences are also thought to play a role, and much research is geared toward understanding how genes and environments interact to produce disorders. Similarly, research in personality development shows the importance of individual temperament. Advances in the neurosciences have implicated brain circuits and other bodily systems, and these are also subject to genetic and environmental influence. Moreover, there has been massive growth in pharmacological treatments, as well as in psychosocial treatments each with its own school of thought and practitioners. Complicating matters further, diagnosis and treatment, especially in youth, have become controversial issues. Advances in all these areas have been rapid and have originated from a range of disciplines. As a result, the available information is widely distributed in literature and is so complex that, unless you have some expertise in the field, the general reader is likely to have difficulty integrating the findings.

Beyond questions of causation and techniques to remedy problem behavior, how do mood and the disorders involving mood fit with how we see ourselves as agents in the world? Are we passive and simply subject to our genes and our environments? What role do we play or can we play? Can mood be linked to responsibility? Is there a way to address these questions and unify the above themes to guide the nonexpert?

Despite the breadth and depth of current studies, surprisingly little attention has been paid to the subject of mood itself and mood disorder. Most often, the focus is on emotion and mood is simply subsumed, used interchangeably with emotion, or is subordinated to cognitive activities. This book takes a unique approach by treating mood as a central controlling factor that from childhood becomes the basis upon which we choose and act, and sets the stage for how we are throughout life. The basic idea is that mood connects the person and the world, and this connection is built and shaped over the course of development. How might this work? If we think of mood as a phase of the activity of neural circuits and bodily systems that continually process information about the world, then the feelings of mood and the associated bodily systems provide the mechanism for the connection. They enable the assessment of possibilities and become the basis for action.

Development comes into the picture because genetic and environmental influences starting with the fetus create the underlying systems. The stress response system, which is active when destabilizing events occur, is especially relevant because it has profound influence on developing neural circuits. How this system functions influences the degree to which someone is vulnerable or resilient when something challenging happens. Disorders involving changes in mood emerge as breakdowns in the connections occur, and resilience comes from the connections being able to surmount challenge.

The book is organized as one possible roadmap that ties together the many biological and social factors that not only shape development and functioning but also underlie the emergence of disorders and are key to prevention and treatment. There are four key themes set around two core notions, the importance of the individual and the importance of developmental processes.

The central theme is that mood reflects the way we are tuned into the world, reveals our possible options in a particular situation, and thereby becomes the basis of action. The basic idea derives from Martin Heidegger, primarily his major work *Being and Time*.[5] Although Heidegger did not write about children, we have adopted some of his central insights and placed them within a developmental context. The first theme is nested in a second theme—we are self-constituting. If we consider the self as a way of being, then who we are as agents is realized only by what we do and by what we make of ourselves as we live an active life.[6] Relationships with others are at the core of these processes. Complex interactions between the child, other people, and the world underlie the child's struggles with becoming autonomous and responsible for himself. Mood, by revealing our possibilities, plays a fundamental role in development because development is the step-by-step process of becoming self-constituting. Interactions with others and the world have mood at their core, and they reciprocally are at the core of how mood develops and can be changed.

To illustrate this approach, imagine a child as a stringed musical instrument with its combinations of strings and sounds. The tuning—mood—of the instrument at any given moment is how the child tunes into the world. But the child is a constantly resonating living organism. Therefore, a mood is always present and since a child has many strings and combinations of strings, many moods are waiting to emerge. From the earliest beginning, genetic and environmental influences form the strings, and throughout life continue to influence the strings. The tuning underlies how events appear to a child, rather than being a reaction to an event or how the child thinks about things. When something happens, the child's strings reverberate and the resulting mood depends on the tuning of the individual string. The child's tuning (mood) alerts him to the possibilities present, paving the way for him to choose and act.

Chapter 2 examines mood and what mood does and attempts to differentiate mood from emotion. Heidegger argues that we are not detached beings, observing and making decisions based on what we see and then acting accordingly. Instead, we always already find ourselves in situations that matter to us and that typically involve others around us.[7] Things matter to us because each of us is uniquely disposed or attuned to the world. Our attunement reveals the world to us, and our attunement is mood. He elaborates that what and how we experience is a function of our involvements with things, and especially our involvement with others. Relationships and situations present possibilities, and our tuning differentially disposes us to the possibilities presented. As we interact with the world, our senses provide information. Moods (how you are tuned to the world) also provide information and reveal the situation. They tell us what matters and has significance.[8]

Think of yourself as a very nervous and fearful person, who is walking alone down a darkened street. Certain features, like doorways and shadows, stand out. Your mood (fearfulness) alerts you to possible danger and provides the conditions for you to react with fear (an emotion) should something happen. Mood is like a special sense that not only tells you about your world (the world is frightening, this situation is positive) but also informs you about yourself—you are a happy person, or a fearful person, or you are nervous and not doing well.

But we are not in full control of our situations. The range of possibilities presented to us is limited, and we vary in skill and understanding on how to proceed. This brings us to Heidegger's ideas about fundamental moods and his concept of authenticity,[9] or what is unique and particular to each individual.[10] For the most part, we live life to suit or to meet the expectations of others by following our social and cultural roles and avoid any underlying anxiety about our being. But when critical events occur that bring us face to face with our finite being, the submerged anxiety reveals the fragility of the way we live, and we're faced with making choices. To become authentic we need to act on this realization, becoming responsible for ourselves and choosing our own way to live.[11]

How might tuning develop? Mood is present from the beginning, well before speech and language develop. Parents describe their newborns as "happy," "content," and "fussy" or as "hard or easy to console." They often say their child "was born" that way. Chapter 3 traces the development of key moods and related emotions (sadness, guilt, anger, fear), emphasizing the role interpersonal relationships play. The chapter introduces temperament, a key construct that is partly defined in terms of characteristic moods and forms the building blocks of personality. Later chapters discuss the relation of temperament and personality to the emergence of anxiety, depression, and disruptive antisocial behavior.

The third theme is that mood and tuning arise through the activity of certain neural networks[12] and body systems.[13] The underlying concept is that the body is a framework through which we perceive the world, and the possibilities offered by the world.[14] *Imagine a six-month-old infant lying on the floor and playing with small blocks. The infant grasps a block, stares intently at it, puts in her mouth, exchanges it in a fumbling way for another, drops one, and searches until she picks up another block, which again goes in the mouth while her small hand manipulates it. This infant is experiencing the world of blocks through her bodily senses—touch, sight, and taste. She is forming some rudimentary sense of the possibilities of the blocks, and in so doing of her world.*

Chapter 4 discusses how the nervous system analyzes and evaluates information about the world, enabling and coordinating our reactions and responses by organizing the activity of neural networks involved in mood and emotion.[15] How these networks are made, and how they function, sets the tuning of each child. We can think of the circuits as the strings of the instrument. Assuming the brain's networks function normally, the child will be appropriately happy; sad; or in an average, everyday mood. But if the tuning of certain string(s) is off, then the world may appear scary or highly exciting, and moods may be intense, subdued, or labile as those strings are sounded.

The way a child is tuned emerges over the course of development as genetic (chapter 5) and environmental influences (chapters 5 and 6) combine to form the circuits (the strings of the instrument) and set how they function in daily life and under conditions of stress. Individual differences in behavior reflect functional differentiation within the circuits.[16] The stress response (chapter 6) is a complex array of neurohormonal processes that is activated when a potentially destabilizing event occurs.[17] A variety of genetic and environmental influences affect the stress response, and interactions and relationships with others are crucial influences that are essential for its normal development. How this system responds plays a large part in the development of the personal characteristics associated with resilience and vulnerability.

Not all children who experience stressful events (e.g., parental separation and/or change in schools) become depressed or anxious, nor do all children in a family with familial or genetic risk factors (a depressed or alcoholic parent) develop a disorder. There is a wide range of responses to the environment. Some children (and adults) respond positively and effectively, but others respond in negative and/or ineffective ways. Someone who responds well in one type of situation may not do as well in another. Why do some but not all children at risk develop a disorder? How can we relate how a child is tuned over the course of development to factors such as genes, stress, and the environment involved in mood disorders? Individual differences are key to understanding what happens.[18] Chapter 6 introduces some current models that are helpful in explaining how multiple influences (genetics, early experience, temperament and other characteristics of the child, relationships with others) may interact to leave some individuals vulnerable and others resilient.[19] The models can also be the basis of prevention and treatment efforts suggesting both targets and strategies for intervention.

The fourth theme is that disorders emerge out of the interaction of events and the functional status of neural circuits and systems. When vulnerable children are faced with stressful events, significant alterations may occur in mood, behavior, and biological functions. Particular patterns of dysfunction underlie the principal disorders in youth that are characterized by mood disturbances: anxiety, depression, bipolar disorder, and antisocial/oppositional disorders. Such features tend to cluster, and the clusters are the basis of the diagnostic categories. The diagnostic system is currently in transition. Chapter 7 sketches some key background issues to the diagnostic process and outlines key changes in the new manual.

Chapters 8–10 consider the main disorders that involve mood and mood changes. Although the focus is on youth, the relevance to adults is indicated throughout. In each case, the mood and emotion component is explored along with neural circuitry and the stress response to illustrate from a developmental perspective how the disorders come about and manifest and why they often occur together. It will be seen that in each case, the disorders have typical mood and emotion profiles, physiological changes, and action patterns. They also show substantial overlap; the stress response system has a role in each; and relationships play central roles both by influencing the development of mood and the circuits underlying mood, and by the role they play in precipitating disorders. In each case current research on neural circuits and the stress response are explored, and shows common patterns of activity in circuits related to mood and emotion. Anxiety (chapter 8) is characterized by worry and fear and is concerned with present or future threats of harm. Anxiety disorders reflect dysfunction in circuits underlying fear, manifest the physiological changes reflecting flight or fight, and action is typically avoidant. Sadness and negative thinking characterize depression. Depressive disorders (chapter 9) are concerned with loss, reflect dysfunction in neural circuits involved in mood, manifest physiological changes reflecting altered stress responses, and diminished activity. Bipolar disorder (chapter 10) involves mania and depression. Elated or irritable mood and grandiose thinking characterize mania. It can be viewed as a dysfunction of neural systems underlying reward. The stress system plays a role, and activity levels are increased. This disorder is increasingly and controversially diagnosed in children and adolescents. The background to the controversy is explored, and proposed changes are discussed.

In terms of mood, antisocial and disruptive behavior presents some interesting and challenging issues. Typically, disruptive and antisocial behavior is viewed as not being related to mood but as defiance of authority, rule breaking, disregard of the rights of others, and with aggressive behavior as a characteristic action. However, it is increasingly clear that mood plays a very importance role in antisocial behavior. Chapter 11 addresses the important roles irritability and indifferent mood play, as well as the role of a diminished as opposed to an exaggerated stress response. In contrast to other disorders, it will be seen that a key subset of antisocial youth and adults show a different pattern of dysfunction in mood-related circuits from the other mood-related disorders.

Prevention and treatment approaches are discussed in chapter 12. We evaluate key elements of the most prominent current procedures, examining their stance in light of the themes of the book. What is their approach to mood? How do they deal with relationships with others? What are the effective ingredients? To what extent do they guide the child and family in discovering what matters and in choosing among available options in ways that foster autonomy and learning to take responsibility for one's life?

In addition to psychotherapeutic techniques, a variety of medications are in use (chapter 13), and they are increasingly combined with psychosocial treatments. Medication therapy is discussed in relation to its affect on tuning of the neural circuits and related systems.

Chapter 14 considers medical illness, the diagnosis of which can present significant challenges to affected youth and families. Medical illness can also serve as a model situation to illustrate the application of ideas expressed in this book. Many illnesses present significant burdens for both child and family, as well as the loss of options and the need to reorganize and refocus. Circuits involved in mood regulate the stress response, and these circuits are also involved in the immune response and inflammation. While most children and families surmount the challenges, many illnesses are associated with increased rates of anxiety, depression, and other disruptive behavior.

CHAPTER 2

WHAT DOES MOOD DO?

The central theme of this book is that mood is a central controlling factor that reflects the way we're tuned in the world and how it becomes the basis of choice and action by revealing our possible options in a particular situation. Because of this, mood plays a fundamental role throughout development and in what we become as persons. This chapter explores some of the ideas behind these assertions. The basic ideas derive from Heidegger, primarily his book *Being and Time*,[1] but his approach to mood is also seen in a second work in which he provides a lengthy discussion of boredom.[2] Because Heidegger is notoriously difficult, we also draw on various commentators who have helped clarify his ideas. Matthew Ratcliffe, in particular, critiques and further elaborates on Heidegger's ideas about mood, and so a number of Ratcliffe's ideas are incorporated.[3] To develop the themes, we must first explore issues in terminology. The point is to draw broad distinctions between *mood* and *emotion*, as it will become clear that a settled definition of either term is not available. A key point will be that mood can be thought of as the basis for emotion.

We freely use the terms *mood*, *feeling*, and *emotion* in everyday conversation and generally seem to communicate what we mean when we use them. But once we start examining these words, we run into difficulty, and distinguishing them turns out to be a challenge. The first difficulty is that each one covers a wide range of experience. Consider the following: *She said she had been sad for weeks; He had the feeling something was wrong; I feel I have lost my way; He hates school; You could tell by her behavior how angry she was; I was in such a bad mood; I'm so scared. My heart is pounding, my hands are sweaty; She said she felt numb; He felt tired; He felt a sharp pain; Her mood was infectious; The mood of the crowd made him feel uneasy; The mood of the voters will determine who wins the election.* Which of these statements represent a mood? Most readers will readily identify some as moods. But some will be identified as feelings; others as emotions; some may be difficult to place, and some may fit all three definitions.

Affect is another term widely used, especially in psychiatry. The mental status examination distinguishes between mood and affect. Moreover, older versions of the *Diagnostic and Statistical Manual (DSM)* classified mood disorders as affective disorders. The *DSM-IV-TR*[4] defines mood as an emotional climate: a pervasive and sustained emotion that colors the perception of the world. Affect, on the other hand, is described as the more fluctuating changes in emotional weather. Neither the glossary nor the index has an entry for *emotion*.

So what is mood, and how does mood differentiate from feeling or emotion? We first address feeling and then discuss differences between mood and emotion. All experiences involve sensation, like what is included in the phrase "I feel."[5] There are also multiple uses of the word *feelings*, ranging from the feeling of an itch to feeling sad.[6] We also sense what it is like to experience something. If we pick up an object, we feel that object and the movements we make. According to Laura Sizer, feeling is a phenomenally conscious sensation, a state that one occupies as opposed to an action one performs. This definition not only captures the sensation of an itch or of feeling cold; it also captures "the way things are with you now," the importance of which you will see when we discuss mood.[7] We now see a wide range of experiences that constitute feelings, some of which are moods and others emotions. How can they be distinguished?

WHAT IS MOOD?

According to *Merriam-Webster's Collegiate Dictionary*, mood is a "conscious state of mind or predominant emotion"; a "receptive state of mind predisposing to action"; or a "distinctive atmosphere or context."[8] The *Oxford Companion to Philosophy* says that moods are "states of mind of an emotional cast which are temporary, yet which color a person's responses and reactions quite generally," and whose "focus is on a pattern of behavior manifesting a current state of mind, and not on the intended consequences of the behavior."[9] These definitions indicate that moods are forms of feelings, but while they highlight certain characteristics of mood, the definitions do not fully distinguish mood from emotion.

People are always surprised when it is pointed out that we are always in a mood. But we cannot be in an alert state without being in a mood of some kind. Mood is a property of consciousness that seems to set the tone or flavor of conscious states.[10] You could even argue that moods are present during sleep. We commonly have anxiety-laden dreams and wake up feeling as if we didn't sleep well. Could it be that the child who wakes up grumpy in the morning was in an irritable mood during sleep, and the grumpiness is, in part, a continuation of the mood? Or do we always wake up in a neutral or even a mood-less state, if only for a fraction of a second before a mood then appears?

People are frequently surprised to learn that moods arise outside of awareness. But if you pause to think about it, a mood is already present by the time we become aware of any mood change. We don't have full control over the mood we're in, and we can't easily change our mood. We may not be able to change our mood without taking some action.

Interestingly, while we say we have moods or feelings, we typically say we are in a mood, but we do not say we "mood." Mood, it seems, is something we are in and not something we do. Mood is not an action. Moods monopolize and characterize the total "set" of a person while he or she is in a mood.[11] Emerson said that "life is a train of moods like a string of beads" that "paint the world their own hue," adding that each mood "shows only what lies in its focus."[12] A sad child or person tends to experience everything in a negative light. There is evidence to support this, as mood has broad effects on attention and memory.[13] For example, negative moods narrow attention and focus, while positive moods have the opposite effect.

An interesting characteristic of mood is that a mood may be public and contagious. For example, a room full of people (or a crowd) may exhibit a particular kind of mood. *Members of a large crowd celebrating a team victory may all be in a happy mood; someone who happened by could note the mood of the room and could easily get caught up in that mood.*

Moods can be short-lived or long-lasting. But particular moods or a tendency toward particular moods can be characteristic of an individual. Here mood is a component of temperament (chapters 3 and 4).

If a mood is always present and we can't change it on demand, what are moods about? Moods are not about some particular thing but rather are unintentional (*intentionality* is a philosophical term referring to how "one's subjective state relates one to the world"[14]). One view is that moods relate to everything and capture the whole world as their focus.[15] Ratcliffe suggests that feelings are about how we relate to the world and to the sense that we belong to the world, and moods are in this category.[16] We feel attached to somebody or to some place; we feel bored, we feel alive, we feel connected, we feel lost, and so on. *John always feels uneasy; John was sad and did not know why; John awoke feeling happy.*

WHAT IS EMOTION?

The historical interest in emotion goes back to the ancient Greeks.[17] But despite intense interest from philosophers, psychologists, and neuroscientists, we still have no single accepted definition of emotion.[18] While there is agreement on what counts as emotion (hate, fear, jealousy, or grief), there is less agreement on what an emotion is. *Merriam-Webster's Collegiate Dictionary* defines *emotion* as "the affective aspect of consciousness"; a "state of feeling"; a "conscious mental reaction subjectively experienced as strong feeling"; and "usually directed toward a specific object."[19] In this instance, emotion—like mood—is described as a feeling, but thinking about something and forming judgments are added components. An example from the developmental psychology literature suggests that emotion is "the process of registering the significance of a physical or mental event as the individual construes significance."[20] *Eight-grader John becomes angry and rushes at Tom because of comments Tom made about John's mother.*

Note that, in contrast to mood, we don't say that we are in an emotion, but we do say we emote. Emotions do not just happen but rather tend to be reactions to something. *John was angry because he was given extra homework.* An emotion seems to be something we do,[21] and an emotion has physiological components that reflect the bodily systems involved in processing information and in preparing to or responding to an event. One prominent expert defines emotion as a distinct, integrated, physiological response system, and lists four components: (1) a prototypical form of expression (e.g., facial expression), (2) consistent autonomic changes (e.g., changes in heart rate), (3) a distinct subjective state of feeling, and (4) a characteristic form of adaptive behavior.[22] *When John heard the comments about his mother, he felt his breathing change, his teeth clenched, and his heart raced as he rushed at Tom.*

Emotions typically do not last long, and most subside as soon as the triggering or provoking issue is resolved. *John's anger evaporated when his teacher relented and gave less homework.* Moreover, emotions do not seem to color the entire situation the person is in. *John may say he hates his teacher, but this does not extend to others or to other situations.* Being public is also not readily seen as a property of emotion. *John's friend Mary might witness John's anger over a homework assignment, but Mary would not easily become angry unless John convinces her that the homework is unfair and should be protested.*

Ratcliffe identified feelings about how we are in or attached to the world as existential feelings, and among these are feelings commonly identified as moods.[23] In contrast, he identifies feelings that are directed toward things in the world as emotions: they relate to something specific. *John is angry with Tim; John ran from the room in fear when he saw the dog.* However, we will use *mood(s)* since that is the term referred to in both general and clinical use, and doing so will avoid confusion when discussing clinical disorders.

HEIDEGGER AND MOOD

Heidegger suggested that we always already find ourselves in situations where we are always engaged in practical concerns or projects that matter to us and that offer certain, but not all, possibilities as we plan ahead and look to the future.[24] Crucially, we never view the world as if we were outside looking in or as if we are distant from things in the world where we have a vantage point to understand the world, but instead we experience ourselves as always already situated in our world.[25] Our world is structured in a meaningful way in which we act and live our lives.[26] We are always in a situation where things matter to us.

Where does mood come in? According to Heidegger, we're always disposed in some way toward the world.[27] This disposition or attitude toward things is our mood: the feeling of how we are in the world. He used the German word *Stimmung*, which refers both to mood and to the tuning of an instrument. As a result, the term *attunement* is often used to convey the way we are disposed toward things. According to Blattner, attunement is like a melody that sets the tone, and "we are tuned into the way things matter," and "our tuning, or our temper, is our mood."[28] We adopt this notion of mood as tuning in framing the central theme of the book.

Additionally, Heidegger views the world as arranged in particular ways, with attunements that our attunement can mesh with or not. In other words, not only are we tuned into the world; we are also tuned by the world.[29] This speaks to the way we are connected to the world—not as observers but as part of a whole. Furthermore, in Heidegger's view, moods are not private experiences. They are neither inside us nor outside us but rather act like an atmosphere in which we are immersed.[30] This speaks to the way moods may be public.

In a broader sense, mood can be akin to the sensibility of an age, the culture of a company, the temper of the times, and the mood of an individual at a particular time.[31] For example, cultures have long-standing sensibilities so that people living within a particular society are conditioned to the moods of their culture. We also have social moods, and people of the same culture can adopt the moods of each other. No one is an island or lives in a vacuum.

Heidegger tried to capture what he meant by coining the word *Befindlichkeit*, meaning "how do you find yourself?" or "how is it going with you?"[32] The concept of *Befindlichkeit* is related to our "understanding" or how skillful we are in knowing how to act in a particular situation. We always possess some level of understanding, i.e., some ability or skill to deal with circumstance as we encounter them. We understand our world and ourselves through our practical engagements and the feeling-states that are fundamentally involved with these activities. As Heidegger puts it, every mood has its understanding and every understanding has its mood.[33] The concept of *Befindlichkeit* puts the person, body, and world together.[34] When we look at things this way, the significance of an event comes from the relation of the event to the person and his or her current concerns, and not from the intrinsic properties of the event. Certain feeling-states allow a person to view surrounding things as disclosing some, but not all, possibilities, putting the focus on the actions available to the person at any given time.[35]

From a developmental perspective, there is never a moment when a child is not involved in a situation—be it with family, or friends, or the classroom, or sports activities. At every step, the child possesses a degree of familiarity with, and a growing understanding of, his situations and tasks, as well as of his available options. Even a newborn infant is born into a situation and a world of possibilities. The newborn is born with her own attributes, her own tuning, her own unique degree of preparedness, into a particular family and culture with all the attendant worries, expectations, and hopes. The newborn also is faced with certain tasks, beginning with finding the nipple to nurse and advancing to ever more complex challenges that will be mastered to varying degrees, and at each level of mastery the baby will exhibit her mood.

One consequence of always being "tuned in" is that we experience the world in different ways at different times. What we find significant in a situation is a function of our mood, and our mood affects how we view the experience. For example, a sad or happy or anxious mood will lead us to experience a situation differently at any given time. *As you drive to work along the same streets, the sounds and sights you experience seem different depending on your mood. For a child on the way to school who usually seems carefree and bright, the same streets may appear dull and empty if her mood is sad instead of happy and cheerful.* Our mood also gives life its sense of meaning, informing us about how things matter and how we're doing.[36]

Moods set up the world in which we experience feelings directed toward things or situations—in other words, emotions.[37] The following vignette captures what is intended, and illustrates a way of looking at the relation of mood and emotion. *John, a high school senior, has applied to college. The day for acceptance letters is approaching. He goes to the mailbox every day. He is not a disinterested objective observer of the contents of the mailbox. He is already in a situation. There have been years of preparation, hard work, and his and his family's expectations. He has been anxious for weeks; he approaches the mailbox with a feeling of anxiety and trepidation; he opens the box, and one letter seems to jump out at him. He recognizes the letterhead of his first-choice college. Everything else in the mailbox seems to recede—he does not notice anything about the other contents of the mailbox.*

John's mood has attuned him such that specific events or possible outcomes can and will affect him. Several possibilities are present in John's situation. The letter may say yes, it may say no, or it could say maybe. A "yes" answer would leave him joyous and contemplating a set of new and exciting possibilities, whereas a "no" would leave him disappointed and upset and with a diminished set of possibilities.

There are further implications of this approach to mood: We *feel* the significance of things and situations.[38] Mood provides a background sense of belonging to a world of meaning without which we cannot experience feelings about things, such as emotions.

Imagine a group of people who walk through a mountainous area during the early morning hours. Signs were posted one morning warning of mountain lion activity. One walker has heard of a confrontation between a hiker and a lion in the area. The behavior of the group begins to change: their hearts beat a little faster, their posture and pace change. One, who tended to be anxious and fearful, decides not to walk at that hour. Others carry sticks, and the group stays close together. The mood is fearful; everyone is watchful and alert to shadows and strange sounds. They are ready to respond with fear should anything even remotely resembling a lion appear.

We noted above that the significance of an event does not lie exclusively in its intrinsic properties but in the relation to the individual and the individual's current concern. An important implication of this notion suggests that mood is prior to cognition.[39] As events unfold, our mood (tuning) has already disclosed what is important to us and what possibilities are available before our cognitive processes take over. The implications of this idea for cognitive theories of depression and cognitive behavioral therapy will be discussed in chapter 12.

MOOD, POSSIBILITIES, AND CHOICE

According to Heidegger, we are future oriented. We plan ahead, and in so doing we are moving into our possibilities. But our possibilities are always limited since we're not in full control of our situations. We must choose from the possibilities presented. A child may fail, may succeed, may plan activities with friends, or may make plans for high school or college—some of the many choices a child confronts all along the way to maturity.

Anthony, a high school basketball player, may dream of becoming the starting center of the Los Angeles Lakers. But if he does not grow to the requisite height then it's an unlikely possibility, and at some point he will need to select another career.

We have seen that our mood is intimately involved in determining what is significant versus our possibilities. Heidegger distinguishes between moods in which we are attuned to particular circumstances and fundamental moods in which we are attuned to the world as a meaningful whole.[40] Anxiety (angst) is Heidegger's primary example of a fundamental mood. As noted, we are future oriented (we plan ahead). We move into our possibilities, but our possibilities are limited just as our lives are finite, and we continue to move in the direction of death. How is this relevant to children and adolescents? Issues of mortality and the meaning of life often preoccupy adolescents. By nine years of age children express fears of death, and attempted and completed suicide remain serious problems in youth. Many acute and chronic illnesses of childhood carry the risk of death or shortened life span. Large numbers of children are raised in highly disruptive and broken homes, where they may have been abused and/or neglected. Other children are products of group homes or a succession of foster homes. These children are constantly faced with the questions *Who am I? Do I matter to anyone? Do I matter to myself? Do I have a future?* Some may even be unable to conceive of a future, let alone articulate one. The rates of disorders associated with mood remain very high in these populations.

Heidegger further states that the fundamental mood of anxiety can be awakened by the realization of our finitude, and he shows that mood clues us into our true possibilities. Most of us live in a world comprised by our social and cultural society, and within the confines of our culture we feel comfortable in conforming to the expectations placed upon us. But when situations arise that awaken fundamental anxiety, our world and our very identity seem fragile and vulnerable.[41] We begin to recognize that the usual social structures, rules, and roles are no longer sufficient to guide how we live and that the significance of our world has disappeared or "withdrawn."

Heidegger implies that in these situations we no longer are faced with a set of possibilities and are free to determine our own decisions rather than do what is expected of us. In this form of anxiety the world of possibility is experienced as illusory, and we are free—or enabled—to make our own decisions (which comprise the concept of Heidegger's authenticity). To be authentic, we need to be ready and willing to grasp the fragility of our world and to do so with skill and focus.[42] In Guignon's words, we are "self constituting" and have responsibility for how we live our lives—"what we make of ourselves as we live our lives."[43] The authentic self becomes responsible for itself by how it engages with the world, its concern for others, and its responsibility for articulating its world.[44] This means we live inauthentic lives but need to "awaken" our attunements to attain authenticity.[45] The narrative we construct about ourselves may be right or wrong, and our mood (if we know how to pay attention to it) can and will reveal that something is wrong.[46]

The concept of becoming is borrowed from the writings of the German philosopher Friedrich Nietzsche, who advocated "Become who you are."[47] The process of becoming implies that the individual has characteristics and capacities, which in the interplay with life (making choices in situations) continually shape how a person is in the world. What does it mean for children who exist in the unsettled and unhappy world, as described above, to feel obligated to make choices and take responsibility for their lives? Most treatment interventions are directed toward helping children change behavior so they "fit in," as they are expected to behave in the society in which they live. While this may be essential for orderly function in society, interventions can go beyond this and help children from dysfunctional backgrounds to achieve a more self-constituting life. If the child's sense of what is possible can be changed, then mood can be changed, and if a new world of possibilities can be opened up then a more positive and peaceful mood can ensue.

To summarize, we have sketched how moods are equivalent to the feelings we have about the world around us and our sense of belonging to that world. Heidegger argued that, instead of being detached observers and acting on what we see, we find ourselves in situations that matter to us and where we can interact with others. Mood is what makes things matter, and each of us remains tuned to the world in our own unique way. Our tuning is our mood, and our mood makes things matter by revealing and differentially disposing us to the possibilities presented. How things matter becomes the basis of our decisions, but mood is present before thinking and judging come into play. Conversely, emotions are feelings directed at something specific that go beyond mood in their cognitive and physiological components involving judgments and preparations to respond.

CHAPTER 3

MOOD AND DEVELOPMENT

This chapter highlights the development of moods and corresponding emotions that are relevant to the disorders addressed in later chapters. Particular attention is paid to interpersonal interactions, which are profoundly influential in the development of mood/tuning. By tracing the developmental connections between mood and relationships, especially with key caregivers, we lay the foundation for understanding how pathological moods may be related to the disruption or loss of personal relations. Chapters 4–6 will discuss the influence of relationships on the development neural circuits and the stress response. We also discuss unique and crucial developments in adolescence that are linked to increased rates of depression, especially in females.

INFANCY AND MOOD

We begin with infancy. A wealth of information exists to show that newborns and very young infants have sensory experiences. However, little empirical research has been conducted on infants' moods, since considerable ingenuity is required to determine what an infant is experiencing given their lack of language. It is far easier to study an infant's behavior toward specific objects than it is to study mood. Hence, almost all research on feelings in infancy focuses on emotion.

When newborns are given sweet-tasting substances they behave in ways that indicate acceptance.[1] For example, when a newborn is offered a sucrose solution he will suck in a burst-pause pattern. As sweetness is increased, he adjusts this pattern by sucking at a lower rate with longer bursts, more swallowing and higher heart rate. We can infer from this that the newborn can discriminate degrees of sweetness. But do newborns experience pleasure? Conversely, newborns given sour or bitter-tasting substances[2] or who are exposed to obnoxious odors grimace and attempt to reject them as evidenced by facial expression and tongue and head movement.[3] Their actions suggest distaste and displeasure, but do they experience the corresponding feelings?

Moreover, neither sensory nor motor experiences begin at birth because the newborn already has experienced sensory and motor sensations as a fetus.[4] The fetus touches and grasps itself and sucks its thumb. It also swallows amniotic fluid and will continue to drink if the amniotic fluid is experimentally sweetened. Amniotic fluid also takes on the odor of food consumed by the mother. In addition, the fetus responds to sounds. This gives rise to evidence that fetal sensory experiences influence later behavior. Very young infants show a preference for tastes to which they were exposed during gestation or for a story read to them while still in the womb.[5] There is evidence that prenatal language exposure influences postnatal language preference and development.[6]

These studies suggest that fetal sensory experience registers, but does a fetus have feelings and experience moods that go along with sensory familiarity? We may not be able to answer that question, but are moods available at birth? Parents readily say their babies show typical moods from early on, whether peaceful or fussy, or irritable and cranky. If moods are present in the first few days of life, do they switch on at birth? What seems more likely is that the infant is indeed tuned to the world, and the substrate of tuning emerges in fetal life and continues to elaborate with development.

We can illuminate the issues involved by considering the role played by the sense of touch. Ratcliffe argues that touch is central to feelings about our belonging to the world or our relationship with the world. When we touch something, we not only feel *what* we touch but we also recognize the existence of something else. Perceptions of things that exist outside the body comprise a single experience. Ratcliffe makes the case that existential feelings (the term he uses to replace mood) have an analogous structure. They can be feelings of bodily states and/or ways of experiencing something outside the body.[7]

Similarly, Rochat describes how infants learn about their embodied self through playful self-exploration, which involves multimodal experience of bodily movements and actions they produce themselves. The manner in which infants actively touch themselves by clasping, waving their hands, and kicking and touching their legs and feet while vocalizing forms the basis for the infant's sense of its own body. These experiences also suggest there is an outside world, such as objects in the environment. In addition to what the infant gains from the experience of touch and other senses, it also feels its own changes in state—from calm to excitable, and the beginning of repetitive patterns. Rochat implies that the experience an infant gains about her own body during bodily movement and contact of self-exploration is inseparable from feelings about her own "vitality." Each forms a single experience. Such experience could be the basis for the infant feeling connected to the world and the beginning of feelings of how one is in the world.[8]

Stern also documents "vitality" affects. During the first two months of life, he theorizes that perceptions are "global" and are directly experienced as intensities, shapes, and temporal patterns. Distinctive subjective events accompany the variety of occurrences experienced by the infant. Such feelings arise when the infant moves, is touched, is picked up, is spoken to, or is dressed. Stern calls these associated feelings *vitality affects*, and adds that categorical affects such as joy, sadness, and anger contribute to the experience. The resulting nascent organization and global sense of the world is the basis for the emergence of the sense of self, forming the foundation for later development and awareness.[9]

Tronick is one of the few researchers to study mood in infants, and we note below his studies of the influence of depressed mothers' facial expressions on their infants. Some of his ideas are reminiscent of those derived from Heidegger. He suggests that moods can be organizing processes that structure behavior and experience over time, providing direction to the infant's behavior as he moves into his future. Infants are always cared for by others. They get picked up and held, and are cuddled, nursed, fed, and communicated with through voice and actions. During these connections babies are exposed to the emotions of those around them. Tronick suggests that moods are generated out of the infant's self-organized biorhythmic control processes, which interact with moods of the persons who share these situations with them. At another level, he suggests that moods are cocreated as part of a process of shared meaning with other people. Shared meaning lies in the interaction between the infant and its caregiver.[10] This is consistent with Heidegger's attunement as "the way of our being there with one another."[11]

INFANCY AND EMOTIONS

We saw in chapter 2 that emotions have cognitive and physiological components that prepare the individual to do something in relation to someone else or to a situation. Given a newborn's and infant's limited ability to judge and act, it is not surprising that different views are expressed on whether or not infants possess discrete emotions.

One view holds that distress and excitement can be identified at first, and discrete emotions emerge later as the infant's motor, cognitive, and language capacities begin to develop. An alternate view is that basic, discrete emotions—each with its own profile—are identifiable in very young infants. According to Sroufe, emotions don't arise out of the blue but emerge from prototypic root forms present in pre-emotional reactions within the newborn, and anger, fear, and joy are not accessible to the infant until the end of its first year. Available emotions represent transformations of earlier "nonemotional reactions." The precursors are global reactions (excitement) to a wide range of stimulation that differentiate and become more specific over the first few months. The beginnings of a meaningful connection between stimuli and the infant's reaction result from its connections with the environment. At ten weeks, the relation of the infant to some event stretches beyond mere stimulation, and the infant seems aware of a meaningful relationship.[12] We could argue that the prototypes and precursors discussed by Sroufe represent the laying down of moods that enable the emergence of emotions. This also supports the idea that mood is prior to cognition, since they are present earlier in development.

Sroufe suggests the development of three basic systems: (1) the pleasure/joy system, (2) the fear system; and, (3) the anger system. During the newborn period, a wide range of internal or external events can lead to a physiologic state that is the prototype for each of the three systems.[13] These are the forerunners of later mature reactions. The behavior is reflexive, and one cannot readily distinguish reactions that would later be anger or fear. Sroufe does not consider them emotions proper because of the absence of meaning or subjectivity.

Pleasure, wariness, and frustration emerge after the newborn period. These are precursor emotions that have an element of meaning, and the content of the event plays a role. Diffuse reactions involving the entire body are based on general rather than specific meaning. The general meaning might be recognition or failure of recognition, or the disruption of an established motor sequence. These diffuse reactions can be difficult to distinguish except by intensity. Basic emotions such as joy, anger, or fear emerge during the second half of the first year. They involve an immediate, more precise reaction and have specific meaning. But precursor emotions are not extinguished, and pleasure, wariness, and diffuse frustration continue to occur. If we put this in terms of tuning, then what is happening is the emergence of moods that set the conditions for emotion to be possible as cognitive and motor abilities develop. Tuning becomes more precise and individualized as the infant gains experience, but broader more diffuse tuning is not lost.

In the next section we introduce the important construct of tempera-ment that can also reflect how a child is tuned. Temperament is important for a number of reasons. Mood is a key component, it is the basis of later person-ality, and subtypes of temperament are predictive of later mood disturbance and disorders.

TEMPERAMENT AND MOOD

Even in early infancy, children can be seen to behave in characteristic ways as they interact with caregivers and their environment. This tendency to behave in typical ways while engaging with the world defines temperament. One early description of temperament refers to the "how" as opposed to the "what" of behavior.[14] For example, temperament encompasses how positive a child will be, how readily he becomes distressed, how fearful he is in the present, and how persistent he will be in pursuit of a goal. Temperament is relatively stable over time.[15] Children who tend to be negative in terms of mood and emotional reactions at age three are also inclined to be that way at age six. Conversely, children who tend to be positive follow a similar pattern and remain positive.

The relation of temperament to mood can also be seen in how tempera-ment is measured. Three of six dimensions commonly used to classify tem-perament are indicative of mood: fearful distress/inhibition, irritable distress, and positive affect/approach.[16] Temperament is assessed by measures that tap into these tendencies as well as by measures of cognitive and behavioral char-acteristics. Moreover, these underlying indicators of mood have a relation to emotion, as research shows that there are stable individual differences in the ten-dency to express a corresponding emotion to a temperamental trait. Individuals who tend to be fearful are more predisposed to more intense episodes of fear.[17] The opposite is also true. Individuals who are low in fearfulness are less likely to show fear, or are likely to experience less intense fear. Similarly, individuals prone to irritability are more likely to experience frequent and more intense anger, whereas those low in the trait of irritability are less likely to experience anger and do so with less intensity.

Temperament is often conceptualized as having three components.[18] The first component, positive affectivity (PA), is characterized by positive moods (joy, happiness, enthusiasm, and pride), a high sensitivity to reward, and reflects a tendency to actively engage the world. The second component, negative affectivity (NA), is characterized by negative moods (fear, anxiety, sadness), sensitivity to punishment, and avoidance and inhibition. The third component, constraint or effortful control, refers to the child's ability to suppress responses when there is conflict. This component reflects executive control of attention, the ability to delay gratification, and the capacity to control impulses and emotions.[19] Individual differences in temperament are thought to be present to some extent at birth, but effortful control only emerges at around age three.

Temperament and Personality

Personality speaks to individual differences in social and emotional functioning. Measures of these individual differences predict not only behavior; they also predict the quality of personal relationships and how individuals adapt to life circumstances, as well as happiness and health.[20] The three components of temperament are common to the main theories of personality. One suggestion is that personality is an amalgam of temperament and character, where temperament refers to individual differences in the tendencies underlying basic emotions, and character refers to individual differences in a person's unique goals and values.[21]

McAdams and Olson propose three developmental layers of psychological individuality. The layers are dispositional traits, characteristics adaptations, and integrative life narratives. They define dispositional traits as the broad, internal, comparative features of psychological individuality involved in consistencies in behavior, thought, and feeling across situations and over time. Traits are the fundamental dimensions of psychological functioning and are closely related to temperament. They write that we can look at the development of personality from three standpoints: the person as actor (behaving), as agent (striving toward goals), and as author (narrating). Beginning in infancy, temperament is the basis of later personality traits. In subsequent years, the child begins to develop goals and ambitions, laying the framework for the child as agent. The process continues in adolescence and early adulthood as the capacity emerges to create a narrative identity that helps create meaning in life.[22]

Two models are used to describe the range of identified traits. The Big 5 model has five factors: extroversion, neuroticism, agreeableness, conscientiousness, and openness to experience. Embedded in each factor are more specific traits. The Big 3 model has three factors: positive emotionality, negative emotionality, and constraint. Positive emotionality approximates extroversion, negative emotionality approximates neuroticism, and constraint overlaps with conscientiousness and control. Positive emotions are implicated in depression and manic states, and negative emotion in anxiety and depression, and they have their roots in infant temperament.

We can think of infant temperament as the substrate out of which personality traits emerge.[23] For example, the positive affectivity and approach evident in an early life may be precursors of the extroversion and positive emotionality factors of later personality. Similarly, neuroticism may be presaged by the anxious, fearful, or irritable distress that may emerge in infants. Similarly, the dimensions of early effortful control may presage conscientiousness and constraint.

Not only are individual differences in early temperament predictive of later personality, but they also predict the later emergence of disorders associated with mood disturbance. One particularly interesting group of infants and children is classified as behaviorally inhibited.[24] These infants and children demonstrate fearful distress and reticence when faced with novel or stressful situations. About 15 percent of infants and preschool children fit this category. Follow-up studies of behaviorally inhibited infants show that they are at later risk of developing anxiety disorders and depression. Infants can also be classified as having high-reactive or low-reactive temperament.[25] Highly reactive infants, who comprise about 20 percent of four-month-old infants, cry and arch their back or move vigorously when presented with unfamiliar stimuli in various modalities. About 40 percent of four-month-old infants demonstrate little motor activity or crying when exposed to the same stimuli. The two temperaments showed different patterns of moods and behavior and dissimilar physiological and brain activity. They also are differentially associated with the emergence of mood disorders over time. For example, the high reactive temperament is associated with the development of social anxiety.

In contrast to the behaviorally inhibited temperament, an exuberant temperament has also been identified.[26] The exuberant temperament is characterized by being sociable, a readiness to approach situations, and positive reactions to novelty. Exuberant infants show positive moods and social behavior, but in later childhood exuberance is associated with risk taking, impulsivity, fearlessness, and a tendency to be sensitive to reward. While exuberance is associated with better social skills, there is also a tendency to become frustrated when goals are blocked.

Irritability is another highly relevant element of temperament. Irritability has been measured in newborns[27] and may be prominent in some infants over the first two years. Although considered a principal mood,[28] irritability may be a hybrid of mood and emotion. It refers to being easily annoyed and touchy, but the behavioral manifestations are outbursts of anger and temper. This suggests that it may be possible to separate out a mood state (as defined in chapter 2), from feelings that are specifically directed at someone or some thing, i.e., an emotion. Irritable individuals tend to have a low threshold for frustration, especially when their efforts to reach a goal are interfered with.

Irritability may be a form of tuning that in the face of challenge manifests as anger, aggression, and temper outbursts. That alone will not make a disorder, but should the person also be tuned such that they are fearful, sad, or indifferent, then an anxiety disorder, depression, bipolar disorder, or antisocial behavior— or a combination of these—may emerge. In youth, irritability is included in the criteria for depression, bipolar disorder, anxiety disorders, and oppositional defiant disorder, but not conduct disorder. In adults, irritability is among the criteria for bipolar disorder, generalized anxiety disorder, as well as antisocial personality disorder.

ATTACHMENT AND MOOD

We saw in chapter 2 that we are always in situations that matter to us, and that mood reveals the available possibilities in these situations. Children are always in a situation, especially with others, and newborns enter a situation with total dependence on caregivers. One of the major social developments is the emergence of the infant's attachment to key caregivers. According to Bowlby, the infant has built-in biases to attach to a primary caregiver.[29] The caregiver provides a *felt* sense of security, a secure base, which the infant uses as a platform for exploration and learning. The resulting attachment increases the infant's chances of survival while promoting cognitive and emotional development. The degree to which the attachment is secure or insecure (reflected in the feelings of security) arises out of the interactions with the caregiver over the first few years of life. There is a normal sequence in the development of attachment. At around age four months, "wariness" of strangers emerges. Here the infant appears uneasy and unsettled when strangers appear. The onset of wariness marks a key step in attachment formation and is indicative of how the infant begins to discriminate between caregivers and others. Wariness of strangers is followed at six to seven months by fear of strangers. Infants protest the approach of strangers and typically cling to their familiar caregiver. At around eight months, infants may cry or show signs of fear when separated from their primary caregiver. Here we see indications of the infant becoming aware of the possibility of separation or loss of her caregiver, and these possibilities can be unsettling and uncomfortable. For most infants, separation anxiety increases and then declines by around fifteen months.

Inherent in theories of attachment is the idea that the infant is forming a sense of the possibilities contained in relationships with primary caregivers. These possibilities include that caregivers are present in a regular predictable way; that they're always present when needed; or, conversely, that they are unreliable and may not return. Mood, as we learned earlier, reveals situational possibilities. Thus, the processes involved in attachment play a crucial role in the child's development of her sense of belonging to a meaningful world. There is experimental evidence that by the age of eighteen months infants can consider possibilities and that by three years of age can consider how things might have been different in the past.[30] But it is also possible that infants can consider possibilities at a much earlier age. Consider the following example.

A six-month-old infant meets her grandfather's brother for the first time. The grandfather and his brother are similar in appearance except that the brother has a beard. The infant, relaxed and comfortable in her grandfather's arms, stares at the brother. She then begins to look back and forth at the two faces, her lips tremble, and she looks uneasy and turns in to the grandfather when the brother approaches before tentatively looking back when he stops.

An infant's experience with caregivers has a major impact on the development and the quality of the attachment. Likewise, the degree to which a parent or caregiver is responsive, predictable, and reassuring plays a crucial role in how unsettled the child becomes. The quality of attachment has long-term implications for the development of anxiety and depression.[31] To understand how this is studied, it is helpful to review how attachment has been measured.[32] The classic procedure involves the observation of infants in controlled situations with their mothers and a few toys. First, the mother leaves, then a stranger enters, and then the mother returns. The child's behavior during each condition is recorded and scored. Infants typically fit in one of four categories: The first (and largest) group of infants comfortably explores and plays within their new setting and in the presence of their mother. They may become mildly distressed if she leaves and they are alone or if a stranger enters. Then they resume their happy mood when she returns. These infants are scored as "securely attached." The second group of infants is clingy with their mother, explores less, and becomes distressed when left alone or with a stranger. These are rated as "insecurely attached." Some rebuff their mother when she returns, but others are ambivalent and may ignore her. A fourth group becomes very disturbed in the setting—angry, or aggressive, or they may freeze and not interact.

The degree to which an infant remains calm and is able to explores his environment or shows fearful or separation anxiety is dependent on a variety of factors such as temperament, prior experience, and parenting practices. For example, the behavior of category-four infants is linked to prior abuse.

Early attachment insecurity, as measured by behavior, modestly predicts increased risk for depression/anxiety, and the effects are stronger for preadolescent and adolescent youth.[33] The avoidant attachment subtype is related to later social withdrawal. Cognitive bias, difficulty with emotions, and self-concept may explain the links between attachment insecurity and depression/anxiety. Insecure attachment is also associated with coercive relationships with caregivers and later disruptive behavior.[34]

Irritability in infancy carries implications for the development of attachment. Irritable infants in the context of low social support available to their mother are likely to later be classified as insecurely attached, and they direct attachment behavior more often toward their caregiver.[35] Highly irritable and insecurely attached infants explore less, but interestingly, highly irritable toddlers were less sociable when insecurely attached, but more sociable when securely attached.[36]

Bowlby also identified loss of attachment figures as a potent risk factor for depression,[37] and this has been borne out in subsequent research in adults.[38] Bereaved youth also demonstrate an increased risk of depression,[39] whether or not the bereavement stems from natural causes or from an accident or suicide with the greatest risk occurring following the suicide of a parent.

DEVELOPMENT OF KEY MOODS AND ASSOCIATED EMOTIONS

In this section we sketch the development of some of the moods and their associated emotions that become the central features of the disorders to be examined later. We have seen from well-conducted sensory studies that newborns may experience pleasure, and that smiles may indicate pleasure or happiness. Pleasure is more clearly evident at two months of age when an infant shows delight in response to her actions when pulled strings result in the sound of music.[40] A smile is the easiest and best indicator of pleasure and joy within the context of a positive mood. Smiling also illustrates the role that interactions with others play in shaping mood and emotional development. Smiles are more likely to be elicited by interactions with humans than by other interesting or novel things or activities. Social smiles, or smiles directed at people, are one of the first building blocks in the development of attachment between the infant and caregiver. Brief smiles can be seen during the first two to three weeks, but it is not until the third to the eighth week that discrete smiles in response to stimulation are observed. Social smiles directed at others are evident by the second to third month. This suggests that emotions, as defined earlier, are present around ten weeks. Expressions of joy are apparent by six months.[41] Over the course of the first year laughter emerges in response to a variety of situations, and we can infer that laughter marks an underlying positive feeling or mood.

By two months of age, observers can distinguish sad facial expressions from general distress, and by six months sad facial expressions occur in response to situations that elicit sadness.[42] Tronick showed the close relationship between parent appearance of depression and infant sadness by exploring how the infant's behavior changes when faced with a depressed mother.[43] Videotapes show that as the depressed mother fails to respond to the infant's efforts to engage, the infant begins to turn away, and his facial expression appears sad.

By two months, facial expressions of anger can also be identified and distinguished from sadness, and by four to eight months, anger can be identified as a distinct entity elicited by frustration.[44] Anger becomes increasingly common over the next two years as the infant learns to control her environment and encounters more opportunities to become frustrated. We noted above that infants show delight when their efforts at pulling a string produced music. But infants varied in their responses when their actions no longer produced music, sometimes showing anger and at other times exhibiting fear. One possible interpretation is that the tuning of the infant sets the conditions for her response to unexpected events—an irritable infant might experience anger, or a fearful avoidant infant might show fear. Cognitive development plays an increasing role in constraint.[45] Preschool-age children become angry if a peer harms them, whether or not the harm was intentional, whereas older children are less likely to become angry if the harm was unintentional.

Guilt is a complex emotion when it focuses on something done or on a behavior, involves feelings of remorse and regret, and there is a desire to make up for behavior.[46] Guilt can also be a mood or a feeling that is not explicitly linked to an event or person, and this is often the case in depression. Guilt arises when harm is done to another person; particularly if the harmed person is an attachment figure or someone closely associated.[47] As a result, guilt is frequently associated with estrangement from others or with the threat of loss and the anticipation of being punished or harmed. Studies reveal that guilt as inferred from behavior appears in the second and third year,[48] and children appear to understand the experience of guilt by age three.[49]

Worry and fear are related as both involve anxious thoughts, but they are distinguishable. Worry may be defined as repetitive, intrusive thinking about negative and aversive things that can but probably will not happen—it is concerned with future possibilities.[50] Worries in middle childhood are very common, tending to focus on school performance, dying, health, and social concerns. Fear is primarily concerned with anxiety that is elicited by the actual confrontation with some event or thing—it is concerned with real and present possibilities.[51]

Last has summarized the ages at which common fears become evident in childhood.[52] Before age two, separation anxiety and fear of strangers become prominent. But fear of high places and the fear of novel events (loud noises or looming objects) are also evident. Many of these fears emerge at seven months and decline around twelve months. Between ages two and three, fear of the dark and fear of small animals emerge. By age five, children begin to report fear of bodily harm and of "mean" or "bad" people. By age six, they express fear of supernatural beings, or of sleeping alone, or of events such as thunder and lightning. Between ages seven and eight, children express fears of events reported by the media. By age nine, fears related to school performance and physical appearance emerge. Interestingly, it is also the age when children report fears of death. The most common fears endorsed by nine- to thirteen-year-old children are of animals, particularly spiders, and of being kidnapped or injured.[53] These fears were related to specific incidents, and conditioning (associating the connection between an event and the fear) was the most common mechanism.

RECOGNITION OF MOODS AND EMOTIONS

The ability to recognize the moods and emotions of others is crucial to human behavior and is important to discussions of empathy and concern (see below). The capacity to recognize facial expressions is a key element in the development of this ability.[54] For example, salient expressions of emotion, particularly facial expressions of fear and anger, are rapidly detected and processed by the nervous system. These expressions are prioritized because they suggest the presence of threats to survival. Infants show a preference for faces during the first few months.[55] But infants don't discriminate facial expressions until they're five to seven months old because of functional limitations in the visual system. Interestingly, if both auditory and visual cues are used and not just visual cues, discrimination becomes evident earlier at three to four months.

Some expressions are more salient than others and appear to take precedence.[56] Five- to seven-month-old infants stare longer at facial expressions of fear, and they don't disengage from them even if distracting stimuli are revealed. These discriminatory abilities are shaped by not only the general experiences all infants possess (they see many faces and expressions) but also by specific experiences a particular infant may contain (exposure to abusive or hostile environments).

For example, the facial expression of a depressed mother shapes her infant's experience.[57] Researchers monitored infants interacting with their mothers who were asked to maintain a flat facial expression. Infants of depressed mothers tended to be less active and more withdrawn than infants of non-depressed mothers when they were face-to-face with their mother, and they protested less when their mother wore a flat expression. Experience coupled with genetic influences shape the underlying mechanisms. Individual differences in the degree of shaping may become predisposing or vulnerability factors for the emergence of anxiety and depression.

MOOD AND PRO-SOCIAL BEHAVIOR

The ability to identify and understand that another child or adult is experiencing a particular mood or emotion defines empathy. Empathy, sympathy, and concern are related topics that are basic to pro-social behavior, and are relevant to disruptive and antisocial behavior where mood may be indifferent or callous.

For example, empathy is said to be absent in a particular subset of youth with conduct disorder.[58]

Empathy can be defined by the capacity to experience the "emotional" state that is akin to or consistent with that experienced by another.[59] A child experiences empathy if she feels sad about encountering a sad child. Sympathy differs from empathy in that sympathy is a negative feeling a child feels when concerned about another. According to Prinz, sympathy is a feeling *for*, whereas empathy is a feeling *because*.[60] The experience of each child need not be the same. A child may feel sad because a friend is angry. Sympathy is focused on how the other is feeling. Moreover, he suggests sympathy and empathy are not emotions but rather are a process by which emotions come about and are directed toward something else. Concern is also a negative feeling that arises when another person is perceived to be in a bad situation or predicament. Concern differs from empathy and sympathy since it is directed at the predicament of another individual and not at the emotion or mood of the other person. As a result, Prinz suggests concern may be the more powerful and crucial motivator of helping behavior while empathy may not be a good motivator of pro-social behavior unless concern is also in the picture.

By the second and third years, children show interest when a peer is distressed.[61] But it is not until close to preschool age that clear evidence of helping behavior emerges. Pro-social behavior continues to increase throughout childhood and adolescence. There are strong family influences on the development of pro-social behavior. Modeling and teaching of behavior, providing opportunities to display pro-social behavior, and constructive and supportive parenting all promote sympathetic and empathic behavior. Genetic influences, perhaps mediated through temperament, are also likely to occur.

MOOD AND ADOLESCENCE

Cognitive and social development increases rapidly as the child continues to move into the world. Adolescence is a period of enormous development as adolescents begin to move away from their parents, spend increasing time with peers, and engage in community activities, volunteering, and service.[62] These social changes are linked to mood.

Negative feelings and emotions increase in early adolescence but decline toward late teenage years. Adolescents report they are happier when with their peers, and while early adolescence is marked by increased conflict between teenagers and parents, by late adolescence relationships with parents are less contentious. Why might this be so?

Moving toward peers brings adventure, uncertainty, danger, threat, and excitement, but it also means testing whatever felt security lay with parents and family as the adolescent experiments with new things that begin to matter to them.

Puberty brings about remarkable change. The influence of mood, which is particularly noticeable in early adolescence, may well be linked to pubertal influences. Nelson and colleagues suggest that the hormonal changes of puberty along with the maturation of neuronal processes and learning underlie the remarkable social changes that occur during adolescence.[63] Gonadal steroids influence responsiveness to social stimuli, particularly sexual responsiveness. New things begin to matter—relationships with others, especially romantic ones, but also relationships with peers, teachers, or coaches in which new ideas are tested and identities are forged. In a way, adolescence is a laboratory in which teen tuning (mood) reveals new possibilities, but the teenager's level of understanding and skill at negotiating the new challenges carries its own moods. While parents provide support and guidance, in many areas the adolescent is on his or her own and must decide among the possibilities that present themselves.

Casey and colleagues marshal data that suggests that younger adolescents, in particular, rely more heavily on feelings when determining critical personal decisions even though they may be capable of thinking rationally and logically.[64] Over the course of adolescence there's a gradual but marked improvement in reasoning and processing information that affords them new skills and expertise. The adolescent achieves a more fully conscious, self-directed, and self-regulating mind through the gradual establishment of executive functional capabilities.[65]

Further, a sense of self develops over the course of adolescence, transitioning from childhood and becoming more abstract, differentiated, and better organized over time. Research shows how an adolescent's self-view differs across contexts.[66] They view themselves differently with peers as compared to their view of themselves when in the company of parents or teachers. Interestingly, adolescents may project a false self, depending on the social context.[67] This false self is connected to mood, sometimes to please others, or to embellish their self-esteem, or to experiment with new situations, but if this self cannot be sustained or surmount challenges, then depression and hopelessness may emerge.

CHAPTER 4

MOOD AND NEURAL CIRCUITS

We suggested that mood is a phase of the activity of brain circuits and related bodily systems that are continually active as we go about our activities. The judgments made and resulting actions and accompanying bodily changes make up the emotions. This chapter discusses how information is transmitted in the nervous system, the brain regions and circuits relevant to mood and emotion, and the neurotransmitter systems that modulate the activity of the networks, and also sketches relevant findings on circuit development. In addition, the reader will see how these neural circuits are connected to key functions such as the stress response and the immune system.

We start from the concept that we perceive the world through our body.[1] Information is processed and stored, and action is initiated through the activity of the nervous system,[2] and these activities are performed by means of neural networks rather than through chemical formation and storage. We can think of mood as a functional state of neural networks: tuning/mood arises through the activity of neural networks and related body systems. Mood as a phase of their activity or tuning is always present as the circuits relay information.

While mood and emotion arise from coordinated activity in the circuits of the brain, it is premature to suggest how this happens. Can we separate out circuits for feeling, mood, or emotion as we have defined them? The answer is no. The difficulty partly stems from the fact that available neuroscience research typically focuses on emotion, and feelings and mood cannot be separated out. Can we separate out circuits for cognitive activities such as attention, memory, and problem solving from mood or emotion? Again, the answer is no.[3] Cognition and emotion are integrated in the brain and interact in complex ways. Brain regions viewed as related to mood and emotions are involved in cognition, and vice versa. Neural circuits may act as organized nested loops, and while each set of loops might underlie a particular function, the loops act as an integrated whole, while the individual responds to a situation.[4]

The brain is organized as a hierarchy.[5] More recently evolved cortical and sub-cortical areas participate in overall regulation and decision making. The lower and older parts of the brain regulate physiological and other functions that are necessary to maintain life. Historically, many of the areas thought to be involved in mood and emotion were referred to as the limbic system. This included the amygdala, hippocampus, the cingulate gyrus, and areas of the thalamus. However, the physical and functional boundaries of the limbic system are unclear, and today we know that many areas outside the limbic system are also involved.[6] For example, the prefrontal cortex (PFC) guides attention and cognition and inhibits inappropriate action, but it also regulates emotion. Regions such as the basal ganglia and nucleus accumbens are involved in motivational systems and motor activities.

NEURONS, SYNAPSE, AND CIRCUITS

The basic components of the nervous system are nerve cells or neurons, and nerve cells communicate and interact to form circuits that underlie all the activities of the nervous system.[7] There are a number of crucial ideas that permeate this and succeeding chapters, and they are the principles that guide how we can understand the ways we are connected to the world. Neurons connect at junctions called synapses; the synapse is the hub where change occurs. Vast numbers of interconnected neurons form circuits, and these are brain regions that perform particular functions. Activity in the circuits is regulated, and this regulation is the function of neurotransmitters. Crucially, environmental events not only influence activity in circuits; they also affect the development of circuits. The synapse allows these changes to occur. In other words, mind, body, and world are interconnected and inseparable. This chapter provides more detail on some relevant systems.

Neurons consist of three components: a cell body containing the nucleus; dendrites that carry information to the cell body; and the axon, which carries information away from the cell body. A fatty insulating layer, called myelin, allows an electrical impulse to travel along the axon and determine the speed of transmission. Neurons connect at the synapses, and groups of neurons form circuits. Information passes from neuron to neuron across the synapse and throughout the circuit. Electrical or chemical signals pass the information through specialized sites on the surface of the neuron at the synapse. These receptors recognize particular chemicals (neurotransmitters and hormones). Two neurotransmitters, one excitatory (glutamate) and one inhibitory (GABA, gamma-aminobutyric acid), are directly involved in the transfer of information from neuron to neuron. Transmission of signals—that is, how well a circuit functions—depends on the balance of activity between these two transmitters.

The synapse is central to the brain's functioning. Information is stored by a continual process of change in the relative strength of synapses. It is a hub where critical activities such as learning and memory take place. Mood disorders are treated by medication therapy that acts by changing the activity in the synapses. Plasticity, the capacity for change to occur in the nervous system, arises through activity in the synapses. For example, our ability to experience operates through its effects on plasticity.

OVERVIEW OF SELECTED BRAIN REGIONS

In the following sections, we sketch key features of regions involved in mood and emotion and in disorders that involve mood. Figures 4.1 and 4.2 show the location of these areas in the brain.

Prefrontal Cortex

The prefrontal cortex (PFC) (fig. 4.1) is central to executive functions, attention, coordinating responses to events (including the response to threat), and deciding a course of action.[8] Information about all aspects of the internal and external environment goes to the PFC. This makes the PFC central to intelligence and personality.

The PFC is located behind the forehead and contains specialized subregions that not only connect to each other but that also connect widely to other regions and systems. While medial and central areas may be involved in emotion, and dorsal and lateral areas in thought and action,[9] these functions are likely integrated.[10] PFC connections go to areas involved in autonomic, endocrine, and immune functions to provide bodily responses, and to motor areas to enable a person to act. For example, projections to the locus coeruleus (see below) and the ventral tegmental area (see below) connect the PFC to neurotransmitter systems. The connections are bidirectional, and neurotransmitter systems can influence the function of the PFC. As we will see in later chapters, the PFC is involved in regulating the stress response and is highly susceptible to damage caused by the stress response.[11] The PFC contains a number of regions that are

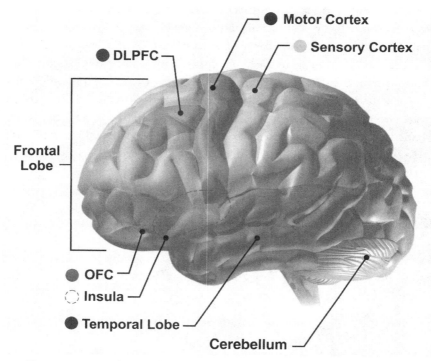

Figure 4.1. Lateral view of the brain showing key landmarks. Frontal area shows the dorsolateral prefrontal cortex (DLPFC) and orbitofrontal cortex (OFC). (Figure created by Dave Cantrell, Biomedical Communications, University of Arizona Health Sciences.)

involved in critical functions related to mood, emotion, cognition, and executive actions, and these are sketched in the next section.

The *orbitofrontal cortex* (OFC) (fig. 4.1) processes the affective quality and value of a stimulus, and influences and tunes perceptual processing in sensory systems.[12] This means the OFC is active when you're dealing with something you want to avoid, or dealing with something you work for or desire, and in learning to associate a stimulus and its reinforcers.[13] Thus, the OFC is involved in motivation (behavior involved in seeking rewards), and as we will see in later chapters this implicates the OFC in depression (decreased motivation) and mania (increased motivation). The OFC has direct connections to the amygdala (see below), is central to mood and motivation, and has reciprocal connections with lateral regions of the PFC, central to executive function.

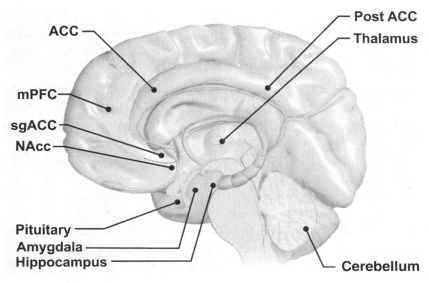

Figure 4.2. Medial surface of the brain showing the anterior cingulate cortex (ACC), posterior cingulate cortex (PCC), and subgenual ACC (sgACC). The medial prefrontal cortex (mPFC) is shown anterior to the ACC. Nucleus accumbens (NAcc) is shown in proximity to the sgACC. The hippocampus is shown in proximity to the amygdala. The thalamus is located centrally. The pituitary is close to amygdala and below the hypothalamus. (Figure created by Dave Cantrell, Biomedical Communications, University of Arizona Health Sciences.)

The *medial OFC* (mOFC) (fig. 4.2) may be involved in positive affective states, while the lateral OFC (lOFC) (fig. 4.1) may be similarly involved in negative affective states.[14] Furthermore, the mOFC may be involved in shutting down the response to fear and therefore implications for anxiety disorders. Not surprisingly, given these properties, the OFC is involved in recognizing emotions from facial expressions.[15]

But how is meaning processed? Roy and colleagues suggest that the *ventromedial* area of the PFC (vmPFC) functions as a hub that integrates information (mood- and emotion-related as well as cognitive and social) from other areas to provide meaning in situations for a person's physical and social well-being and future prospects. They base this notion on patterns of connectivity with other circuits and systems, such as those involved in memory, visceromotor functions, sensory information, and determining goals.[16]

Executive functions are processed in the *dorsolateral PFC* (DLPFC) (fig. 4.1), which is involved in setting goals and in working memory. Because of connections to the motor cortex and hippocampus, it plays a key role in coordinating behavior with circumstances in the environment.[17]

The *anterior cingulate cortex* (ACC) (fig. 4.2) further illustrates the complexity of the PFC. This is an area that can be thought of as a site where affect and cognition are integrated, and it further functions as a higher-level area where the physiological responses necessary to support cognitive and affective responses are generated.[18] The ACC in conjunction with the OFC and mPFC may be involved in processing the physical or physiological changes that accompany experiences with significant mood or emotional components. The ACC connects to the autonomic and endocrine systems involved in bodily symptoms that are associated with negative feelings and moods. Negative affect, pain, and cognitive control functions activate an area of the upper ACC, and information about reinforcers may be linked through this area to motor areas expressing affect and executing goal-directed behaviors.[19] The ACC may monitor the emotional salience of stimuli, influence the autonomic nervous system and cognitive activity, and as a result may influence responses when challenging events occur.[20] An area of the lower anterior portion of the ACC, the *subgenual* ACC, is implicated in depression and bipolar disorder (chapters 9 and 10). The involvement of the ACC in cognitive control or in constraining behavior implicates the ACC in temperament (see below).

Amygdala

The amygdala (fig. 4.2) lies in the medial temporal lobe close to the anterior tip of the hippocampus, and because of its many connections, the amygdala serves as a hub in mood, emotion, and social behavior.[21] The amygdala is a collection of nuclei with different connections.[22] The lateral nuclei are involved in processing input, learning connections, and associating events. The central nucleus connects the amygdala to areas in the cortex serving cognitive and executive functions, to systems regulating visceral or bodily functions, and to the motor systems serving action. Broadly speaking, novel and biological events are given affective significance in the amygdala, and although the amygdala preferentially participates in a range of negative experiences, it is also activated by positive experiences.

The amygdala gets information from the senses about the environment, as well as input about the internal state of the body. The input is multimodal, and may include facial expressions, vocal sounds and intonation, posture, and movement.[23] The amygdala also connects back to sensory systems influencing sensory input and cortical processing of sensory input (e.g., the reading of facial expressions). The dopamine system (see below), the PFC gate sensory input to the amygdala,[24] and individual differences in these mechanisms may be related to mood.

The amygdala is primed to participate in tuning, to reveal situational possibilities and set the stage for how a person acts in situations. Consistent with this view, Cunningham and Brosch suggest that the amygdala is involved in determining the relevance of a stimulus and is activated depending on needs, goals, or values of the person.[25] Indeed, recent research suggests the amygdala is activated by the impact or subjective significance of events to the person. Moreover, it is closely associated with cortical regions thought to be involved in registering meaning in situations.[26] This finding is relevant to the idea (chapter 2) that mood makes things matter and reveals the significance of events.

Fear processing is one of the best-studied aspects of the amygdala's role in processing emotional expression.[27] This is an essential, rapidly processed component of the response to threat or danger. When a threat is perceived, the amygdala may inhibit the prefrontal cortex so that only essential responses occur. Cortical connections with the amygdala help take the context of the threat into consideration and may override any initial fear response. This ensures that the fear response is limited, and that the person does not live in a constant state of fear.

Not unexpectedly, the amygdala plays a key role in the processing of facial expression, especially expressions of fear, making the amygdala and its connections highly relevant to anxiety and antisocial behavior.[28] The subject need not be aware of the stimulus presented, and other indicators of fear, such as body posture or vocal expressions also activate the amygdala.

The amygdala, through its central nucleus, plays a crucial role in the response to stress and in regulating the neuroendocrine component of the stress response.[29] Circuits link the amygdala to visceral responses, the autonomic nervous system, and the stress response system (chapter 6). These connections may account for the physical or visceral sensations associated with anxiety, fear, and the response to stressful events.

Another way to look at the amygdala and tuning is through its connections to temperament.[30] There is strong evidence linking the amygdala with the tendency to avoid or to be inhibited and sensitive to negative aspects of situations. This suggests that individual differences in the excitability of the amygdala and its connections may underlie temperament. It also supports the idea that individual differences in how the amygdala and related circuits function are key to the understanding of mood in the life of an individual.

Nucleus Accumbens

The nucleus accumbens (NAcc) (fig. 4.2) is a crucial component of the motivational reward system.[31] It serves as a crossroads between the limbic, cognitive, and motor systems through links to prefrontal cortex, amygdala, hippocampus, thalamus, and motor areas. Strong connections to the dopamine system (see below) give the NAcc a central role in positive states. The NAcc is activated by toned situations (humor, positive pictures, and verbal stimuli), and the anticipation of reward, which implicates circuits involving the NAcc in mood disorders.

Insula

The insula (fig. 4.1) may be involved in monitoring both the emotional and cognitive aspects of events. Craig has proposed that the insula in partnership with the ACC is responsible for our sense of awareness of others and of our environment and our sense of self.[32] Internal visceral sensations project to the insula and are then remapped as bodily feelings. This means the insula is involved in how aware we are or how sensitive we are to gut sensations, e.g., in anxiety or fear.

Hippocampus

The hippocampus (fig. 4.2) is a folded area at the base of the brain in the medial temporal lobes that controls short-term memory and conversion to long-term memory, and involves intellectual and emotional response.[33] The lower area of the hippocampus is primarily involved in behaviors related to anxiety, while the upper area is involved in the memory of facts and events. The amygdala connects to the hippocampus and may relay memories (especially emotionally charged ones) to the hippocampus for later retrieval. The hippocampus and amygdala play related, albeit different, roles in fear and anxiety as well as in negative affectivity associated with increased hippocampal activity.[34] It also plays an important role in the stress response (chapter 6).

Hypothalamus

The hypothalamus is a cluster of nerve cells that controls appetite and sexual and mood responses, located close to the pituitary gland (fig. 4.2).[35] It receives information from the amygdala, the cingulate cortex, the hippocampus, and also directly from the senses before transmitting signals to the endocrine and autonomic nervous systems. These connections allow the hypothalamus to integrate and coordinate essential life functions while offering explanations for body functions, which are altered in mood disorders.

Thalamus

The thalamus (fig. 4.2) is a paired structure close to the center of the brain.[36] Sensory information en route to the cortex passes through the thalamus where it is processed and organized into nuclei that process input from specific sensory or motor systems. The thalamus features in many key neural circuits because of the importance of its role in processing sensory information. Two circuits implicated in mood disorders link the thalamus, amygdala, cortex, and motor areas with other connections to the hypothalamus and autonomic nervous system.[37]

NEUROTRANSMITTER SYSTEMS

Neural circuits must respond and adjust rapidly when events occur. How is their activity adjusted? Neurotransmitter systems are mechanisms that have evolved to rapidly adjust the activity of neural circuits.[38] A neurotransmitter is a biochemical substance released by nerve endings that chemically transmit nerve impulses. Although these systems may originate in sites far from the brain, their transmitters are released in response to signals from the amygdala, OFC, ACC, and other areas. Widely distributed in the body, they work together by offering broad influence on the activity of neural circuits while ensuring that they play an important role in regulating body functions and response to stress. Psychotropic medications act through neurotransmitter systems (chapter 12).

Dopamine System

Dopamine is one of the most studied neurotransmitters in the brain. The dopamine system modulates the tendency to actively engage the world, affects sensitivity to rewards and the tendency to experience a wide range of positive moods.[39] As a result, dopamine is implicated in anhedonia (loss of interest and pleasure) and in motivation. The cell bodies begin in the ventral tegmentum, and overlapping dopamine pathways project too many key areas.[40] The mesolimbic (or reward) pathway projects to the nucleus accumbens, amygdala, anterior cingulate cortex, and prefrontal cortex. These areas are involved in monitoring the internal and external environment, generating moods, and corresponding emotional responses. As a further result, dopamine modulates the positive affectivity component of temperament.

Dopamine is released in the NAcc when significant events require engagement and adaptive responses.[41] The ACC receives more dopamine projections than any other area of the brain, while contributing to the ACC's role in approach behavior and the monitoring of rewards. Excess dopamine in the amygdala may heighten the response to threat while diminishing the influence of the PFC on the amygdala. This result could activate heightened fear responses. Individual differences in the capacity of the amygdala to store dopamine may also influence emotional processing in the amygdala and upper ACC.

Dopamine is also involved in the control of movement, and its depletion can lead to Parkinson's disease and motor function disorders. Its role in movement is important in producing side effects of psychotropic medications.

The dopamine transporter regulates the level of dopamine in the synapse. Certain enzymes, e.g., monoamine oxidase, metabolize dopamine, and genetic variations of these enzymes have important interactions with the environment that are linked to mood and other disorders.

Serotonergic System

The serotonergic system is involved in mood, learning, memory, and regulating vigilance.[42] This system begins in the midbrain and sends projections upward to a variety of structures that include the cerebral cortex, PFC, limbic areas, hippocampus, and thalamic nuclei, where the transmitter serotonin is released by nerve endings. The serotonin transporter is under genetic control[43] (chapter 5) and results in a short and long form of the serotonin transporter. Significant interest has been focused on the short or "s" allele. Those with the "s" allele show reduced volumes of the ACC and amygdala. Having the "s" allele increases vulnerability to stress (chapters 5 and 6) and makes the amygdala more responsive to input through its effects on the circuit-linking PFC and the amygdala. A more responsive amygdala is receptive to environmental input that can lead to increased anxiety or sadness. The "s" allele is associated with depression in the context of early abuse, neglect, and traumatic events.

Noradrenergic System

The noradrenergic system (NA) helps maintain vigilance, facilitates shifts in attention and memory, is active when an individual is adapting to a changing environment, and helps regulate the fear response.[44] The noradrenergic system originates in the midbrain as a group of neurons called the locus coeruleus (LC). The LC connects to the spinal cord and brain stem, as well as to the thalamus, hypothalamus, hippocampus, and cortex. Norepinephrine is increased during stress (chapter 6), and chronic stress sensitizes the response with the result that subsequent acute stress produces a more intense response. The LC has significant influence on the amygdala, where it can lower the threshold for future activation.

CIRCUITS RELEVANT TO TUNING

There is a voluminous and ever-expanding literature on the relevance of brain areas and systems to mood, emotion, and behavior. One prominent approach is that of Price and Drevets.[45] They describe two basic systems, which serve essentially as an input and an output system. The input system (or orbital network) is comprised of areas in the orbital PFC, receives sensory input, assesses objects, and is also critical in anticipating reward. The output system (medial prefrontal network) includes areas in the medial prefrontal cortex as well as some areas in the OFC, ACC, and the vmPFC. As an output system it connects to neuroendocrine and autonomic systems and to motor systems. The amygdala and other limbic structures have critical bidirectional connections with the medial network. This framework provides a structure illustrating how these areas collaborate to maintain normal function, and it provides a basis for understanding how the various clinical symptoms and behaviors of the disorders involving mood emerge.

We can also think in terms of interconnected systems that generate mood and emotion, regulate the processes that underlie them, and underlie reward-seeking behavior.[46] The medial prefrontal cortex, anterior cingulate, and OFC are involved in processing emotion and in the automatic regulation of emotion. Cognitive control and effortful regulation of emotion involve the lateral PFC, including the ventrolateral and dorsolateral areas. The amygdala and ventral striatum are involved in reward processing as well as emotion. The connections among these areas result in a medial prefrontal-limbic network that includes the amygdala, anterior cingulate, and medial prefrontal cortex. This system is modulated by serotonin. A second system can be conceptualized as a reward network system and includes the ventral striatum, orbitofrontal cortex, and medial prefrontal cortex. The reward system is modulated by dopamine.

Fear Circuit

Circuits underlying fear are among the most researched and important circuits in the nervous system. They underlie the systems involved in processing threat and are involved in anxiety disorders.[47] Key components include the amygdala, an area called the bed nucleus of the stria terminalis (BNST), and areas of the prefrontal cortex. The amygdala appears to be critical for the production of fear as part of its overall role in processing mood and emotion. The amygdala in this context seems to be necessary for learning the associations between stimuli and reinforcement. The BNST appears to be involved when fear is sustained over time and is also involved when threats are less specific and less predictable. The PFC participates in both automatic regulation and when effort is required to regulate responses. With regard to fear, the vmPFC is involved in inhibiting conditioned fear and in the extinction of conditioned fear. Lateral areas of the PFC (e.g., DLPFC) participate in regulating fear responses through their role in attention.

The circuits involved in fear arise through connections between these areas, as it is thought that the PFC modulates the amygdala. Anxiety disorders are hypothesized to result from an imbalance between production of fear through the amygdala and inadequate regulation through the PFC (chapter 8).

Reward Circuit

The reward system underlies motivation, goal seeking, novelty seeking, and reinforcement of behavior and is centered on dopamine, the nucleus accumbens, and their connections.[48] Dopaminergic projections originate in an area known as the ventral tegmentum (VTA) and go to the nucleus accumbens, prefrontal cortex, amygdala, and hippocampus. The VTA is modulated by input it receives from the nucleus accumbens, prefrontal cortex, and amygdala. The serotonin system also modulates the dopaminergic projections through projections to the nucleus accumbens and the VTA. The nucleus accumbens in turn projects to the globus pallidus in the basal ganglia, and projections then go to the thalamus and back to the prefrontal cortex. These circuits underlie positive emotions and have become a critical focus in understanding the emergence of mood disorders and anxiety in adolescents.[49]

Decision Making and Executive Action Circuits

In making decisions we not only draw on our past experience and our current goals but we also anticipate future outcomes. Decision making is a complex process and is influenced by emotional tone and cultural context. A number of models of decision making have been proposed. For example, Rosenbloom and colleagues suggest decision making involves circuits in the cortex and their connections to the amygdala, hypothalamus, striatum, thalamus, and other areas.[50] Within the cortex, the key areas are the OFC, the ACC, and the DLPFC. The OFC monitors rewards and punishment, and different subareas are specialized for different levels of reward, and it is involved in networks responsible for emotional processing. The DLPFC participates because it is involved in planning and other executive functions. The ACC is involved when situations are conflicting and choices are ambiguous. The OFC has outgoing connections to different areas of the amygdala that lead in one case to autonomic arousal by disinhibiting the hypothalamus and a second output leads to inhibition of the hypothalamus. Further connections go to the striatum, which connects to the thalamus and back to the cortex. Lesions in this circuit may lead to disinhibition, lability of behavior, alterations in reward-seeking behavior, and apathy.

TEMPERAMENT AND NEURAL CIRCUITS

Temperament (chapter 3), or the tendency to behave in typical ways while engaging with the world, is an important construct. From early infancy, children can be seen to behave in characteristic ways as they interact with caregivers and their environment. Temperament becomes a significant component of later personality. As we have seen, temperament is related to mood. Temperament is also a model situation illustrating how neural networks might combine to produce the mood and behavioral tendencies that make up temperament types. To recap, temperament is often thought of as consisting of negative affectivity, positive affectivity, and constraint or control. Whittle and colleagues propose that specific neural circuits underlie temperament, and individual differences in the dimensions of temperament may depend on how the connections function.[51] Negative affectivity, or expressed or felt frustration/anger when limits are set, is associated with a circuit linking the amygdala and lower ACC with structures in the right hemisphere. These include the hippocampus, the upper ACC, and dorsolateral PFC. The amygdala and lower ACC are involved in the production of affective states, as well as the appraisal and regulation of autonomic responses to affective experiences. The right hemisphere structures are more involved with executive functions, integrating cognitive processes, affective input, and the effortful regulation of affective states. Whittle and colleagues established that smaller volumes of regions in the ACC were linked to negative affectivity in adolescents.[52]

Positive affectivity is associated with a left-sided circuit based on the NAcc getting input from the amygdala, and with the hippocampus and lower ACC being less involved. Projections from the NAcc to left PFC (including upper ACC and dorsolateral PFC) promote conscious feelings of pleasure, and they influence the drive to engage in pleasurable activity. The prefrontal regions in return regulate affective processing in the NAcc and amygdala. In adolescents, the volume of ACC subregions was linked to seeking out and enjoying intense experiences and affiliative tendencies.

The circuit underlying constraint or effortful control is hypothesized to involve some or all of the above structures. They suggest that constraint is positively related to how much inhibitory control is exerted on the amygdala and NAcc by the dorsal ACC, DLPFC, and lateral OFC.

CHAPTER 5

GENES, ENVIRONMENTS, AND NEURAL CIRCUITS

I n this chapter we consider the role played by genes in forming the circuits underlying tuning and then examine how genes and environments interact in shaping circuits and the way they function. First, we sketch the basic principles of how genes operate, and then we discuss current thinking about how environments and genes interact, especially in development. This will give insight into processes underlying individual differences in tuning that are important to the development of resilience, vulnerability, and mood disorders. We will see the important role relationships play in these interactions.

GENES AND WHAT THEY DO

Genes encode for proteins (strings of amino acids) that form the building blocks of the body, regulate the function of neurons, and make peptides that are the means of communication within and between cells.[1] Variations in these genes have a profound influence on development and function. Current evidence suggests that the environment regulates the cellular signals controlling the genome such that the way cells function is the result of a constant dialogue between the genome and its environment.

How does this work? The basic genetic information is carried in the DNA. The DNA is contained in the cell nucleus in forty-six pairs of chromosomes, each pair made up of a chromosome from the mother and one from the father. The information is contained in long strings of chemical bases arranged in a double helix. There are only four bases (adenine, thymine, cytosine, guanine) arranged in sets of three. The three base sequences make up the code (the instructions) to make proteins or peptides. A gene refers to a section of the string of bases that contains particular information.

Protein manufacture begins with DNA directing the synthesis of messenger RNA. An exact copy of DNA nucleotide sequence information is read. This process is called transcription. The messenger RNA then directs the synthesis of amino acids leading to the formation of proteins. This process is called translation. Both transcription and translation are key to our understanding of how change can occur in neurobiological function.

Gene expression refers to the selective activation of genes and involves both transcription and translation. Genetic and environmental factors influence the processes involved in transcription. Genetic influences that affect transcription are referred to as the "promoter." These are sequences of bases that can regulate a gene. Changes in gene expression can result from mutations where bases are deleted or otherwise modified. While only one gene codes for a particular protein, there are multiple genetic influences on its transcription and expression. The same gene can also produce a number of different proteins via a process known as splicing. Genetic polymorphism refers to changes in the bases coding for a particular protein.[2] These genetic polymorphisms may give rise to different amino acids and can change the way the protein functions. Because of this, polymorphisms play very important roles. For example, the effects of polymorphisms on brain circuits and synaptic activity are the basis of genetic influences on the stress response and gene-environment interactions (see below).

But changes in gene expression can also be brought about without changing the underlying DNA sequence. Environmental (nongenetic) influences can change gene expression. Epigenesis refers to modifications made to the DNA or to regions surrounding the DNA by chemical means. For example, adding methyl groups to a base affects the transcription of a gene. Epigenetic processes are important because they are the means whereby environmental influences work. Early life events can influence the epigenetic state of parts of the genome, modifying the way genes build proteins.[3] For example, animal studies suggest that a mother's behavior toward her offspring can bring about stable changes in gene expression. Such epigenetic influences may become the basis for individual differences in behavioral and neuroendocrine response to stress in adulthood,[4] and subsequently may result in individual differences in the risk for psychopathology. This important work shows that relationships play vital roles at the very basic level of gene expression, and that they thereby influence neural circuitry that underlies mood.

Of further importance, gene expression is specific to periods of development as well as to specific issues.[5] Certain genes are activated during fetal life, leading to the formation of new nerve cells. Genes regulating the development of connections between cells are active during early infancy. Other genes are activated during adolescence when further brain growth occurs. The early construction processes seem to be primarily genetically controlled, while the later processes of connecting and expanding are more influenced by the environment. The next section explores key issues in how genes and environments interact and the differential effects of environmental influences in infancy and early childhood and adolescence.

GENES AND ENVIRONMENT

Genes and environmental factors play a role in producing individual differences in behavior.[6] All children in a family share certain things, but each child will also share unique environmental influences. It appears that it is these non-shared environmental influences that are important in making children different. Environmental influences (e.g., parenting or social support) also have strong genetic influences because we select, modify, and construct our own world experience. Genes and environments also interact where there is differential exposure to experiences, and this type of interaction is the basis of diathesis-stress models (see below). Genetic factors that affect one trait may also affect other traits, and recent studies of the strength of this correlation have led to the idea that there are generalist and specialist genes.[7] The basic idea is that certain genes have broad effects, and the unique environments individuals experience determine final functioning. For example, in relation to the focus of this book, studies show that psychopathology can be divided into two broad domains of internalizing disorders (anxiety, depression) and externalizing disorders (disruptive behavior), and these broad domains share common genetic factors. The notion is that generalist genetic factors lead to the broad dimensions, and then other genes provide the specialist environments that shape the final form of the disorders that present in a particular individual. The overlap of anxiety and depression, the overlap of irritability and disruptive behavior and depression, and the overlap with disruptive and antisocial disorders are three areas relevant to mood where such ideas may apply. These ideas can be construed as consistent with tuning, with generalist genes setting the basic templates of the range of moods we experience, and specialist genes influencing the particular mix of moods that are characteristic of a given individual.

GENES, ENVIRONMENT, AND NEURAL CIRCUITS

With this background on genes and environments, we can now consider the development of neural circuits that are the basis of tuning. The growth of circuits depends on genes and environmental input working together, and neuroplasticity allows the connections (and communication) between neurons to respond to experience.[8] The next chapter considers how stress affects circuits and development.

Two great developmental events occur during the growth of neurons and their connections.[9] Massive growth occurs before birth and continues into maturity, but more connections than necessary are established during this time frame. Two waves of pruning occur. About 40 percent of synapses are pruned back in the early wave in infancy, and a second wave of pruning occurs during adolescence. The process of pruning has significant implications for our understanding of the effects of experience. While genes control brain growth, pruning is influenced by experience. The effects of experience on brain development can be classified as experience-expectant plasticity and experience-dependent plasticity.[10]

In experience-expectant plasticity, the brain "expects" certain experiences to occur. Every infant and child are exposed to a myriad of experiences that shape the structure of the brain. For example, infants are picked up, they hear, see, smell, and touch things, all of which affects brain growth. Connections between neurons that are most used survive, and those that are less active are pruned. Experience-expectant plasticity offers both a positive and a negative side. While the brain can recover from damage by having other areas take over functions, the absence of expected experiences leaves the developing brain vulnerable to damage. For example, there are sensitive periods during which exposure to certain experiences need to occur. Otherwise, the circuits do not develop normally and the relevant functions do not emerge. The classic example is the effect of experience on the developing visual system, where, for example, exposure to horizontal lines during a certain period is critical, otherwise the animal loses the ability to see horizontal lines later.[11]

In experience-dependent plasticity, the unique experiences of each infant or child affect brain growth. Here, the neural connections are made and reorganized based on the individual's unique experience. For example, being raised in complex environments leads to greater and stronger connections and improved performance. But if a child is exposed to an impoverished environment, deleterious effects are likely.

With this background understanding of genes and gene-environment interactions, we can consider the development of key regions and circuits that are involved in mood and emotion.

DEVELOPMENT OF CIRCUITS INVOLVED IN MOOD

The amygdala steadily develops throughout gestation, and there is evidence that it is well formed and functional at birth.[12] By ten months of age, connections between the amygdala and the cortex are myelinated. This early myelination of the connections between the amygdala and the cortex coincides with the emergence of stranger fear and separation anxiety in infants. Moreover, the development of connections between the amygdala and orbitofrontal cortex (OFC) is related to infants' capacity to recognize facial expressions as they are exposed to social signals.[13] The neural circuitry enabling a child to recognize facial expressions appears to be active early in infancy.[14] Over the course of childhood, the developing amygdala is involved in learning the meaning of facial expressions. This is especially relevant for expressions of fear, anger, and threat. The volume of the amygdala continues to increase during adolescence and into the twenties. Between four and eighteen years of age there is a significant increase in the volume of the right amygdala in boys, but not in girls.[15]

Growth of the prefrontal cortex (PFC) follows a protracted course, and reward-related circuits involving the PFC show marked changes during adolescence.[16] The frontal cortex grows rapidly from mid-childhood until adolescence, mirroring cognitive development and emerging executive functions. Synapses in the PFC proliferate during childhood and on into puberty, and the second wave of reorganization and pruning occurs in adolescence. Myelination also increases into adolescence, and the combined processes lead to improved prefrontal connectivity.[17] Larger volumes of left OFC and hippocampus are associated with higher effortful control or the capacity to constrain behavior in adolescents.[18] We saw in chapter 4 that the anterior cingulate cortex (ACC) is an important region of the PFC, but although it is identifiable at eighteen weeks gestation, little is known about the development of the ACC in humans, except it appears that myelination in the ACC continues throughout life.[19]

The relative rates of development of different regions have interesting implications, as presented by Casey and colleagues.[20] For example, ventromedial areas of the PFC develop earlier than lateral prefrontal areas, suggesting that areas processing meaning, significance, or the impact of events develop before executive control. Furthermore, although connections between the amygdala and the PFC develop rapidly during adolescence, development of the frontal cortex lags behind the amygdala. The protracted development of the PFC is associated with the decrease in impulsivity that occurs with increasing age, spanning across childhood and adolescence, leading to the interesting proposal that greater risk taking in young adolescents relative to children or adults is related to the relatively greater development of the amygdala and associated circuits in early adolescence. A further suggestion is that the nucleus accumbens, involved in reward circuitry, is activated along with the amygdala when adolescents make risky choices and may play a role in risk-taking behavior that is especially high in the presence of peers.[21] Supporting this notion is the observation that when adolescents are engaged in a task where reward is anticipated, relatively greater activation occurs in the nucleus accumbens relative to the prefrontal cortex.

Pubertal influences also come into play. Gonadal steroids regulate neurotransmitters, thereby affecting circuits involving the amygdala and social behavior.[22] The earlier development of the ventromedial PFC relative to lateral PFC areas is dependent on experience and is less influenced by gonadal steroids.[23] The late maturing of prefrontal regions in adolescents (and, therefore, lessened capacity to self-regulate or exercise control) may leave adolescents vulnerable, particularly to the emergence of anxiety.[24]

Neurotransmitter systems regulate circuits and also show developmental patterns. For example, the dopaminergic system develops substantially in adolescence.[25] The developments mirror the pattern of growth and pruning as projections to PFC increase and are pruned. But pruning is less pronounced in the PFC, and this results in a relative dominance of the mesocortical connections, involved in motivation. One result is that the adolescent can now become motivated by more abstract and complex goals and rewards.[26]

The relation of infant characteristics to adult brain function can also be seen in studies of infant temperament. Infant temperament measured as early as four months of age is related to structural differences in the orbital and ventromedial PFC of adults.[27] Infants with low-reactive temperament compared to infants with a highly reactive temperament showed greater thickness of the left OFC, whereas highly reactive infants showed greater thickness in the right ventromedial PFC. Moreover, a highly reactive infant temperament predicts greater amygdala reactivity to novel faces in adults.

GENES AND SUSCEPTIBILITY TO PSYCHOPATHOLOGY

The genes that bring about susceptibility to psychopathology are very common.[28] They are normal alternate gene variations or alleles. The risk associated with these allelic variations is low and is on a continuum rather than acting in an all-or-none fashion. Linking genes to discrete psychiatric disorders, however, is extremely difficult. We have seen how complex mood and emotion are. Behavior also is complex, and psychiatric disorders are heterogeneous, making measurement extremely difficult. Moreover, genes act on molecular and cellular mechanisms of information processing in circuits,[29] and as a result, the effects of genes on behavior are indirect. The next section examines the role of genetic polymorphisms.

Polymorphisms and Neural Circuits

Studies linking common polymorphisms to neurotransmitter function are one widely used pathway relevant to understanding how tuning comes about. The neurotransmitters serotonin and dopamine have been the subject of many studies.[30] For example, a common polymorphism resulting in short and long alleles occurs in the promoter region of the serotonin transporter protein 5-HTT. These alleles, short and long 5-HTT, produce their effects by regulating the amount of serotonin in the synapse, where the efficiency of serotonin regulation is affected by the short allele. Serotonin neurotransmission is also dependent on a monoamine oxidase A (MAOA) enzyme for which polymorphisms exist, one of which produces a low-activity enzyme. Dopamine neurotransmission in the prefrontal cortex is affected by a polymorphism in the gene for an enzyme, catechol-O-methyltransferase (COMT), which inactivates dopamine, potentially affecting cognitive function and decision making. One allele produces a low-activity enzyme. A second key polymorphism occurs in the dopamine D4 receptor and may affect behavior related to reward seeking.

Another way polymorphisms can act is through effects on the amygdala and other brain areas involved in mood and emotion. The short allele of the serotonin transporter protein has been linked to reduced volume of gray matter in the amygdala and cingulate cortex, and it has also been linked to the degree to which the amygdala is activated by negative stimuli and to the degree to which the amygdala is coupled to PFC activation.[31] The low-expression MAOA polymorphism is also associated increased responsivity of the amygdala but reduced reactivity of prefrontal regions.[32] Of further relevance to the idea that our tuning reveals what matters to us and the possibilities in situations, polymorphisms affect the circuitry that underlies responses to fearful and angry facial expressions. For example, those with one or two copies of the short allele of the 5-HTT polymorphism showed greater amygdala activation to threatening facial expressions than did those homozygous for the 5-HTT long allele.[33]

Polymorphisms and Temperament

The complexity of gene-environment interactions can also be seen in the development of temperament and in the role temperament may play in the emergence of disorders. While individual differences in temperament are partly due to genetic influences, the environment plays a large part in determining whether children with a particular temperament get into difficulty or develop a disorder. Moreover, personality development appears to be a lifelong process that is subject to genetic and environmental influences.[34] The environmental influences on personality vary by age and include changing social roles (e.g., entering the workforce, marriage) and individual life experiences. Genetic influences may be more important in the early decades, and environmental factors play a role throughout.

Polymorphisms are relevant to temperament. Individual differences in aspects of temperament have been linked to two important receptors in the brain.[35] Infants who have the short rather than the long allele of the dopamine DRD4 gene are rated by their mothers as higher in negative emotionality at two and twelve months of age, and infants who have the short 5-HTT allele tend to be more behaviorally inhibited and show heightened fear. Infants with the short form of both alleles show more negative emotionality than infants who carry only one risk allele. The principle that genes appear to have indirect effects and that they produce their full effects only in the presence of particular environments is relevant here, and we again see the influence of relationships. The child's relationship with her parents and the parents' socialization practices play an important role in shaping a child's temperament.[36] For example, children who tend to be in negative moods and who are also avoidant and sensitive to punishment do less well if their parents are punitive and rejecting.

CHAPTER 6

WHEN EVENTS THREATEN STABILITY—THE STRESS RESPONSE

I n this book we suggest that moods emerge out of coordinated activity of neural networks that are constantly working as we interact with the world. We examined aspects of the development of circuits and the ways genes and environments function and influence circuits. We now consider what happens when events threaten stability, and how such stressful events shape neural circuits. First, we outline the stress response and key factors that influence the development of the response. We examine the effect the stress response has on neural networks, vulnerability, and resilience. Here we see that relationships with others are among the more profound influences shaping the stress response and, therefore, on the neural circuits and the moods they support. Moreover, we will see how the stress response plays crucial roles in the emergence of individual differences in key systems.

WHAT IS STRESS?

Stress is a subjective sense we have that something adverse is likely to happen and that our well-being is threatened.[1] It is important to note that any event, positive or negative, is potentially a stressor if the event is likely to disrupt a person's overall balance or homeostasis. A change of job or school might be a stress for one person, but not for another. The loss of a loved one or even the possibility of the loss of a relationship that matters to us, or changes in health or status, or expectations placed on us are stresses just as much as are physical threats to safety. Threats may be imminent (the sudden appearance of a snarling dog), requiring immediate action, or they may be in the future (consequences of illness) and require a change in future behavior to prevent something from happening.

Coping with the range of possible threats to well-being requires a system that is flexible and able to mobilize bodily resources. Ideally, the response to threat should not be too easily activated, and it should be capable of turning off and returning to baseline once the threat has receded or has been dealt with. The response should match the event so that we respond to the appropriate degree. In other words, we should not be in a constant state of alertness or vigilance, where we respond to the slightest hint of danger. How well the system is able to achieve these goals reflects our tuning and sets the tone of our everyday behavior.

THE STRESS RESPONSE

A highly coordinated symphony-like system has evolved to deal with events experienced as stressful.[2] Dysfunction in the circuits involved in the stress response system can create vulnerabilities that interact with life events to lead to disorders. However, it is important to remember that most individuals adapt well to stress. This ability to be able to resist stress, or resilience, is equally important to consider and likely involves active neurobiological processes and is not just the absence of vulnerability.[3]

We can look at the overall response to real or potential threats as a two-part system.[4] The first system appraises the threat, scans the environment (including the body or internal environment), and detects and evaluates danger. The system compares the current situation to past situations, decides what to do, and initiates appropriate action. This component employs circuits underlying mood, judgment, and memory, and sets the stage for decision making. Tuning comes into play here, revealing how events appear to us, alerting us to the possibilities present, and paving the way for us to choose among the possibilities and take action. In other words, an emotion may be generated. Fear is the classic example, and we can consider the degree to which we are fearful as the underlying tuning or mood. The second component of the system mobilizes the body for action and uses highly coordinated neurotransmitters, peptides, and hormones. The two components, threat appraisal and stress response, are tightly and reciprocally connected.

When stressful events happen, sensory systems take in information, and a complex array of highly coordinated processes mobilizes the body for action.[5]

The stress response system is regulated so that the system can return to baseline once the threat is dealt with. This counterbalancing prevents us from living in a constant state of fear and vigilance. However, events can alter the response system such that it overshoots, does not return to baseline, or is too easily evoked or exaggerated.

The key elements of the stress response originate (figs. 6.3 and 6.4) at the level of the anterior cingulate cortex (ACC), orbitofrontal cortex (OFC), amygdala, and hippocampus, areas we have seen are involved in processing of information, assigning affective significance, memory, and decision making. Signals from these regions are sent to the *hypothalamus*, where responses are integrated and coordinated. The hypothalamus utilizes two main systems to orchestrate the response, and both use products secreted by the adrenal glands.

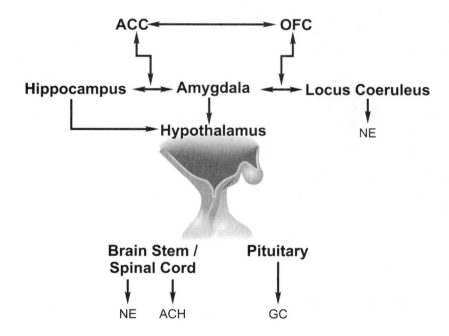

Figure 6.3. Illustrates the regions involved in regulating the stress response. Regions have reciprocal interactions. Output from the hypothalamus to the brain stem/spinal cord and pituitary are illustrated. (Figure created by Dave Cantrell, Biomedical Communications, University of Arizona Health Sciences.)

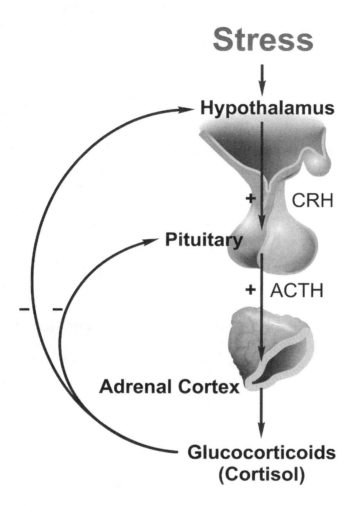

Figure 6.4. Illustrates the HPA (hypothalamic-pituitary-adrenal) axis and feedback loops. (Figure created by Dave Cantrell, Biomedical Communications, University of Arizona Health Sciences.)

The first component is the *sympathetic-adrenomedullary system* (SAM), which, as its name suggests, uses the sympathetic division of the autonomic nervous system (ANS). The sympathetic system prepares the body for action when a threat is perceived and helps regulate the flight-or-fight response pattern. It does this by stimulating the medulla of the adrenal gland to secrete adrenaline (epinephrine). Adrenaline increases the blood supply to the brain and muscles, and increases glucose necessary to supply energy. The second division of the ANS, the parasympathetic system, which under normal conditions maintains physiological function—e.g., resting heart rate—counterbalances the SAM system response. The locus coeruleus (LC) (chapter 4) releases norepinephrine throughout the brain leading to increased vigilance and arousal, and helps direct attention toward what is immediately important.[6]

The second component is the *hypothalamic-pituitary-adrenal* (HPA) system (fig. 6.4), which, as its name implies, connects the hypothalamus to the adrenal gland via the pituitary gland. Corticotrophin-releasing hormone (CRH) from the hypothalamus causes the pituitary gland to release adrenocorticotropic hormone (ACTH), and ACTH in turn activates the adrenal glands to release cortisol, a glucocorticoid. Cortisol is widely known as the stress hormone. Glucocorticoids enter cells in the brain as well as the body. They act on two receptor types, glucocorticoid and mineralocorticoid receptors. Crucially, these receptors regulate the transcription and expression of genes. In other words, they influence the production of proteins and therefore can change the structure of circuit components. As a result, the effects of the HPA system response are slower and last longer than the effects of the sympathetic system response. The HPA response, like the SAM response, is counterbalanced. Once cortisol reaches a certain level and the threat has receded or been dealt with, a series of feedback loops attempt to rebalance the system. The feedback may be immediate or delayed, and it is mediated through receptor effects in the hippocampus and medial prefrontal cortex.

REGULATING THE STRESS RESPONSE

The amygdala, hippocampus, and OFC modulate the stress response.[7] This means that the circuits involved in mood are integrally involved. Corticotrophin-releasing hormone is the crucial mediator. For example, CRH expressed in the amygdala is involved in both the SAM response and the HPA response. It seems to be particularly important in activating long-term fear responses, and it also influences the LC. The LC may enhance the role of the amygdala, resulting in a more intense fear response, while lowering the threshold for the amygdala to respond, thus making it easier for future threats to activate the amygdala. The LC also helps regulate the SAM system through the actions of norepinephrine.

Input from areas of the prefrontal cortex (PFC) reduces the reactivity of the amygdala and LC. The parasympathetic system also reduces the reactivity of the amygdala and LC. Further counterbalancing occurs through the action of neurotransmitters. Both the HPA axis response and the sympathetic nervous system response are under the influence of serotonin and gamma-aminobutyric acid (GABA). Serotonin activates the system, and GABA inhibits it. Without these counterbalancing forces, the child or adult could well be in a constant state of threat. Moreover, if rebalancing does not happen and stress continues, the HPA activity and continuing glucocorticoid production can damage organs, leading to a variety of medical disorders.[8] Reactivity to threat rests on how well these activating and counterbalancing influences function, and individual differences in how activation and counterbalancing occurs are an integral part of the structure of tuning. How does this come about?

DEVELOPMENT OF THE STRESS RESPONSE

As discussed in chapters 4 and 5, developmental events and genetic influences shape the development of the brain regions that comprise the circuits determining how the threat appraisal system functions. The stress response system also has a developmental course. As in the case of the circuits underlying the threat response system, early life events interact with genetic influences to shape the developing stress response system, setting the stage for how the system responds to future as well as immediate threats. Individual differences in the responsivity of the stress response system, therefore, become part of the child's—and later the adult's—unique tuning.

In adults, cortisol levels rise at night and begin to fall from high levels in the morning to low levels in the afternoon/evening. While this pattern emerges early, it does not begin to appear in infants until they are about three months of age, and it does not resemble the adult pattern until after the infant gives up daytime naps.[9]

Until the infant is about three months of age, cortisol typically increases in response to acute stresses such as physical examinations (blood draws), however, over the next year or so cortisol does not increase even if the infant is distressed.[10] As discussed further below, this pattern is dependent on the security of the relationship with caregivers and how supportive caregivers are. Cortisol will increase and match behavioral distress in infants who are insecurely attached. Secure infants may cry and fuss, but without increases in cortisol. The basal level of cortisol rises throughout childhood into adolescence, until increased cortisol responses to stress become more like the pattern in adults.

RELATIONSHIPS AND THE STRESS RESPONSE

Recall that we always find ourselves in situations where things matter to us, and our situations involve others around us. It turns out that relationships, beginning in earliest infancy, play an important role in the stress response and underlying circuitry. A series of studies by Gunnar and colleagues show that significant change occurs in how reactive the HPA system is in the first two years of life, and there are important individual differences in the degree of cortisol response. More specifically, the quality of maternal care is among the important influences on how stress affects neural circuits. These studies are outlined in the following paragraphs.[11]

Early in the first year, cortisol levels increase when an infant is stressed, e.g., by being taken to well-baby checkups or given inoculations. Over the next year or so, brief separations or doctor visits result in progressively less change in cortisol until little or no increase is detected at about fifteen months of age. Even though the infant may cry and fuss and show behavioral evidence of distress, cortisol levels do not rise. Cortisol levels begin to rise again in response to stress in later childhood into early adolescence. But some infants show little or no change in cortisol, whereas others show a marked and easily elicited response.

The presence of a parent (caregiver) is critical to the degree to which cortisol increases. The crucial factor seems to be a secure attachment relationship and supportive caregiving. Sensitive, responsive, and supportive care produces minimal or no HPA axis response and offsets the effect of stress. Less sensitive and less supportive care is associated with greater cortisol responses. The temperament of the child may also play a role, and the role temperament plays may also be dependent on the available environmental support.[12] For example, behaviorally inhibited children may show increased cortisol levels when entering daycare or in laboratory settings. Children rated as having a negative emotional temperament seem to have a more robust cortisol response when they are in unsupportive caregiving situations.

The influence of relationships on the developing stress response system is also evident in the effects of maternal distress. The influence of maternal distress may be seen as early as prenatal life,[13] as maternal anxiety and depression during pregnancy is related to offspring cortisol levels throughout childhood. Maternal distress during the child's infancy may also shape the reactivity of the stress response in ways that influence reactivity during later childhood and adolescence.[14] For example, children whose mothers were stressed during the child's infancy showed higher cortisol levels later in childhood. Maternal depression in the child's first year is also related to higher cortisol levels in preschool children and even as late as early adolescence. These changes also predict adolescents' depression.

Moreover, the influence of social relationships on cortisol responses goes beyond the immediate family. Peer relationships also elicit cortisol responses, possibly because of the challenges these relationships pose.[15] For example, children who are rejected and those who are neglected by peers show elevated cortisol levels.

Finally, the impact of relationships on the development and function of the stress response system is evident in the effects of neglect and deprivation. Severe deprivation and neglect is associated with reduced cortisol levels.[16] Severe neglect has also been associated with diminished diurnal variation in cortisol and low resting cortisol. These findings are significant because a diminished stress response and low cortisol are associated with certain forms of disruptive and antisocial behavior characterized by callous and unemotional behavior. This topic will be examined further in chapter 11.

STRESS AND NEURAL CIRCUITS

Baram et al. suggest that fragmentation and unpredictability of early life experience, specifically maternal sensory signals, may sufficiently alter developing circuits to lead to vulnerability or resilience to later disorders.[17] While these suggestions are based on animal data, they are relevant to our discussion. Acute and chronic stress may have different effects on neural circuits and the processes they serve.[18] Chronic stress or adversity may be particularly important in affecting circuitry and hence tuning. While acute stress may enhance learning, the functional effects of chronic stress may include increased sensitivity of the stress response, and later events may more easily trigger the stress response. Early adverse life events may also blunt the stress axis response. As noted above, we will see in chapter 11 that early adversity and low cortisol response can be associated with antisocial behavior, whereas increased HPA axis responses are associated with depression (chapter 9). But one interesting recent study found that when healthy young adults without psychiatric illness were given a laboratory stress test involving public speaking and arithmetic, those who had experienced more stressful events (separation or loss of a parent) before age fifteen showed blunted heart rate and cortisol responses.[19] Thus, the effects of early adversity may be linked not just to risk but to resilience.[20]

The timing of stress during development also influences how the response system is affected. There may be early sensitive periods when stress-induced glucocorticoids damage specific structures, e.g., by reducing volume or interfering with synaptic reorganization.[21] The greatest impact occurs if structures are developing at the time the stress occurs. There are also important developmental differences in the growth of areas important to the stress response.

Besides affecting the SAM and HPA responses, corticolimbic structures are also affected. These effects could set the stage for anxiety and depression. Stress affects the growth of the amygdala and is linked to increases in amygdala volume and size. Studies using functional magnetic resonance imaging (fMRI) have shown that early maltreatment is associated with adults with increased excitability of the amygdala in response to negative but not positive facial expressions.[22] Hyperresponsiveness of the amygdala could bias attention to negative situations. Similar findings have been reported in children and adolescents with a history of early deprivation or neglect.[23] Chronic stress may activate the amygdala, as well as the bed nucleus of the stria terminalis (BNST),[24] and appears to enhance synaptic plasticity and the function of amygdala neurons.[25] This enhancement may lead to faster and more intense responding by the amygdala in the face of threat.

Early stressful experiences or chronic, repeated stress can reduce the volume of the hippocampus, impair synaptic plasticity, and damage the ability of the hippocampus to produce new neurons.[26] This may be one way early life stress becomes linked with vulnerability to depression. For example, both depressed adolescents and adolescents at risk of depression because they had a depressed parent had significantly smaller hippocampal volumes than control subjects.[27] Adverse early life events were associated with smaller hippocampal volumes.

Both acute and chronic stress affect the PFC, resulting in cognitive changes found in mood disorders, including distractibility, inattentiveness, and memory difficulties.[28] Moreover, chronic stress may damage the structure of neurons and/or affect neuroplasticity in the PFC and leave the individual susceptible to the influence of later events.

Adolescents exposed to early and continuing adversity show higher base-line cortisol levels and more pronounced responses to stress.[29] There is evidence that early continuing stress alters gray matter volume and neuronal integrity in the frontal cortex of adolescents and reduces the volume of the ACC. Healthy adults who experienced more than two early adverse events (e.g., loss of a parent, witnessed domestic violence) showed reduced volumes of the ACC and caudate nucleus.[30]

RESILIENCE AND VULNERABILITY

Although vulnerability models have been the dominant force in child psychiatry, interest is increasingly focused on resilience and related concepts.[31] Vulnerabilities can be viewed as the attributes or ways of functioning that lead a person to have a poor outcome when stressors occur.[32] There are many ways to think of how someone might be vulnerable or susceptible to stress. Vulnerabilities could be biological (illness, genetic), social (not having friends), cognitive (tending to think negatively), or related to mood (tending to be sad or irritable). Having a particular temperament (tending to be in negative moods, being avoidant or sensitive to punishment) could be a form of vulnerability. On the other hand, resilience is defined after the fact. Rutter defines resilience as reduced vulnerability to environmental risk experiences, the overcoming of a stress or adversity, or a relatively good outcome in the face of risk experiences in comparison to others facing similar adversity.[33] There is no resilience without adversity or risk. Resilience results from the interaction with the risk environment. Like vulnerability, resilience can be described in terms of characteristics of the individual and the underlying neurobiological characteristics. Because of this, both vulnerability and resilience can be viewed through the lens of tuning. A variety of psychosocial characteristics have been identified in resilient children: positive emotions, optimism, social competence, the ability to regulate emotions, flexible thinking, being open to and able to use social support, a tendency to view events as less threatening, and the ability to reframe or reappraise events.[34] In adults, resilience is associated with spirituality, having a moral compass, and having a purpose in life (all of which emerge in youth).

Studies in primates, children, and young adults suggest "steeling" or strengthening effects in the development of resilience.[35] Although exposure to stress or adversity in some individuals may lead to vulnerability because the events have a sensitizing effect such that later events lead to distress or dysfunction, in others adversities may lead to a strengthening effect. Children who are successful in overcoming an adverse event may develop a sense of efficacy that changes their outlook and enables them to better surmount later events. We might argue that this is a function of tuning. For any given child, the child's tuning will reveal the possibilities in situations as they come up. What the child chooses to do in the context of the available supports and the child's ability to take advantage of the supports will determine the outcome.

Viewing resilience as a dynamic and ongoing process has significant implications for concepts of both mental and physical wellness, and once again relationships are key.[36] Being resilient, that is, being able to maintain a purpose in life, use social support, and maintain competence while remaining positive and flexible in terms of attitudes, rests on having positive ties to others.

GENE-ENVIRONMENT INTERACTIONS AND ADVERSITY

Gene-environment interactions are central to understanding the role of adversity. A key finding is that being reared in adverse environments, e.g., exposure to distress in a parent or abuse by a parent is critical in determining if children with risk alleles become depressed, anxious, or aggressive. For example, one notable study found that the short version of the serotonin transporter gene is associated with the onset of depression in children, but only for children exposed earlier to adverse life events.[37] Despite controversy that has risen, it appears that the effect is real, particularly for early maltreatment.[38]

Diathesis stress models for various disorders are the mainstay of many current formulations, pulling together the multiple influences involved in how disorders could come about. The basic idea is that each individual has vulnerabilities that interact with stress to increase the vulnerabilities or act as a trigger leading to dysfunction.[39]

These models, however, tend to focus on the negative, and there is a case to be made that there has been too much focus on the negative side. It may not just be a story of inevitable negative outcomes for at-risk children: the outcome can be much more positive if they are exposed to positive, nurturing environments.[40] For example, while children with risk alleles (e.g., the DRD4 gene) who were exposed to insensitive mothering showed later behavior problems, those with the risk allele exposed to sensitive mothers showed the fewest problems. This evidence suggests that while some children are most at risk in negative environments, they may also be more likely to have positive outcomes if they are exposed to positive environments. Infants rated as having difficult temperaments at six months show more behavior problems in early childhood if they experience poor parenting, but they show fewer behavior problems and more social skills than other children if they are exposed to higher-quality parenting or daycare. Another example found that highly fearful fifteen-month-old infants experiencing coercive paternal behavior were more likely to cheat at a task at thirty-six months, but if they received caring, nurturing parenting they were the most likely to follow rules.[41] These studies suggest that plasticity allows the possibility for positive outcomes given the right environment or intervention.

These results led to the view that there is also a positive side to plasticity, that while most research has focused on the vulnerability in the effects of negative environments, vulnerable children placed in positive environments may actually do very well.[42] Recently researchers have combined two independently derived theories of how and why some children are not only susceptible to stressful environments where they do badly, but they also seem to be highly susceptible to positive environments where they may do unusually well.

The first of the biological sensitivity to context theories was based on observations that differences in children's autonomic and adrenocortical reactivity to stress identified children who did poorly in adverse environments but did unusually well in positive environments.[43] Other evidence showed that some sensitive, avoidant children subject to negative moods showed more problems when exposed to negative parenting, but did very well in nurturing environments. Similarly, some infants with difficult temperaments at six months showed more behavior problems in early childhood if they experienced poor parenting, but they showed fewer behavior problems and better social skills than other children if exposed to higher-quality parenting or daycare.[44] These researchers developed the differential susceptibility theory, which argues that differential susceptibility to rearing environments is an evolutionary adaptation to hedge bets where the future is uncertain.

A recent study examined the relationship of the way a child and teacher interact in first grade to the development of depression and anxiety by seventh grade. These researchers studied behavioral (temperamental inhibition or disin-hibition) and physiological markers. While they did not find clear support for differential susceptibility in the case of the physiological markers, they found clear support using the indicators of temperament. They suggested that the salient aspects of social environments differ with the temperament of the child, and these aspects of the environment are most salient because they are the ones to which the child is "most attuned and responsive."[45] This approach suggests that genetic influences are on susceptibility to environments and experience and not just on vulnerability.[46]

CHAPTER 7

ISSUES IN PSYCHIATRIC DIAGNOSIS

CATEGORICAL VS. DIMENSIONAL APPROACHES

Before discussing clinical disorders we need to first sketch some background issues in psychiatric diagnosis.[1] Psychiatric diagnoses are based on the presence or absence of certain signs and symptoms essentially obtained by taking a history and examining the person concerned. The diagnostic system in current use is a categorical system, meaning that someone does or does not have a disorder. The categories are based on clinical similarities because we do not know either the underlying mechanisms or what causes disorders. Committees of experts drawn from research and clinical disciplines decide the categories, and they are field tested and reviewed by clinicians and others before they are finalized, and a manual is produced and made available. As such, the manual, the *Diagnostic and Statistical Manual of Mental Disorders* (*DSM*), is a bridge between researchers and clinicians that serves as a clinical tool to help clinicians decide the categories that best fit the particular symptoms a person presents with, and it also serves as a research tool to continue to refine the clinical, epidemiological, and etiological understanding of the various disorders.[2] The impetus for the current system in large part came from the Washington University School,[3] which emphasized delineating disorders by clinical description, family history, course, and outcome as a means of getting to the etiology of disorders. Currently the *DSM* is in transition from *DSM-IV-TR*[4] to its fifth iteration, the *DSM-5*.[5]

The basic format is that each disorder has a core criteria of which one or more must be present and a set of additional criteria of which a certain number must be present in order for a diagnosis to be made. A person may have as many diagnoses as criteria present warrant. The *DSM-IV-TR* is a multiaxial system that takes into account personality, medical conditions, environmental influences, and overall level of functioning. Axis I is the primary diagnosis, axis II is for any personality disorders present, axis III is for any medical conditions, axis IV is for environmental variables, and axis V is a measure of global severity.

One significant problem with the current approach is that criteria are treated as equivalent so that any two persons with the same diagnosis—for example, depression—might have quite different symptoms. A second problem is that the boundaries between diagnostic classes are often unclear and are rarely mutually exclusive.[6] A person may meet criteria for more than one disorder, and typically does. This comorbidity may not represent how things are in nature but may in part be an outcome of the way the diagnostic system is set up. Other problems are that variations in severity in the different phases of a disorder are not taken into account, nor is etiology(with few exceptions) taken into account. It is also difficult to incorporate the developmental nature of many disorders or the burgeoning influence of research findings in neuroscience.

The categorical approach focuses on the disorder. The objective is to determine which if any disorders are present. With the recent changes in health-care delivery, where clinicians often have little time with the patient, it is easy to reduce the diagnostic workup to checking items off on a list in order to fit the person into a diagnostic category and then pick a treatment (medication or therapy or both) to fit that diagnosis.

The *DSM-5* represents an attempt to move away from a predominantly categorical system and to include dimensional aspects of disorders. Why dimensions? A growing body of research suggests an alternative view of the underlying structure of psychopathology. Studies in children[7] and adults[8] suggest that two broad correlated dimensions underlie psychopathology. An internalizing factor includes depression and anxiety, and an externalizing factor includes antisocial personality disorder, conduct disorder, and substance abuse. The internalizing factor can be broken down into distress disorders (major depression, dysthymia, and generalized anxiety disorder), and fear disorders that include the other anxiety disorders. Furthermore, there is evidence from twin studies in adults that two genetic factors load on the internalizing and externalizing dimensions, and that environmental experiences load on three factors.

The dimensional approach brings certain implications and advantages over the categorical approach.[9] The focus of the dimensional approach is on the individual components or symptoms, how they relate to each other, and on the degree of severity. The origin of the symptoms and how they came to be rather than the category in which the individuals can be placed become the focus. It opens the door to bringing etiology into the equation, improves the understanding of comorbidity or co-occurrence of disorders, allows scaling of symptoms, and more readily allows a developmental perspective. In other words, the emphasis is no longer on the disorder but on the person and the implications and consequences of the disorder for that person. Individual differences can now be a focus, and factors leading not only to susceptibility but also to resilience can be taken into account. This approach more readily leads to choosing a form of therapy and a treatment plan tailored to the individual.

DSM-IV-TR AND *DSM-5*

The fifth edition of the *DSM* (*DSM-5*) is the current version. There are significant changes from the previous edition, the *DSM-IV-TR*, and they are indicated where relevant in chapters 8–11 of this book. The changes reflect the accumulated new research or attempts to clarify areas of particular clinical difficulty and relevance.[10]

The *DSM-5* incorporates aspects of the dimensional approach by providing for various specifiers that can be added. For example, specifying the degree to which anxiety is present in depression. The axis format is abandoned, some new disorders have been added in the chapters on mood disorders, and some disorders previously in the mood disorders or anxiety disorders chapters have been moved to their own chapters. The section of *DSM-IV-TR* on disorders specific to childhood has been eliminated. Instead, these disorders appear in their own relevant chapter, e.g., anxiety or depression, or as separate chapters. Thus, the developmental nature of disorders is acknowledged.

With regard to anxiety disorders, obsessive-compulsive disorder has been placed in its own section along with related disorders, such as trichotillomania, and with another new disorders characterized by hoarding behavior. Post-traumatic stress disorder has also been moved out of the anxiety disorders section, and is now grouped with other trauma and stress related disorders. These changes reflect the emerging evidence of the unique circuitry involved in these conditions. A third major change is that agoraphobia has been separated from panic attacks, and panic attacks are now included as a specifier across the range of anxiety disorders. A fourth major change is that separation anxiety disorder is no longer viewed as specific to childhood and is now included with anxiety disorders to acknowledge that it occurs in adults.

There are also significant changes to the chapter on depression. One change acknowledges that depression can be severe and persistent, and replaces the old diagnosis of dysthymia as a separate disorder with a new diagnosis of persistent depressive disorder. This new entity captures both dysthymia and chronic forms of major depression. A second new disorder is disruptive mood dysregulation disorder. This diagnosis applies to children who display extreme irritability without the mood changes characteristic of bipolar disorder. This change is proving to be controversial. In the *DSM-IV-TR*, the presence of grief could exclude the diagnosis of major depressive disorder, but this exclusion has been removed in the *DSM-5*. The intent here is to allow those experiencing severe and persistent depression following bereavement to be diagnosed and treated. Clinicians will have a "mixed-state" specifier for situations where symptoms of depression and mania are both present. A specifier is also added for severity of any anxiety present. Bipolar disorder is no longer included with depression but has its own chapter, and the criteria now include both changes in mood and changes in activity or energy.

In contrast to *DSM-IV-TR*, in which attention deficit hyperactivity disorder was grouped with oppositional and conduct disorder as disruptive disorders, a new chapter recognizes oppositional, conduct, and impulse-control disorders as disorders reflecting problems in emotional and behavioral control, and so groups them together. Also, antisocial personality disorder is placed with them (as well as with personality disorders), thus recognizing the developmental connections.

OVERVIEW OF CLINICAL CHAPTERS

Chapters 8–11 of this book discuss anxiety disorders, depression, bipolar disorders, and disruptive/antisocial disorders. The focus is on children and adolescents, but reference to adult studies are made as needed to show relevance. The chapters are organized around a common formulation based on the notion of tuning. The idea is that each person has a unique tuning (moods and associated neural circuitry), formed by genes and environments interacting during development, and that is the substrate for how they experience the world. Tuning may be the basis for vulnerability that leads to disorders involving mood when events threaten well-being, or they may become the basis of resilience. Multiple influences may play a role, and among influences relationships are critical. While there are common pathways, each individual has his or her unique tuning, experience, genetic influences that interact with the threat/stress response system in forming tuning. Each person is more or less fearful, more or less timid, more or less unhappy, and what evokes timidity or fear in one may not trouble another. Everyone has these moods and dispositions, but each has his own unique complement that are the basis of personality and that determine how a person will fare. Disorders arise if these systems are dysfunctional and stressful events occur. Life events and stress play similar roles across the disorders, but the nature of the threat plays a role shaping the response. Gene-environment interactions are similarly crucial, with certain polymorphisms involved across disorders.

The chapters are organized to examine disorders through the lens of tuning and to trace how mood and neurobiological circuits relate to the many aspects of the disorder. The core issues in each disorder category are identified and sketch how development, life events, genetic influences, and relationships interact with the underlying neural circuits and lead to the emergence of the various disorders.

We can think of disorders as having certain components. Each disorder has typical moods and different emotions associated with those moods. For example, there is fearfulness and then fear in anxiety. Each is also associated with typical actions and behaviors (e.g., avoidance in anxiety, diminished activity in depression, excessive activity in mania, aggression in antisocial behavior), cognitions (e.g., judgments about others, negative thinking, changes in attention), and physiological changes (heart rate, breathing, or gastrointestinal changes) that go along with the actions. Note that these are also the components of an emotion. This also reflects themes of the book. Tuning is the substrate such that when something happens, assessments and judgments are made (cognitions), preparation for action occurs (physiological changes), and some form of action is taken.

For example, some develop anxiety disorders because they are fearful, worry, and readily experience fear. Experience leads them to have difficulty learning to distinguish signals of safety from those signaling threat, and they fail to suppress these associations when there is no longer a threat, and consequently they avoid situations (chapter 8, anxiety disorders). Others tend to be sad, irritable, and unhappy, and become vulnerable to the loss of and threats to relationships, whether with others or relationships reflecting personal agency. They become sad, depressed, lose interest, and withdraw (chapter 9, depression). Others show signs of dysregulation of systems underlying drive, goal seeking, and positive emotions, and events related to personal commitment and effort may lead to elation, high energy, sleep disturbance, and increased activity and impulsivity (chapter 10, bipolar disorders). Others may readily perceive threats and respond with aggression. They may be indifferent to the situation of others and appear unmoved by consequences of their actions, or are motivated to act by their own uncomfortable mood (chapter 11, disruptive/antisocial disorders).

Since the chapters address investigations of brain function, some cautions are in order regarding methodological issues common to all. All the issues are amplified in youth because of changes due to development. Disorders are heterogeneous, and subjects may vary considerably in their symptoms. For example, whether a person is currently depressed or euthymic, in a first episode or with a history of multiple episodes, is medicated or unmedicated are all variables that may influence results. Years of illness might well change how circuits are involved. The likely presence of comorbid disorders also presents significant problems. Efforts to understand the circuits involved in bipolar disorder, for example, are complicated by the fact that the classic disorder has three phases. Subjects might be manic, depressed, or euthymic. Further complications are presented by hypomania, mixed states, previous episodes, medication, and comorbid disorders.

Another major issue is the type of task being used in imaging studies, as the nature of the task will engage different circuits to different degrees. Some tasks may involve judgments or decisions about faces showing emotion (fear, sadness) or neutral expressions. Other tasks are cognitive with no overt emotional content, but may be designed to frustrate or challenge the subject. What the subject is asked to do is a critical variable.

CHAPTER 8

WHEN MOODS ARE WORRIED AND FEARFUL— ANXIETY DISORDERS

Julie, an eight-year-old girl, worries all the time. She is often fearful and irritable. Bed times are protracted, and she insists her mother stay with her until she falls asleep. She often comes to her parents' room at night. She delays in the morning and consequently is often late for school. She worries that something will happen to her mother. She talks about a school friend whose parents recently divorced. While in school she complains of stomachaches and, almost daily, has to go to the nurse's office. Julie's mother has been treated for depression and had been anxious as a child.

Frank is a sixteen-year-old adolescent male. For some time he has been troubled by thoughts that keep intruding into his mind. Often these are images of something bad happening, such as a car accident. He worries that some contaminant has gotten on his hands. He washes multiple times a day to the extent that his hands are now excessively dry and chapped. He finds he is unable to finish his homework because he has an urge to keep checking his math. The result is he often fails to complete his assignments. He is also starting to feel that he has to perform particular actions when he sees certain numbers or letters. He has family members who are anxious.

The above vignettes describe typical presentations of anxiety, and variations on these stories can be found across the lifespan. Anxiety disorders are extremely common. Almost 30 percent of people have an anxiety disorder at some point in their lives, and most anxious adults first experience symptoms in childhood.[1] Anxiety disorders are the most common psychiatric disorders in youth. At any given time, 2.5–5 percent of children and adolescents have one or other anxiety disorder, the risk in females is twice that in males, and from 40–60 percent of anxious children have more than one anxiety disorder.[2] The twelve-month prevalence of any anxiety disorder in adolescents is 25 percent.[3] A child diagnosed with an anxiety disorder is likely to continue to meet criteria for that disorder as he or she grows into adolescence, and many continue to have anxiety as an adult.

Anxiety disorders are very common in family members (see below), and this has implications for how anxiety is transmitted in families. Moreover, they often accompany other disorders, especially depression. This is true in both adults and youth. Depression and anxiety overlap significantly in youth, and anxious youth are very likely to have depressive disorders as adults.[4] Almost 60 percent of adults who ever have depression also have an anxiety disorder.[5]

What is anxiety about? Anxiety is concerned with present or future threats of harm and may have evolved to help detect or deal with threats to life.[6] Although a quick reading of the vignettes suggests that anxiety disorders are distinct and different, closer examination reveals worry and fear as the central issues. We can distinguish worry and fear based on future or present concerns (chapter 3). Worry is concerned with preparing for future possibilities, and appears as repetitive, intrusive thinking about negative and aversive things that can but probably will not happen.[7] Fear is an alarm response elicited by the actual confrontation with some event or thing.[8]

Worry and fear can be moods, i.e., feelings that are not about something specific. They can be a vague feeling of unease or fearfulness. But worry and fear have the characteristics of emotion when they are about something specific. Here, they are reactions to something, e.g., a threat (angry dog); they involve judgment (I am in danger), physiological changes (heart racing, sweating), and action (avoidant behavior). There may be fear of a particular object or situation (e.g., animals, the dark, heights), fear of losing control, fear of social occasions or situations where performance is expected. For others, there is excessive worry about real-life circumstances or catastrophes, war or disasters. Some children and adults may experience excessive anxiety about separation from others. Worry and fear are often found together, of course, as are the feelings of being uneasy or fearful. The anxiety disorders have common physiological elements that are the bodily changes involved in preparation for action needed to deal with threat, i.e., increased heart rate, shortness of breath, muscular tension. Finally, the actions typically chosen in anxiety are avoidance of and withdrawal from situations.

Our working premise (chapters 2 and 3) is that tuning as a construct refers to mood as the felt aspect of how we are in the world, and is a phase of the activity of neural circuits and body systems through which we experience the world and its possibilities. Anxiety as a mood is the felt aspect of a complex neurobiological system whose job is to help detect, anticipate, and avoid danger. It's like a radar system that is always switched on, and most people most of the time are unaware it is there until it begins to signal. Some individuals are more prone to be fearful and worried, and are overly sensitive to possible threats, with the result they are more likely to respond with fear in the face of threat. The system is tuned too high, responds too quickly, is slow to shut off, or too readily associates cues with danger. The resulting tendency toward worry and fearfulness becomes a controlling factor and the lens through which they experience the world. The result may be pervasive anxiety, hypervigilance, fear, constant worrying, and avoidance and withdrawal from activities, as a result of failure to distinguish signals of safety and signals of threat, and failure to recognize when danger has passed.[9]

HOW ARE ANXIETY DISORDERS CLASSIFIED?

The following descriptions broadly reflect the descriptions provided in *DSM-IV-TR*[10] and *DSM-5*.[11] The descriptions are not intended to be complete but highlight the mood, emotion, physiological, and action components to show the common pattern.

Panic attacks refer to discrete periods of intense fear or discomfort that reach a peak within ten minutes. The fear may be of losing control. Panic disorder is diagnosed if frequent attacks recur unexpectedly and are accompanied by worry or concern about having another attack or about the implications or consequences of an attack. Palpitations, sweating, and dizziness are typically present. Behavior may change significantly. Panic disorder is more unusual in childhood, and the typical age of onset for panic disorder is late adolescence or early adulthood.

Agoraphobia refers to worry and fear about being in places or situations from which escape might be difficult or embarrassing, or where help may not be available should a panic attack arise. The result is avoidance of situations, and agoraphobic adults may feel that they cannot leave their home. Agoraphobia is no longer coupled with panic attacks in the *DSM-5*, a change from the *DSM-IV-TR* that recognizes that agoraphobia often occurs in the absence of panic.

Specific phobia refers to a persistent, unreasonable fear of a particular object or situation, such as animals, the dark, heights, or medical procedures. Intense anxiety and fear or panic-like responses occur in the presence of the threatening event or thing or even when the event is anticipated. Again, the action chosen is avoidance. Phobic adults recognize their fear is unreasonable, but children may not.

In social phobia, the fear is of social or performance situations in which embarrassment may occur. Anhedonia or lack of interest or pleasure in activities may be present in addition to worry and fear. Children, again, may not recognize that their fear is excessive or unreasonable. Situations are avoided or endured with great distress, leading to significant impairment in functioning. Feared situations can be restricted to particular activities, but they can be generalized to a variety of situations.

Generalized anxiety refers to excessive worry about real-life circumstances that is present more days than not for at least six months. Irritability may be present in addition to worry and fear. Children and adolescents may worry about performance or competence at school or sports. But they may also worry about catastrophes, war, or earthquakes. Difficulty in concentrating is common, and it is difficult to control the worries. Physiological symptoms may include accelerated heart rate and sweating. Fatigue, disturbed sleep, restlessness, and muscle tension may be associated. In the case of children, only one physiological symptom is required for diagnosis, but three are required in adults.

The essential feature of separation anxiety disorder is excessive anxiety regarding separation from home or attachment figures. In the case of children the anxiety is developmentally inappropriate. Previously classified as a childhood disorder, it is now recognized in adults. Features include worrying about possible harm to or about losing key attachment figures; excessive worry that something bad will lead to being separated from a major attachment figure, such as being kidnapped or getting lost. Physical symptoms can include headaches, stomachaches, or other symptoms when separation is anticipated or imminent. Active resistance and signs of distress are commonly seen. Children may refuse to go to school or elsewhere if separation is involved. Commonly children become reluctant to sleep alone and refuse to remain in their own bedroom.

Obsessive-compulsive disorder (OCD) and post-traumatic stress disorder (PTSD) are grouped with the anxiety disorders in *DSM-IV-TR*, but they have been given their own chapters in the *DSM-5*. This revision acknowledges that the anxiety disorders have to do with fear circuitry, and OCD and PTSD have their own patterns of neural dysfunction. However, marked anxiety and distress are common.

Obsessive-compulsive disorder refers to the presence of recurrent obsessions or compulsions that take up more than an hour a day or that cause significant distress or impairment. Obsessions refer to persistent ideas, thoughts, impulses, or images that are experienced as intrusive and inappropriate and cause marked anxiety or distress. Common obsessions include recurrent thoughts about contamination, doubts, needing to have things in a particular order, aggressive impulses, or sexual images. The person may avoid touching doorknobs or shaking hands. Compulsions are repetitive behaviors that are designed to prevent anxiety or distress. The aim of the compulsion is often to reduce the stress of an obsession or to prevent some dreaded event or situation from happening. Typical compulsions include excessive hand washing, repeatedly checking whether a door was locked or a light was turned off, the need to count a certain number of times or repeat some other action, such as tying and untying a shoe. The behaviors are often done in secret. Avoidant behavior commonly results as the person seeks to avoid situations where they feel they may be exposed to contaminants.

Acute stress disorder refers to the development of characteristic anxiety, dissociative, and other symptoms within one month after exposure to an extreme traumatic stressor. This is also placed along with PTSD in a new chapter of the *DSM-5* and not with the anxiety disorders. Symptoms of acute stress are brief, lasting no more than four weeks. The precipitating events, which may be directly experienced or witnessed, involve actual or threatened death or serious injury, or a threat to the physical integrity of self or others. During or after experiencing the distressing event, the individual also experiences at least three indicators of dissociative symptoms that may include a sense of numbing or detachment, reduction in awareness of surroundings, derealization or depersonalization, or failing to recall important features of the event. The event is also persistently reexperienced as recurrent images, thoughts, dreams, or flashback episodes, or as a sense of reliving the experience. Stimuli that arouse memories of the traumatic event are avoided, and symptoms of anxiety or increased arousal are present.

PTSD essentially refers to an acute stress reaction that persists for more than four weeks. Characteristic symptoms follow exposure to an extreme traumatic event that involves actual or threatened death or serious injury or other threats to a person's physical integrity. PTSD may also result from witnessing such an event or learning about the experience of a family member or close associate. In children, there may be disorganized or agitated behavior, repetitive play that expresses themes or aspects of the trauma, frightening dreams without recognizable content, or trauma-specific reenactment may occur.

ANXIETY DISORDERS AND NEURAL CIRCUITS

Underlying the features of the anxiety disorders are dysfunctions in neural circuitry, especially circuits related to fear and the stress response (chapter 4). The involved circuits include the amygdala, prefrontal cortex (PFC), nucleus accumbens, hippocampus, insula, thalamus, and hypothalamus.[12] These areas are also involved in the stress response system (chapter 5), linking circuits involved in anxiety to environmental events.

The amygdala is involved in processing the significance and impact of what is happening (chapter 4) and can be considered the central relay point for the fear circuit that underlies the anxiety disorders.[13] It participates in the learning of associations and fear conditioning as well as the expression of fear responses. The connections the amygdala has with other areas illustrate the pivotal role it plays in anxiety. Connections to the prefrontal cortex allow for the cognitive modulation of anxiety. Connections to the ventromedial PFC (also involved in the significance of events) and hippocampus provide context and links to memory—for example, indicating that previously threatening events are no longer threats. Connections to the anterior cingulate cortex (ACC) serve as a mediator between cognitive and mood-related aspects of anxiety, and connections to the insula facilitate processing of internal bodily states. Connections to the basal ganglia enable processing of facial expressions and body movements associated with fear.

There is significant overlap in areas and circuits involved in the stress response and fear/anxiety.[14] Amygdala connections to the stress response system lead to physiological changes and immune system activation, and the amygdala also helps regulate the stress response. The hypothalamic-pituitary-adrenal (HPA) axis is particularly sensitive to life events, and corticotrophin-releasing hormone (CRH) plays a key role in both. Early life trauma and abuse are commonly found in anxiety disorders and are associated with hyperresponsivity to the administration of CRH. However, they are not necessarily activated together, as feeling anxious and fearful is not inevitable when the HPA axis is activated.

Neurotransmitters modulate activity in the neural circuits, and variations in areas activated and transmitter activity may underlie the various anxiety disorders.[15] For example, the locus coeruleus (LC)/norepinephrine system is involved in the flight-or-fight response (chapter 4), and individual differences in the responsivity of this system are likely important in anxiety.

Both early acute stressful events and chronic adversities interact with genetic influences to alter the function of many of these areas and the circuits they form. For example, the development of the amygdala and its connections is highly subject to environmental events (chapter 6), and both acute and chronic stress can markedly affect how responsive the amygdala is over the course of development.

Neural Circuits and Specific Disorders

The central finding is that amygdala hyperresponsivity appears to be a consistent characteristic of the anxiety disorders, appearing in panic disorder, social phobia, and possibly generalized anxiety disorder.[16] In panic disorder, the brain stem in also hyperresponsive; in social phobia, the rostral ACC and insula may be hyperresponsive; and in specific phobias, the dorsal ACC (dACC) and insula may be hyperresponsive. This would account for many of the characteristic findings in anxiety (for example, vigilance, fear, and bodily sensations).

A stable finding in adults with PTSD is that the amygdala is hyperresponsive, but the medial prefrontal cortex (mPFC), including the rostral ACC, is hyporesponsive. The result is failure to damp down or inhibit the amygdala. In addition, the dACC and insula may be hyperresponsive. The volume of the hippocampus appears to be decreased, and while hippocampal function is abnormal, it is not yet clear what the direction of the abnormality is.[17]

OCD appears to be the exception to the above findings. Core OCD symptoms do not appear to be mediated by the circuits involved in fear. Instead, circuits involving the thalamus, cortex, and striatum appear to be involved.

A variety of neurotransmitters are involved in anxiety.[18] For example, gamma-aminobutyric acid (GABA), the inhibitory transmitter in the synapse, may be involved in panic disorder. Glutamate, the excitatory transmitter in the synapse, has also been implicated in anxiety, and the balance between GABA and glutamine receptors may be a key factor. The success of the serotonin reuptake inhibitors in treating anxiety (chapter 12) suggests that serotonin is implicated. Dopamine may be involved because of its role in social withdrawal and the reward system (chapter 4).

ANXIETY, NEURAL CIRCUITS, AND YOUTH

Studies of neural circuitry of anxiety disorders in adolescents are in the early stages and show similarities to the findings in adults.[19] Initial results suggest greater activation of the amygdala in adolescents with anxiety disorders compared to healthy controls when they are asked to focus on their own sense of fear while viewing fearsome faces. Another study of adolescents with generalized anxiety disorder found evidence for disruptions in the connections between the amygdala and prefrontal cortex, insula, and other areas. Anxiety severity was correlated with functional connectivity between the amygdala and insula and superior temporal area.[20]

The relative course of development of brain regions presents some interesting issues in adolescents as illustrated by the research of Casey and colleagues.[21] When the amygdala is detecting signals of safety and threat, it can signal the visceromotor PFC (vmPFC) of the significance of cues, and the vmPFC can in turn dampen the response of the amygdala. But the amygdala and related structures develop earlier than the slower and later-developing PFC, and this creates an imbalance. Casey and colleagues suggest that early adolescent behavior is more "feeling driven." In one study, in which adolescents faced a possible threat, e.g., viewing images of fearsome faces, the initial response showed exaggerated amygdala activity. The responses were exaggerated compared to the responses of children and adults but were not correlated with trait anxiety. When the fearsome face was presented repeatedly, the response diminished and was correlated with self-reported elevations of everyday anxiety. Suppression of the response over time was lowest in individuals with higher trait anxiety. Moreover, the greater the response or activation of the vmPFC, the lower was suppression of the amygdala response. Casey and colleagues suggest that the initial emotional reactivity indicated by the exaggerated amygdala response is typical or normal for adolescents, but failure of this response to decline over time as the threat recedes may be atypical and suggestive of anxiety.[22]

Studies in children are also under way and also show amygdala activation.[23] There are consistent findings in children with generalized anxiety disorder of increased amygdala activation when the children are viewing negative emotional expressions, but there are inconsistent reports of PFC activation. There is also evidence of increased functional connectivity between the amygdala and the insula in anxious children compared to healthy controls. Increased amygdala activation is also reported in children with social phobia or those at risk of social phobia. Children with social phobia also show activation in the nucleus accumbens and related components of the reward system in response to rewarding incentives.[24] Similarly, increased amygdala activation was found in separation anxiety disorder.

In summary, anxiety and the anxiety disorders involve dysfunction in fear circuits, centered on the amygdala, which is hyperresponsive. This dysfunction gives rise to the complex of features seen in anxiety: worry, fear, withdrawal, avoidance, and the physiological changes needed to prepare for action.

EMERGENCE OF ANXIETY DISORDERS

The following sections consider how anxiety disorders emerge. First, we consider the characteristics of the individual, notably temperament. Next, we consider genetic influences and how genetic and environmental influences interact to produce anxiety disorders. Two important issues are the roles of stress and relationships.

Characteristics of the Child

We can approach the emergence of anxiety disorders by first considering characteristics of the child that might be related to anxiety and fearfulness. Temperament (chapter 3), in particular inhibited temperament, is a risk factor for the development of anxiety disorders. Behavioral inhibition as a temperamental style and anxiety share many features (avoidance of the unfamiliar, attentional bias to threats) and patterns of physiological responses (heart rate variability, increased salivary cortisol). There is a strong predictive link between early behavioral inhibition and social anxiety in both children and adolescents,[25] and behavioral inhibition is also found in the children of adults who have anxiety disorders.[26]

Negative affectivity (the tendency to be fearful, anxious, or sad; to be sensitive to punishment; and to be avoidant and inhibited) also overlaps with behavioral inhibition, and it, too, is linked to the later emergence of anxiety disorders.[27] But negative affectivity is also linked to depressive disorders (chapter 9), providing one condition for the overlap of anxiety and depressive disorders. Behavioral inhibition and negative affectivity in infancy may predict the emergence of anxiety disorders because they share risk factors.[28] But we can also think of them in terms of tuning, where they may each be reflecting different aspects of underlying patterns of tuning. A particular infant experiences the world as uncertain, fearsome, and threatening, and may be unhappy to different degrees. The experience is mediated by the mood component. Then, depending on the quality of caregiving, available supports, and unique life events, the infant's tuning becomes the condition for disorders to emerge.

Anxiety sensitivity, or the belief that anxiety sensations indicate harmful physiological, psychological, or social consequences, is a third construct related to the emergence of anxiety disorders in youth. Such misinterpretations of bodily signals may lead to a "fear of fear" cycle.[29] The fear produces anxiety, which then increases the frequency and intensity of physiological sensations in the face of environmental events and fosters apprehension or fear regarding the significance of the bodily sensations. The result may be panic attacks. Anxiety sensitivity could also be thought of as an aspect of tuning since the higher a person's level of anxiety sensitivity, the more likely the person is to experience anxiety symptoms as threatening.

Furthermore, anxious youth are thought to have information-processing biases toward threat, and this is also found in anxious adults.[30] Even young infants give more attention to potential threatening stimuli (chapter 3). We do not know what role the infant's mood plays in the development of this apparent bias, but there is some evidence that clinically anxious children have a bias toward threat. However, it is not yet clear if this is true of children at risk of developing anxiety disorders. Moreover, abnormal fear safety learning in child-hood may help establish these biases toward threat.[31]

Gene-Environment Interactions

Gene-environment interactions play a part in the emergence of anxiety dis-orders, as constitutional and/or prior experiential factors are likely to be important. Rapee and colleagues suggest that environmental experiences may be processed through "a personality" filter, a suggestion that is consistent with the idea of tuning.[32] Fears may also become the basis for specific anxiety disorders, depending on the characteristics of the child and the child's experiences. For example, phobias may arise through conditioning, associating the connection between an event and the fear. Since fears and worries vary by age or developmental periods, then the form of anxiety disorder that emerges will vary.[33]

Genetic Influences

There is substantial evidence that anxiety disorders run in families.[34] Twin studies suggest that there is a genetic component for anxiety disorders that does not appear to be significantly different across the disorders. There is also evidence that non-shared environmental factors (those that differentially affect siblings) have a considerable influence on the development of anxiety, but there is mixed evidence regarding shared environmental factors, e.g., parental psychopathology or family stress.

Chapter 5 sketched how genetic polymorphisms, especially the short allele of the serotonin transporter (5-HTT), influence the responsivity of the amygdala and cingulate cortex that are involved in mood, emotion, and the response to fearsome and angry expressions.[35] There is evidence that amygdala responses in anxious adolescents are related to whether the individual has the short or long 5-HTT allele.[36]

A link to anxiety can be seen as early as infancy, when the short allele of the dopamine DRD4 gene is linked to higher negative emotionality, having the short 5-HTT allele is linked to increased behavioral inhibition and heightened fear, and having both short alleles is linked to greater negative emotionality.[37] The short 5-HTT allele also plays a role in anxiety sensitivity. College undergraduates with the short allele who had experienced childhood emotional abuse showed higher levels of anxiety sensitivity.[38]

Environmental Influences and Stress

Although research is limited and it is difficult to tease out the effect of events, independent life events are likely to precede anxiety disorders. Chronic adversities early in life may also be related to the emergence of anxiety disorders.[39] The nature and meaning of events bear on the disorder that emerges. In adults, events suggesting loss and danger are associated with pure generalized anxiety disorder, but events signaling loss and humiliation predict pure depression or mixed depression-anxiety.[40] Similar effects can be seen as early as the preschool years. For example, in a study of early traumatic events, violent behavior directed at or witnessed by a child was associated with separation anxiety, post-traumatic stress disorder, depression, and disruptive behavior, but non-interpersonal traumatic events were only associated with phobic anxiety.[41] Events involving separation in early childhood (along with behavioral inhibition and parental generalized anxiety) are specifically linked to generalized anxiety disorder, but not depression in youth.[42]

In the next section we examine the role of relationships. They have been looked at in two ways. One is through the effects of parenting style and the other is through attachment relationships.

Relationships and Anxiety Disorders

Parenting Style

There are a number of ways that parental behavior plays a role in the emergence of anxiety disorders in youth.[43] One way is for the child to simply learn to be anxious from observing the parents' own anxious behavior or from listening to their parents' verbal expressions of anxiety. But overprotective parenting seems to have the most powerful effects on childhood anxiety (see below). The direction of the effect is not clear, however, since it is plausible that anxious children elicit overprotective parenting. In contrast, negative or critical parenting is more strongly related to the emergence of depressive disorders.

Attachment

Recent reviews suggest that insecure, ambivalent attachment may be a general risk factor for anxiety (or internalizing symptoms, including depressive symptoms).[44] The link with anxiety seems to be stronger for adolescents than for children, possibly because adolescents have a more stable internal working model of attachment figures, but methodological and cultural factors may be critical.[45] How might insecure attachment be related to tuning? Recall (chapter 3) that attachment refers to a *felt* sense of security. If the infant is unsure because his caregiver is unpredictable, experiencing his own uneasiness or fearfulness could lead the infant to cry and seek out his caregiver, and to do so persistently. There is evidence that insecurely attached infants direct more behavior toward the caregiver. There may also be an overlap with irritability. Irritable infants whose mothers have low social support are likely to later be classified as insecurely attached.[46] The infant is likely to be frustrated by failure to get the desired response, and a pattern may then be established.

Brumariu and Kerns offer some further interesting speculations regarding the link between insecure attachment and anxiety disorders. For example, over-controlling and overprotective parenting (parent may be anxious) may lead to thoughts of physical or psychological threat, vigilant attention to threat, and a perceived lack of control in the child. If the insecurely attached child is not allowed to explore and learn, the child may develop a reduced sense of autonomy, self-control, or self-efficacy. The result might be that the child develops a negative perception of her own efficacy and self-worth. Modeling of parental behavior may simply compound the child's difficulty. These authors suggest that two other child characteristics may explain the link between attachment and anxiety and depressive symptoms. First, the child may have cognitive biases that manifest as inaccurate beliefs or interpretations, or as attributions and expectancies in relation to particular events. Second, the child may have problems identifying and understanding emotional states and consequently may adopt fewer constructive coping strategies.[47] But recall the idea that mood is prior to cognition (chapter 2). The insecure child could experience the world as fearful and threatening, and overprotective and anxious parents might be unable to provide the conditions necessary for the child to learn to identify and label her moods and resulting emotions, and do what is necessary to replace them.

In summary, individual differences as shown by particular temperaments and the presence of genetic polymorphisms create the conditions for anxiety in the context of traumatic events, parenting style, and disturbed attachment relationships.

The next section explores how early anxiety disorders may appear. First, we look at symptoms, then the constellation of symptoms that form discrete disorders.

Appearance of Core Symptoms of Anxiety

How early do the core symptoms of anxiety appear? As noted above, worries are anxious thoughts about negative future events that may happen, whereas fears are anxious thoughts about threatening events that are happening now. Worries in childhood are very common (chapter 3). In one community-based study, 70 percent of children aged eight to thirteen years reported at least one worry. The study found that worries tended to be self-referent and were related to school performance, social contacts, health, and dying. The majority of children were unable to identify threatening or aversive events that led to the worry. Interestingly, almost one in four children said that their main worry served a positive goal, meaning that worrying helped them deal with potentially difficult future events. The frequency of worrying was correlated with a measure of trait anxiety, and in addition worry, trait anxiety, and depressive symptoms were correlated.[48]

A similar community-based study on fears found that the most common fears were different from the most common worries. The most common fears were of animals, fear of the unknown, fear of danger and death, medical fears, and fear of failure and criticism. Fears were commonly accompanied by physical symptoms, negative thoughts, and avoidant behavior. Almost 90 percent of children reported that they had heard frightening things about the event or thing that they feared the most. However, almost a third of children had no clear idea about how their particular fear began.[49]

Fears emerge as early as the first year of life, and the nature of the fears track emotional, cognitive, and social development as the child ventures out into the world[50] (chapter 3). Before age two, separation anxiety and fear of strangers become prominent as part of the normal developmental sequence in attachment. Fear of high places and of novel events (loud noises or looming objects) also emerge around seven months and decline around twelve months. Again, this reflects the normal sequence of perceptual and cognitive development. Between ages two and three, fear of the dark and of small animals emerge. Other fears emerge as children grow and attend school and their world expands. Separation anxiety appears. Children report fears of bodily harm and of "mean" or "bad" people by age five. Fears of supernatural beings and events such as thunder and lightning appear by age six. By age nine, fears related to school performance emerge. Fears about physical appearance are present, and interestingly, it is also the age when children begin to report fears of death. Fears related to specific incidents involving animals or insects are most commonly seen in nine- to thirteen-year-old children. While specific phobias may emerge at any age, social phobias are more common in adolescence when greater demands are placed on appearance, attractiveness, and performance.

Appearance of Anxiety Disorders

How early can the grouping of symptoms into the pattern of anxiety disorders be seen? The constellation of symptoms that form the anxiety disorders appears early. Côté and colleagues tracked the emergence of symptoms of anxiety and depression in a representative sample of over two thousand infants in the province of Quebec.[51] Mothers were annually asked to rate their children on being nervous, fearful, not happy, and having difficulty having fun. Symptoms were rated annually to age five. Almost 15 percent showed high rates of symptoms at eighteen months of age, and in this group the frequency of symptoms increased over time. Fifty-five percent showed moderate rising levels of symptoms over time, and 30 percent of children showed low, stable rates of symptoms over the five-year period. Even in two- to three-year-olds, anxiety symptoms grouped into patterns consistent with separation anxiety, social phobia, generalized anxiety, and obsessive-compulsive disorder.[52]

Finally, we consider some issues in the overlap of anxiety with other disorders, especially depression.

ASSOCIATION OF ANXIETY WITH OTHER DISORDERS

The comorbidity of anxiety with other disorders can be viewed through the lens of tuning, where the nature and meaning of events is mediated by the moods and the status of the underlying circuits that comprise the child's (or adult's) tuning, and that are the product of genetic and environmental influences. This would be in line with the idea that there are general or common factors that are shared by all (all have the same moods, at least in the same culture), but we are shaped in unique ways (we each have our characteristic moods). With regard to depression and anxiety, congruent with the idea that threats may not only signal danger but also loss, threatening events may lead to anxiety, depression, or both depending on the nature and meaning of the event. Kendler and colleagues found that, in a very large sample of adults, events suggesting loss and danger were associated with pure generalized anxiety disorder, but events signaling loss and humiliation predicted pure depression or mixed depression-anxiety.[53] If the events signaled entrapment, only mixed episodes were predicted. In adolescents followed for a year, anxiety disorders tended to appear in time before depressive disorders and predicted later depression.[54] But certain features specifically predicted anxiety, others predicted depression, and yet others predicted both. Lower self-esteem (feelings of dissatisfaction with self, including body parts and physical appearance) was a specific predictor of anxiety. Specific risk factors for depression were a negative attributional style and a history of subthreshold depressive symptoms. Worry predicted later anxiety and depression. Also, loneliness (feelings of solitude, disconnection, and lack of closeness), emotional reliance (desiring access of support and approval from others, being anxious about being alone or abandoned, and being sensitive in interpersonal situations), and difficulties in relationships with family and peers increased the risk for both anxiety and depression.

Other studies of the comorbidity of depression and anxiety in children and their parents suggest that depression and anxiety may be different phases or alternative expressions of the same disorder.[55]

SUMMARY

Anxiety is concerned with present or future threats of harm that can be considered an alarm system to help detect and deal with threats to life. The anxiety disorders are a group of symptom complexes that often overlap and are all associated with avoidance behavior and physiological changes necessary for action needed to deal with threats.

The underlying moods of fearfulness and worry are the basis of fear, and the underlying circuitry centers around the amygdala and brain regions involved in the assessment of threat and preparation for action. The most consistent finding is increased amygdala activity, and a more easily activated and persistent fear response. The result is that events and situations appear threatening, and this effect may be pervasive, leading to symptom complexes that range from simple phobias (fear of spiders), to separation anxiety (fear of separation), to a state of generalized anxiety. Anxiety disorders first appear in early childhood, and there's considerable continuity across the life span. Early adversity, genetic influences, temperament, and psychosocial influences combine to set the stage for the elaboration of the disorders.

CHAPTER 9

WHEN MOODS ARE LOW— DEPRESSION

John, an eight-year-old boy, has become irritable, cries easily, and wakes at night. This behavior began over five or six weeks. Prior to this, he was a robust, happy child. Now, he has become listless and uninterested in activities and is no longer interested in playing with friends. He is having trouble concentrating at school, and his grades are slipping.

Mary, a fifteen-year-old adolescent, is always sad and is often irritable and cranky. She is losing interest in school and is spending less and less time with her friends. She is losing weight. She lies awake at night worrying about her family. Mary's mother has rheumatoid arthritis, and so Mary has to do extra chores and care for younger siblings. There is concern that her father will be laid off. A number of Mary's relatives have been treated for depression, and an uncle committed suicide.

The vignettes describe common presentations of depression, and, as with anxiety disorders, variations on these stories can be found across the life span. Depression, like anxiety, presents with particular mood, emotion, cognitive, physiological, and action components. Furthermore, as seen with anxiety disorders, depression may begin early in life; a depressed person is likely to have encountered distressing life events and difficult family circumstances at some point, to have a family history of related disorders, and to have other psychiatric disorders.

Depression in adults is associated with impairment equivalent to that associated with many chronic medical diseases.[1] In the National Comorbidity Survey, the lifetime prevalence of depression was 16.2 percent,[2] and the age of onset spanned adolescence and early adulthood. Current data shows that depressive disorders in youth are also common and have significant consequences. Thirty to sixty percent of youth attending mental health clinics report significant depressive symptoms, and

25–50 percent will have major depressive disorder (MDD).[3] According to community studies, the one-year prevalence of MDD in children ranges from 0.5–2.5 percent, but in adolescents it ranges from 2–8 percent.[4] Fourteen percent of adolescents will experience an episode of depression over their lifetime, and 20 percent of adolescents will experience an episode by the time they reach eighteen years of age. The sex ratio is equal before puberty, but depression is twice as common in females after puberty, and it remains that way throughout adulthood.

Depression and anxiety are very commonly seen together. Close to 60 percent of adults who have ever been depressed will also be diagnosed with an anxiety disorder.[5] Moreover, up to 50 percent of youth with depression will also be diagnosed with two or more other disorders.[6] Anxiety disorders (separation anxiety, panic attacks, generalized anxiety) are very frequently present, and social anxiety often precedes depression. Other associated disorders are disruptive behavior disorders, substance abuse, and eating disorders.

In youth, both the length of episodes of depression and the frequency of relapse and recurrence can be surprisingly high.[7] Overall, 6–10 percent have a protracted course. Forty to sixty percent of depressed youth relapse, and 20 to 60 percent have a recurrence of depression within one to two years of recovery. A full 70 percent have a recurrence after five years. Depressed children are four times more likely than controls to have an episode of depression after age seventeen years, and furthermore, 20–40 percent in some studies are diagnosed with bipolar disorder in five years. Major depression is highly likely to occur within two to three years of the onset of dysthymia (see below).[8]

What is depression about? Whereas we can think of anxiety as concern with present or future threats of harm, we can think of depression as concern with loss or something that has already happened. Relationships and loss are central to many hypotheses about depression and the evolutionary significance of depression.[9] One prominent hypothesis is that depression is an adaptive response to perceived threats of exclusion from key social relationships. The critical relationships are those that signal attachments and that reflect agency as expressed in social standing, reputation and well-being. We can expect depressive symptoms to arise in situations that reflect loss or threatened loss in these two areas. This is consistent with the ideas expressed in chapter 2, wherein we discussed how Heidegger argued that we are not detached observers of our world but instead are always engaged in practical concerns, or projects, that matter to us and offer certain possibilities, and where, crucially, many of our most important situations involve others.

And since we have already seen that anxiety arises in situations where our well-being is threatened, we should not be surprised that anxiety and depression often occur together. Moreover, we will see that mania (chapter 10), which along with depression forms bipolar disorder, is also linked to systems underlying agency and our capacity or drive to seek rewards and to do things.

HOW IS DEPRESSION CLASSIFIED?

Clinical features, pattern of recurrence, and course define depression.[10] Depressed mood is one of two core features of depression, and depression may occur in episodes or it may be long-lasting. Mood may be depressed, sad, hopeless, discouraged, or one may describe oneself as feeling "down in the dumps." The second defining feature is anhedonia, or the loss of interest or pleasure in nearly all of one's usual activities. Certain adjustments to the criteria for a major depressive episode in adults are allowed in youth to account for developmental issues. The key change is that irritability can be substituted for sad mood, but otherwise the criteria are essentially the same.

To qualify as a major depressive episode, at least one of the two core features must be present most of the time nearly every day during at least the same two-week period. In addition to the core mood disturbance, at least four additional symptoms must be present nearly every day. Because a diagnosis requires the presence of some but not all symptoms drawn from a list, the clinical presentation of depression can vary widely across individuals. And since the symptoms are in different domains (e.g., cognitive, physiological), the problem of heterogeneity is compounded. The result is that any two depressed individuals might have very different presentations.

Some of the additional symptoms are related to mood. There may be a feeling of worthlessness, or a feeling of excessive or inappropriate guilt. Recurrent thoughts of death (as distinct from a fear of death) may be present and may extend to thinking about or planning suicide. Cognitive changes include difficulty concentrating, being less able to think, and being indecisive. Physiological changes may include significant change in appetite or weight, insomnia or hypersomnia, fatigue, and loss of energy. Motor changes may include purposeless and excessive activity associated with inner tension, or a sense of physical and mental heaviness or slowing manifested as slowed movements and speech. All symptoms must represent a change from previous functioning, cause clinically significant impairment, and not be due to substances or medical conditions. While bereavement was an exclusion criterion in *DSM-IV-TR*, it has been removed in *DSM-5*.[11]

Not all depression occurs in episodes. A new diagnosis of persistent depressive disorder has been added to the *DSM-5* to address the issue of prolonged, chronic forms of depression. Some individuals present with depressed mood for prolonged periods but with few additional symptoms, but nonetheless they may be significantly impaired. Previously, this clinical picture was called dysthymia. Others, however, might begin with a major depressive episode, but episode(s) persist and become chronic.

Other forms of depression in which there are insufficient symptoms present to meet the criteria for an episode are variously named depending on whether there is a clear reason why insufficient criteria are present. An adjustment disorder is present if the depressed mood arises within three months of a directly related stressor and interferes with functioning. Finally, depressed mood maybe judged to be a direct physiological effect of a medical condition or a substance (e.g., medication, drug, toxin).

DEPRESSION AND NEURAL CIRCUITS

Where do the features of depression come from? In essence, depression emerges out of the interplay of current and past events and the functional status of certain neural circuits and the threat/stress response systems. We will see that either dysfunction in circuits generating mood, emotion and reward seeking or failure of executive circuits to regulate appropriately or some combination of these two are the critical issues. The clinical features of depression require the involvement of extensive networks that include medial prefrontal cortex (PFC), amygdala, medial thalamus, striatum, and hypothalamus, as well as the neurotransmitter systems that modulate the networks. The vegetative features of depression (weight change, appetite change, sleep disturbance) likely reflect abnormalities in the stress response.[12]

A number of studies, including neuroimaging studies, suggest that overall there is increased activity in networks that process mood and emotion and reduced activity in circuits involved in voluntary or effortful regulation of emotional responses.[13] Specifically, there is increased activity in the amygdala, subgenual anterior cingulate cortex (ACC) and insula, and decreased activity in the lateral PFC and the upper ACC (figs. 4.1 and 4.2).

In depression, processes are biased toward the negative and away from the positive.[14] Neuroimaging studies show abnormally increased activity in the amygdala, ventral striatum, and medial PFC when the tasks involve negative emotional stimuli such as fearsome faces. These findings are similar to findings in anxiety studies. In addition, there is reduced activity in the reward circuits (ventral striatum, nucleus accumbens) when the tasks involve positive emotional or reward-related stimuli. Additional evidence that the amygdala shows abnormalities suggestive of a negative processing bias,[15] comes from studies showing an exaggerated amygdala response to sad words or sad faces that may be present even in recovered depressives. This suggests that the exaggerated amygdala response may be a trait marker in depression.

Furthermore, neuroimaging studies suggest abnormalities in the dorsal and lateral PFC in depressed patients performing tasks that test executive function.[16] Similarly, there is evidence for abnormalities in hippocampal function that may be related to memory problems. These findings correlate with the inattentiveness, indecision, and memory problems often seen in depression.

Similar to what has been noted among adolescents with anxiety disorders,[17] there is greater activation of the amygdala in adolescents with MDD compared to healthy adolescents when they were viewing faces that expressed fear and were focusing on their own sense of fear.

Left-sided orbitofrontal cortex (OFC) abnormalities are present in depressed children, and these findings are consistent with models postulating that the left PFC (mediating positive emotions) is underactive, whereas the right PFC (mediating negative emotions) is hyperactive in depressed adults.[18] There is evidence of similar changes in depressed preschoolers. A small group of depressed preschoolers were asked to look at images of faces with expressions that were sad, happy, or neutral, as well as images of their mothers.[19] Amygdala activation occurred in response to sad faces, and severity of depression was positively related to amygdala activity. A second study, in a small sample of preschoolers who had a history of depression, reported increased activity in the amygdala and limbic areas but decreased activity in the PFC, while the children participated in a procedure that induced sadness.[20]

The Stress Response and Depression

There is considerable evidence that the stress response is involved in depression.[21] Increased activity of the stress response as shown by increased cortisol, and corticotrophin-releasing hormone (CRH) is often found in those with depression. Increased secretion of CRH, especially if depression persists, may account for abnormalities in the hypothalamic-pituitary-adrenal (HPA) axis found in those with depression.[22] Early life stress profoundly affects the system (chapter 6). The increased secretion of CRH can result in structural changes in developing neural circuits. The result can be a sensitized stress system that is more easily triggered and more resistant to counterbalancing.

Reward System and Depression

We noted above neuroimaging evidence linking depression to abnormalities in the reward system. The dopamine reward system involving the nucleus accumbens is implicated in the reduced motivation and anhedonia of depression.[23] The dysfunction may be related more to the onset or first episodes of depression than it is to recurrence.[24] Functional studies show that the degree of activation of the nucleus accumbens in response to reward is greater in adolescents than in children or adults, but it is deactivated in depression.[25] Interestingly, young adolescent girls at risk of depression, but who were not depressed, showed anomalies in the reward system (striatum and dorsal ACC) in tasks involving reward and loss. Moreover, there is evidence of reduced activity in reward systems in at-risk children,[26] consistent with evidence of reduced positivity in children at risk of depression.[27]

Neurotransmitters and Depression

We saw in chapter 4 that change in the nervous system occurs through activity in the synapse, where the availability of norepinephrine, serotonin, and dopamine is crucial to how circuits function. An intricate series of processes in the synapse have been identified in depression.[28] Evidence that neurotransmitters are involved in depression comes from a variety of sources.[29] There is the evidence that antidepressants that increase serotonin and norepinephrine availability and dopamine transmission effectively treat depression. Levels of metabolites and receptors of these transmitters also suggest a role in depression. As we have seen, the short allele of the serotonin transporter gene promoter area is associated with vulnerability to depression in those with an early history of abuse or neglect. Dopamine is also implicated because of its role in the reward system.

In summary, evidence is emerging across the life span that depression results from dysfunction in circuits involved in mood, reward-related activity and motivation, executive function, and the stress response.

EMERGENCE OF DEPRESSION

In the following sections we examine how depression emerges. First, we consider characteristics of the individual, notably temperament. Next, we consider genetic influences and how genetic and environmental influences, particularly stress and relationships, interact to produce depression.

CHARACTERISTICS OF THE CHILD

There is evidence that temperament is related to the emergence of depressive symptoms. Difficult temperament as rated at five months by report of mothers was the best predictor of depressive symptoms in young children.[30] Irritability (the tendency to be easily annoyed and touchy) is a criterion for depression where it can be substituted for sadness in youth. Irritability in oppositional defiant disorder (chapter 11) is a specific predictor of depression and generalized anxiety disorder,[31] and the specific prediction to later depression holds for depression and dysthymia twenty years later in adults (where irritability is not a criterion for depression).

GENE-ENVIRONMENT INTERACTIONS AND DEPRESSION

Although there is wide variation in study methods, there is evidence for gene-environment interactions in youth depression.[32] Early traumatic events are associated with depression later in life. But, as we have seen, not all persons exposed to traumatic or stressful life events become depressed.

Chapter 4 discussed a number of issues relative to gene-environment interaction and the role of genetic polymorphisms, especially the serotonin transporter gene alleles. There are also genes involved in the stress response that can confer vulnerability to depression in the context of early life stress.[33] Depending on which polymorphism or how many copies the person has confers resistance or vulnerability. These polymorphisms involve the CRH type I receptor, which mediates the response to stress, as well as polymorphisms of brain-derived neurotrophic factor (BDNF) gene, which is important in plasticity. These polymorphisms are associated with structural and functional changes in the amygdala, hippocampus, and prefrontal cortex. These alleles are implicated in depression in children who have been subject to early abuse and maltreatment, but, crucially, only those who experienced maltreatment and had copies of the alleles became depressed.[34] In one study of adolescents at risk of depression, carriers of the Val66Val BDNF polymorphism with higher morning cortisol levels were at increased risk of depression.[35] Moreover, amygdala responses in depressed (or anxious) adolescents are related to whether the individual has the short or long allele of the serotonin transporter gene.[36]

The characteristics of the individuals and their social context are also important determinants of whether or not depression occurs. For example, the quality of peer and love relationships, personality types, and perceived positive parental care are associated with resilient outcomes in at-risk children.[37] However, studies of at-risk children show that having two copies of the long allele of the serotonin transporter gene confers resistance. Resilient children, or those at risk for depression, who did not become depressed, also show personal characteristics that appear to confer resilience.[38] They appeared to be more aware of their limits in relation to the parent's illness and were able to maintain a focus on goals and accomplishing goals. Aspects of relationships were important, particularly the recognition that the parents were committed to parenting and the relationship. Parental support and peer support, and the capacity to elicit and engage support are also important. One crucial component is the capacity to take action, whether through social interaction or involvement in activities. The child being able to self-regulate his or her own emotions and behavior is crucial. This capacity could well rest on the individual child's tuning.

LIFE EVENTS, RELATIONSHIPS, AND DEPRESSION

While it has long been noted that major stress often precedes the onset of depression, it appears that stressful events are most likely to occur before the first episode of depression, but not before subsequent episodes.[39] Moreover, not everyone exposed to stress becomes depressed, and stress alone is insufficient to cause depression in many cases. About one in five adults exposed to stress become depressed, and it is clear that other factors must be involved. But are all life events the same, or are there characteristics of life events more typically associated with depression?

Negative events that have interpersonal content are particularly overrepresented in depression. In a large sample of adult twins from a population-based registry,[40] events related to loss and humiliation predicted pure depression and mixed depression/generalized anxiety, whereas events associated with loss and danger predicted the onset of pure generalized anxiety. Death of a partner and separation initiated by the respondent predicted pure depression, but not pure generalized anxiety. Mixed episodes were predicted by high ratings of entrapment. Events that combined humiliation as well as loss were more likely to predict depression then were pure loss events.

Stressful events occurring in close relationships and social networks among adolescent girls are highly predictive of depression.[41] The characteristics and behaviors of depressed adolescent girls may contribute to this effect by creating life contexts that increase the likelihood that depression will reoccur.[42] For example, these adolescent girls may select into long-term relationships or marriages with partners who are prone to coercive behavior, and who may themselves be unhappy and dissatisfied. In time, dysfunctional behavior may spill over into child-rearing practices.

The death of a parent, physical or sexual abuse, or removal from the home was more common in depressed preschoolers than in preschoolers who did not have psychiatric symptoms.[43] But parental separation or divorce, death of a pet, birth of a sibling, or a change in daycare or preschool setting did not distinguish the groups. In another study, preschoolers exposed to violence were likely to be depressed, but they also showed separation anxiety, post-traumatic stress, and disruptive behavior.[44] In contrast, exposure to non-interpersonal traumatic events was only associated with anxiety.

RELATIONSHIPS AND RISK FOR DEPRESSION

There are many ways issues in relationships are risk factors for depression in childhood.[45] Parental separation and divorce, particularly if there is conflict involved, family moves, and social isolation have all been linked to depression. Bereavement is a particularly potent risk factor for depression. Parenting style is also a factor. Overcritical parenting is linked to depression, whereas anxiety is linked to overprotective parenting.

But while having a depressogenic cognitive style and a prior history of depression[46] are specific risk factors for depression, the strongest risk factor for the development of depression is having a parent with a depressive illness.[47] There is 30 to 50 percent more prevalence of depression in family members of depressed youth, and more than half of parents bringing their depressed adolescents to clinics themselves have mood disorders. Children of depressed parents have about a two- to fourfold increased risk of developing depressive disorders. But family members also have high rates of anxiety disorders, alcohol abuse, substance abuse, and personality disorders, and in addition to depression, offspring also have other disorders, e.g., anxiety disorders and disruptive disorders, and they are at risk of having more social and academic difficulties.

Children at risk for depression because of parental history of depression show less positive affectivity than controls, and continue to do so over time. Of further interest, at-risk children showed more negative affectivity,[48] although this is less clear at younger ages and is a less consistent finding than the finding of low-positive affectivity. This again may reflect tuning, as at-risk children before they become symptomatic are less likely to be rated as showing positive mood.

Côté and colleagues found that lifetime maternal depression was the most important predictor of depression and anxiety symptoms in young children. The second most important predictor was difficult temperament. In addition, having a mother who had a low sense of self-efficacy and greater levels of family dysfunction distinguished children who showed higher and increasing levels of depression and anxiety symptoms from five months to five years from children showing fewer symptoms.[49] This study highlights the need to address maternal depression, self-efficacy, and family dysfunction in the prevention and treatment of depression and anxiety in youth.

The effects of maternal depression can be observed in early infancy, when the facial expression of a depressed mother influences the infant.[50] When a depressed mother failed to respond to her infant's efforts to engage, the infant began to turn away and his facial expression appeared sad. In addition, infants of depressed mothers were less active and more withdrawn than infants of non-depressed mothers when they were situated face-to-face with their mother, and they protested less when their mother had a flat expression.

ATTACHMENT AND DEPRESSION

Insecure attachment may be a general risk factor for internalizing symptoms[51] (chapter 8). The link is modest, with no clear connection to potential moderating factors such as clinical versus nonclinical status, or gender,[52] and three child characteristics may explain the link between attachment and depressive and anxiety symptoms. The characteristics are cognitive biases (inaccurate beliefs or interpretations, attributions or expectancies in relation to particular events), difficulty identifying and understanding emotional states, and poor self-concept or perception of one's own efficacy and self-worth.

How might this be related to tuning? We might ask what is the experience of the insecurely attached infant? Surely the insecure infant feels—that is, experiences—her mood and behaves accordingly. Experiencing her own uneasiness or fearfulness could lead the infant to cry and seek out her caregiver. There is evidence that insecurely attached infants direct more behavior toward the caregiver, and this may overlap with irritability (chapter 3). These experiences then become the basis of further development. Indeed, Brumariu and Kerns hypothesize pathways connecting attachment, dysfunctional parent-child relationships, and depression.[53] Parental rejection may predispose the insecurely attached child to infer he is to blame for the parent behavior, to feel responsible for the interactions, and to begin to attribute negative outcomes to internal factors. In other words, the interactions mark the beginning of the negative attributional style that is a core feature of cognitive behavioral theories of depression. The researchers also speculate that in these situations children may learn to overregulate their own emotions for fear of rejection by parents, to have difficulty understanding their emotions, and as a result to develop ineffective coping strategies. The final outcome is the development of negative self-image and low self-worth.

In summary, individual differences in temperament and genetic influences create the conditions for depression in the context of traumatic events, especially loss or the threat of loss in attachment relationships.

As in the previous chapter we consider here the emergence of symptoms and then the symptom complex that constitutes depression.

How early do symptoms of depression appear?

Symptoms found in depressive disorders appear early in life. Recall that we suggested in the previous chapter and in chapter 3 that the experiences every infant has are conditions that often signal potential danger and potential loss—the conditions for anxiety and sadness. Therefore, everyone is tuned such that particular experiences make both anxiety and depression likely. The younger the child, the more difficult it may be to distinguish between the two disorders, and the more likely they are to occur together.

Developmental data suggests that from infancy to early childhood there is an increase in positive affectivity (smiling, laughing, playing), and a decrease in negative affectivity (crying, sadness, anger, fearfulness).[54] Conversely, negative affect (items indexing frustration, sadness, and fear) decreases from infancy up to late childhood, but, depending on items measured, there is variability among the youngest ages. For example, fear increases and anger shows a u-shaped function across time. The intensity of negative affectivity declines from the early school years up to early adolescence.

By two months of age, observers can distinguish sad facial expressions from general distress in infants. By six months sad facial expressions occur in response to situations that elicit sadness. Facial expressions of anger can be identified and distinguished from sadness as early as two months (chapter 3). By four to eight months, anger can be identified as a distinct entity that is elicited by frustration. Over the next two years, anger becomes increasingly common as the infant grapples with learning to control his or her environment and as opportunities to become frustrated are more common.

Guilt appears in the second and third year, and children appear to understand the experience of guilt by age three. Guilt arises when harm is done to another, particularly if the harmed person is an attachment figure or someone closely associated with the child (chapter 3). Because of this, guilt often arises in the context of loss and estrangement from others and the anticipation of being punished or harmed.

*How early does the symptom complex
of depression appear?*

We noted in chapter 3 that symptoms of depression and anxiety emerge early.[55] High rates of not being happy and having difficulty having fun (along with anxiety) were noted in almost 15 percent of a large sample of young infants, and the frequency of symptoms increased over time. Other researchers have focused on preschool children diagnosed with depression. One group is systematically attempting to validate the diagnosis in preschoolers by establishing that it may be reliably distinguished from other disorders, is transmitted in families, has distinct biological correlates, and takes long-term course.[56] For example, preschoolers were identified who met criteria for depression using age-appropriate manifestations, although the two-week *DSM-IV-TR* duration criterion was set aside.[57] Depressed preschoolers were older, averaging about four and a half years of age, and showed significant impairment. Extreme fatigue and guilt were highly specific to the depressed group. Irritability did not distinguish the depressed children from those with other disorders. Anhedonia was present in both depressed and anxious children, but not in primarily disruptive children. Depression in preschoolers also predicted depression up to two years later.[58] A family history of depression was a strong predictor of later depression. Disruptive disorder at baseline also predicted later depression. Links between irritability and disruptive behavior are addressed again in chapter 11.

SUMMARY

Depression is concerned with the loss of, or the threat of loss in, key relationships. Especially important in childhood are relationships that signal attachments, and this may create the template for depression later in life, when losses in other domains become important. The principal mood associated with depression is sadness, but irritability is often present, especially in youth. Dysfunction in circuits generating mood, emotion, and reward seeking; failure of executive circuits to regulate appropriately; or some combination of these two are the critical issues. Depression emerges out of the interplay of current and past events and the functional status of these circuits, as well as the threat/stress response systems. The strongest risk factor for the development of depression is having a parent with a depressive illness. Early life stress, particularly involving relationships, contributes risk for depression by altering neural circuits. Gene-environment interactions, involving genetic polymorphisms, especially the serotonin transporter gene alleles, as well as genes involved in the stress response, can confer vulnerability to depression in the context of early life stress.

CHAPTER 10

WHEN MOODS ARE HIGH AND LOW— BIPOLAR DISORDER

Bipolar disorder is among the most severely impairing psychiatric disorders, it is one of the leading causes of disability worldwide, and affected individuals spend approximately half of their lives in a symptomatic state.[1] It is not a new disorder. The ancient Greek physicians and philosophers took note of bipolar disorder, and Hippocrates provided the first systematic description of mania and melancholia.[2]

The following vignette illustrates a classic fairly uncommon presentation of mania in youth.

Celia was a twelve-year-old girl admitted to a children's psychiatric unit with a week- long change in behavior that included insisting she was a pop star, singing in public, and not sleeping for almost a week. She spoke rapidly and forcefully, and jumped from topic to topic so that it was difficult to follow her train of thought. She showed near-constant excessive energy.

A second vignette illustrates a different but much more common presentation, and shows why bipolar disorder is among the more controversial diagnoses in child psychiatry.

John, a young adolescent, who had a long history of attention deficit hyperactivity disorder, angry and destructive outbursts, and periods of unhappiness, was admitted during the night to an inpatient psychiatric unit after he broke some furniture at a group home. By morning, he was calm and friendly. When he was asked what was going on he replied, "It's my bipolar." But when asked what that meant he said he had no idea except that he was told that's what he had, and that was why he behaved in the way that he did. After we talked about what had happened, we read and discussed the diagnostic criteria for some disorders in the DSM-IV-TR (with the section headings occluded). He asked a number of questions to clarify some

117

technical terms, and then, suddenly, he looked up and said, "Damn, I'm ODD. I'm not bipolar."

As the name suggests, there are two poles to bipolar disorder, with mania sitting at one pole and depression at the other. Mania, like anxiety and depression, has mood/emotion, cognitive, physiological, and action components. Adults with bipolar disorder often report experiencing their first symptoms in adolescence or childhood. Furthermore, as is seen with anxiety disorders and depression, stressful life events, a family history of related disorders, and comorbid disorders are commonly observed.

According to the National Comorbidity Survey, about 2 percent of the population have bipolar I or bipolar II disorder (see classification below), and over 2 percent have sub-syndromal forms of bipolar disorder.[3] Bipolar I disorder may be equally common in males and females, but bipolar II disorder may be more common in females. Bipolar disorder is highly heritable, and heritability estimates from twin studies may be as high as 85 percent.[4] As many as 50 to 66 percent of affected adults report their first symptoms before age twenty, and between 15 and 28 percent reported they first had symptoms in childhood.[5] The first symptoms are often depression, but anxiety may also feature in the early history (see below).

The reported prevalence and incidence of bipolar disorder in youth have varied widely, and very large increases have occurred in rates of diagnosis both in outpatient clinics,[6] and in hospitalized youth.[7] However, a recent meta-analysis of epidemiologic studies found bipolar disorder occurs in 1.8 percent of youth in community studies in America and Europe.[8] Higher rates were observed in studies with more adolescents, and lower rates in those with more prepubertal children. Follow-up studies in youth show that this is a severe illness with lengthy episodes and high relapse rates[9] that are conditioned by family (intact or non-intact) and relationships (degree of maternal warmth) factors.[10]

Bipolar disorder, like the anxiety and depressive disorders, is commonly associated with other disorders. In adults, anxiety disorders, substance abuse, attention deficit hyperactivity disorder (ADHD) are often associated with bipolar disorder.[11] Antisocial and personality disorders may also be present. In youth, the most common comorbid disorders are anxiety disorders, ADHD, oppositional defiant disorder (ODD), conduct disorder, and substance abuse.[12]

This chapter will focus primarily on manic states, since the issues related to depression were covered in the previous chapter. Can we identify and trace tuning that leads to mania and to factors that influence its development and expression?

What is bipolar disorder about? Mania can be looked at as a state of heightened awareness of positive signals and a heightened drive toward goals, achievement, and reward, even when there are negative consequences to behavior.[13] Having goals, a drive to achieve, and a tendency to seek out and approach situations could be considered adaptive, and the positive moods and associated emotions could be self-reinforcing.[14]

There is evidence that risk for mania in adults is associated with elevated positive emotion,[15] whether the stimulus is related to reward, achievement, or prosocial activities.[16] For example, there is excessive motivation to engage in reward-related and goal-oriented activities, and mania may represent a breakdown in the underlying mechanisms leading to exaggerated and dysfunctional versions of the behavior. Individuals with bipolar disorder highly value goals, and they may be overly ambitious and tend to undervalue threats. They attend to positive emotional aspects of situations, selectively direct attention toward the positive aspects of situations, and overgeneralize those aspects. Those at risk of bipolar disorder tend to behave impulsively when experiencing strong positive emotions. But negative biases and attitudes are also present, and appraisals may shift depending on the underlying mood. Depending on the phase of illness, activity levels and impulsivity increase, and inattention and distractibility worsen. In this context, life events may activate positive dysfunctional beliefs and lead to manic episodes, whereas negative dysfunctional beliefs lead to depression.[17]

Depressed individuals tend to participate less in positive activities and show less inclination toward positive approach behavior. We noted previously that loss of interest in pleasurable activities is a central criterion for depression. This may extend as far as actively avoiding activities associated with positive mood. Depressed persons tend to have a selection bias for negative events or stimuli and the corresponding lack of attention to positive events or information. They also tend to make automatic negative appraisals, for example in ambiguous situations, and have difficulty in reappraising their impressions. We noted in chapter 8 that depression is concerned with loss of attachment relationships or with relationships reflecting our agency in social standing, reputation, and well-being, and may be an adaptive response to perceived threats of exclusion from key social relationships.

If mania results from a breakdown in the mechanisms underlying approach behaviors and reward-related activities, then depression in bipolar disorder might result from the loss of agency, from the frustration when goals cannot be achieved, or because of exclusion from others because of manic behavior, as was described for depression in the previous chapter. The loss or threatened loss of attachment figures might feature in both.

Moreover, we could expect irritability and anger (often the result of frustration of blocked goals) to be present in mania in addition to the expected elevated mood. Indeed, manic states can be mixed with irritability as a prominent feature. We might also expect anxiety because anxiety is concerned with detecting threats and preventing harm. In addition, anxiety disorders (social anxiety, agoraphobia, and generalized anxiety disorder) may be associated with disturbance in positive emotion (anhedonia and avoidance of positive and approach-related activities) (chapter 8).

HOW BIPOLAR DISORDER IS CLASSIFIED

The classification of bipolar disorder hinges on whether mania or hypomania occurs.[18] Basically, bipolar disorder consists of repeated episodes in which mood and activity levels are disturbed, and the phases shift from elevated mood and activity to lowering of mood and activity.[19] Although the two phases should be distinct, with clear shifts between them, this is not always the case. Episodes can be mixed, the phases can alternate rapidly or infrequently, and sometimes only mania occurs. Revisions have been made in the *DSM-5* classification, and they are noted below.[20] An important change pertains to children and adolescents where there has been much controversy and concern about over diagnosis and treatment.

Mania is defined as a distinct period of mood disturbance lasting at least a week (or less if the person is hospitalized) where there are no drugs or medical condition involved and the person's ability to function is impaired. The disturbed mood must be abnormally and persistently elevated, expansive, or irritable. The *DSM-5* elevates increased energy/activity as a primary criterion. Other features must be present during the period of mood disturbance. The associated features include inflated self-esteem/grandiosity; decreased need for sleep; being more talkative/pressured speech; flight of ideas/racing thoughts; distractibility; increase in goal-directed activity or psychomotor agitation; excessive involvement in pleasurable activities that have a high potential for painful consequences. Four of these features must be present if the disturbed mood is only irritable; otherwise three must be present.

Hypomania is diagnosed if the criteria for mania are met but have been present for less than a week but more than four days. Also, symptoms must not cause marked impairment or lead to hospitalization, but the change must be observable to others and there must be an unequivocal change in functioning that is uncharacteristic of the person when he or she is not symptomatic.

Sometimes episodes include both manic and depressive symptoms, or there are insufficient symptoms present to meet the criteria for one of the primary forms. The *DSM-5* includes a new "mixed state" specifier for situations when symptoms of depression and mania are both present, a specifier for severity of any anxiety present, and a specifier for when insufficient symptoms are present.

Bipolar disorder is subdivided based on the presence or absence of mania. In bipolar I disorder there are one or more manic or mixed episodes, but episodes of depression are not required. But depression is not excluded, and one or more depressive episodes may have occurred. An important point is that the first episode may be depression, and this has treatment and management implications since mania may occur in the future. In bipolar II disorder there are not manic or mixed episodes, but there must be at least one episode of hypomania and one or more depressive episodes.

Cyclothymia refers to fluctuating mood disturbance where there may be numerous episodes of hypomanic symptoms and numerous episodes of depressive symptoms.[21] Cyclothymia is of interest because it may be a precursor of bipolar disorder and because of its relation to the construct of affective temperaments. Changes in state are frequent, and symptoms are often present for less than a week. Mixed depressive and hypomanic symptoms are common. Irritability, anxiety, impulsivity, guilt, feelings of low self-worth, insecurity, impulsivity, and agitation are common in cyclothymia. For a diagnosis of cyclothymia, symptoms must be present for two years in adults or one year in youth, and they must represent a change from baseline.

The prevalence of cyclothymia varies from 0.4 to 2.5 percent and may be more common in females. Up to a third of adults with cyclothymia go on to be diagnosed with bipolar disorder. Conversely, up to a third of those with either bipolar I or II report a history of cyclothymia. Moreover, there is evidence that 50 percent or more of adolescents with cyclothymia or a cyclothymic temperament later have bipolar disorder.

BIPOLAR DISORDER AND YOUTH

Bipolar disorder in youth has been highly controversial, in part because of concerns over diagnosis and increased use of medications. The background to the controversy involves questions of diagnosis, including symptom definition, diagnostic boundaries, the definition of episodes and cycles, and whether and how the criteria used in adults should be applied. Part of the difficulty is that investigators have used different approaches in recruiting subjects, different diagnostic methodologies, varying levels of expertise in interviewers, and different informants (parents only, adolescents only, or both parent and child). Moreover, the reader will note that in studying the criteria for mania and hypomania there are many areas where diagnostic difficulties could arise in youth. Elation, grandiosity, or pressured speech could be difficult to distinguish from normal developmental phenomena in childhood. Think of the grand boasts of a young child dressed in a Superman outfit, or a highly excited and talkative child eagerly describing some lofty event or scheme. Now put this behavior in the context of a distractible, active child who is prone to temper tantrums.

In one review of the phenomenology of bipolar disorder in youth, only two mood-related features were highly specific to bipolar disorder. Elated, expansive, euphoric mood was highly specific, but average sensitivity across studies was 70 percent. Labile mood (or mood swings) was highly specific, and it was also highly sensitive. In contrast, irritability showed low specificity, but an average sensitivity was 81 percent. Grandiosity was moderately specific but was also strongly associated with conduct disorder.[22]

In response to the controversies, an NIMH expert panel proposed an alternate classification with three categories. The first or narrow type essentially delineated the classic form of illness. Here either hypomania or mania is present with full-duration episodes and hallmark symptoms. In the second or intermediate form, either hypomania or mania is present, but with neither meeting the narrow-type criteria, or a predominantly irritable hypomania or mania may occur. The third or broad type is characterized by severe mood dysregulation (SMD), marked by chronic, severe irritability and anger, and hyperreactivity to negative emotional stimuli.[23]

Severe mood dysregulation has received a lot of attention because a great many children and adolescents present with a mix of anger, high energy, and hyperactivity. SMD has two components: developmentally inappropriate, frequent, and extreme temper outbursts, and anger or sadness between outbursts.

Almost all children with SMD have persistently angry mood between outbursts. The chronic nature of the irritability distinguishes SMD from the narrow type of bipolar disorder, where mood disturbances are episodic. The criteria for SMD also include symptoms common to ADHD and ODD. These features place SMD at the intersection of bipolar disorder, ADHD, and ODD and speak to the difficulty of separating out these disorders in childhood.

Available evidence suggests that the long-term outcome of SMD is not bipolar disorder but increased risk of major depression, dysthymia, or generalized anxiety disorder.[24] Similarly, in young adolescents, irritability (defined as temper tantrums and anger by parent report) predicted depression, dysthymia, and generalized anxiety disorder twenty years later, but not bipolar disorder.[25]

In response, a new disorder called disruptive mood dysregulation disorder has been added to the *DSM-5* with the hope and intent of reducing over-diagnosis and overtreatment of bipolar disorder in children (chapter 7). This new disorder is aimed at children who show persistent irritability and frequent temper outbursts for more than a year, and who have been the source of diagnostic controversy. Note, the disorder has been added to the chapter on depression and not the chapter on bipolar disorder. However, in one recent study, children fitting the disorder criteria could not be distinguished from children with disruptive behavior disorders, and the diagnosis was not associated with a family history of mood or anxiety disorders.[26]

BIPOLAR DISORDER AND NEURAL CIRCUITS

Research into the neural circuits underlying bipolar disorder has flourished, but methodological problems (e.g., phases of illness, medication status) have led to conflicting results. An expert workgroup has addressed these issues and provided a summary.[27] The general consensus is that bipolar I disorder emerges from abnormalities in the both the structure and function of networks regulating emotional processes. They suggest that abnormalities arising during development lead to decreased connections among ventral prefrontal networks and limbic regions, especially the amygdala. The abnormalities might be structural (failure of the amygdala to develop normally) or functional (abnormal processing of significant events). Failure of the ventral prefrontal networks to regulate the limbic regions might then lead to mania. While the available results were inconsistent regarding the amygdala response, the consensus view was that activation of the amygdala varied as a function of mood state. For example, increased activation occurred in mania but not in euthymia, and how the amygdala responded might vary depending on the salience or valence of the stimulus (whether fearsome or sad faces were being viewed). However, the prefrontal cortex (PFC) response typically shows hypoactivation regardless of the phase of illness. These abnormalities become evident by adolescence, where decreased amygdala volumes have been consistently reported.

As noted above, the amygdala shows increased activity during the manic phase, a finding that has been noted in a number of studies,[28] but the PFC remains hypoactivated across mood states or the phases of the disorder.[29] These findings are consistent with the amygdala being involved in the response to environmental stimuli and are also consistent with the clinical features of mania: inattention and distractibility, irritability, euphoria, and sleep disturbance. These findings may also be interpreted as indicating that the amygdala response depends on the phase of bipolar disorder, but the way the PFC areas and the amygdala connect may represent an underlying trait.[30] Phases of the disorder would then reflect dysfunction in connections between prefrontal areas and the amygdala, with the orbitofrontal areas unable to sufficiently regulate the amygdala, and with overregulation in the depressed phases.

Bipolar Disorder and Reward Circuits

In the introduction to the chapter, bipolar disorder was viewed as a disorder of motivational systems and their regulation. Evidence consistent with this has been reported in euthymic bipolar patients and relatives.[31] Moreover, a circuit involving the amygdala-striatum (putamen)-insula was implicated in another study.[32] Subjects with current bipolar depression, current bipolar hypomania or mania, euthymic individuals, and healthy control were asked to match faces depicting anger or fear. Increased activation in the striatum occurred in all clinical groups, and the investigators reasoned that this reflected an underlying trait abnormality in reward behavior and motor activity. While further study is needed, the involvement of these areas reflects the clinical features of bipolar disorder: mood disturbance, poor judgment, increased reward seeking, anxiety, physiological changes, and motor disturbance.

BIPOLAR DISORDER, NEURAL CIRCUITS, AND YOUTH

A number of studies have found structural and functional abnormalities in the amygdala of adolescents with bipolar disorder.[33] Children and adolescents with bipolar disorder tend to have smaller amygdala volumes. However, the amygdala is typically enlarged when the disorder has an adult onset. Why this difference occurs is not clear, but it may be related to the use of psychotropic medications. Functional studies where subjects view images with a negative tone or faces displaying fear or anger consistently show increased activation of the amygdala in bipolar disorder regardless of the age of the subject. Youth with bipolar disorder may also show increased amygdala responses to a wider range of facial expressions than adults.[34] Furthermore, irritability may mediate misidentification of sad, fearsome, or neutral faces in youth with bipolar disorder.[35]

There is evidence that youth with bipolar disorder and youth with SMD show increased attention to negative emotional information, but the neural circuits involved may be different in the two groups.[36] The investigators used an attention task where in one condition subjects were told they were too slow and had lost money when in fact this information was independent of the subjects' response time. Youth with SMD had more intense negative responses than those with bipolar disorder, although both groups were less happy than controls. SMD youth showed greater activation in the anterior cingulate cortex and medial frontal gyrus than controls. Bipolar youth, on the other hand, showed greater frontal gyrus activation and decreased activation of the insula when they were given negative feedback. These results suggest that while both SMD youth and bipolar youth showed heightened attention to negative emotional information, the neuronal circuits involved may be different in the two groups.

STRESS RESPONSE AND BIPOLAR DISORDER

There is substantial evidence for abnormalities in the hypothalamic-pituitary-adrenal (HPA) axis in bipolar disorder. Increased cortisol is a recognized finding in depression, where it is thought to be involved in the cognitive deficits of depression, and manic episodes are similarly associated with increased cortisol and cognitive deficits.[37] Increases in adrenocorticotropic hormone (ACTH), and cortisol may also precede mania, and higher levels may be associated with more severe mania. Evidence also shows that increased ACTH and cortisol precede mania. While studies have been complicated by the phase of illness, medication status, and subject sampling, there is some suggestive evidence that excessive HPA-axis secretion may be a trait marker. For example, HPA axis dysregulation has been found in remitted patients and is associated with risk of recurrence.[38]

Studies of offspring of adults with bipolar disorder suggest that increased HPA activity may be a marker of sensitivity to stress. One study reported that the offspring of parents with bipolar disorder showed a greater cortisol rise in the morning if they experienced high as opposed to low interpersonal chronic stress. Those experiencing severe stress also exhibited higher daytime cortisol than those reporting mild stress. None of these relationships held in a comparison group who did not have a family history of mood disorders.[39] In another study, offspring with a family history of mood disorders continued to show elevated cortisol levels two years later.[40]

In summary, bipolar disorder emerges from abnormalities arising during development that lead to decreased connections among ventral prefrontal networks and limbic regions, especially the amygdala, that regulate emotion, as well as from abnormalities in circuits related to reward and the stress response.

THE EMERGENCE OF BIPOLAR DISORDER

In the following sections we examine how bipolar disorder emerges. First, we consider characteristics of the individual, notably temperament. Next, we consider genetic influences and how genetic and environmental influences, particularly stress and relationships, interact to produce bipolar disorder.

Temperament

An important historical strand has been the recognition from earliest times of "affective temperaments," for example, hyperthymia and cyclothymia.[41] While the concept of affective temperaments was first mooted by the ancient Greeks and has enjoyed a long clinical history, there are few studies of early temperament and bipolar disorder. Cyclothymia may be a precursor of bipolar disorder and has been identified in a number of studies before the onset of bipolar disorder in youth.[42] It also occurs in the relatives of affected persons. Similarly, cyclothymic temperament has been noted in depressed children who later developed bipolar disorder.[43]

Little is known about temperament in youth bipolar disorder or about temperament as a risk factor. Bipolar youth compared to healthy controls show greater novelty seeking, more harm avoidance, more fantasy, but they score lower on persistence, reward dependence, and being cooperative.[44] Consistent with these findings, high-risk infants who were behaviorally disinhibited (a temperament feature characterized by high approach and novelty-seeking behavior) showed increased rates of mood and disruptive behavior at age six years.[45]

The behavioral activation system (BAS) is important to consider in relation to temperament and mania. The BAS is an attempt to conceptualize the neurobiological systems that link personality traits, behavior, and psychopathology,[46] through the interaction of three systems, a behavioral activation system, a behavioral inhibition system (BIS), and a fight-or-flight system.[47] The BAS is conceptualized to underlie approach behavior and incentive motivation (wanting something). Included in the BAS are the circuits involved in the reward pathways as well as those involved in motor activity.

It is possible that there are individual differences in these systems, i.e., the systems could be more or less sensitive in a given person. A hypersensitive BAS might characterize a person who is very sociable, gregarious, motivated to seek rewards, and tending toward positive moods. Such individuals might also be more inclined to work hard to achieve, and in the face of rewards or anticipated rewards might be driven to excess. But they might also more easily become discouraged, disinterested, and apathetic if their efforts are blocked or if they fail to achieve their goals. For these reasons, BAS sensitivity is thought to be highly relevant to bipolar disorder.[48] Specifically, persons who have bipolar disorder or are at risk may have an overly sensitive BAS that is easily activated by signals suggesting reward.[49] The relevant rewards are those involved in working for and attaining goals. Symptoms of mania or hypomania including euphoria, increased energy, irritability, and excessive optimism could be precipitated. On the other hand, if goals are not achieved or are blocked, then depressive symptoms including anhedonia or lack of interest in wanting something, decreased energy, hopelessness, and sadness might occur.

Gene-Environment Interactions and Bipolar Disorder

There is considerable evidence that genes play a major role in determining the susceptibility to bipolar disorder.[50] The lifetime risk in first-degree relatives of a person with narrowly defined bipolar disorder is 5 to 10 percent compared to the general population risk of 1.5 percent or less. Heritability in twin studies has been estimated to be over 80 percent. Current data are consistent with multiple genes, each with a small effect. Studies of polymorphisms involved in neurotransmitter systems show mixed results. Clock genes involved in circadian rhythms have also been studied, and genome-wide association studies have identified genes involved in calcium channel activity.

In examining life events and bipolar disorder, it is important to not only consider effects on the overall disorder but also to also consider separately the effects of life events on the depressed phase and the manic phase.[51] Independent, severe negative life events adversely affect the course of bipolar disorder. They appear to predict faster relapse and slower recovery. Interpersonal events are important, but surprisingly, there is some evidence that social support does not offset the effects of life events.

Environmental factors play an important role in precipitating both mania and depression. The kindling hypothesis posits that major life stress triggers initial episodes of mania and depression, but over time episodes become independent of life events.[52] But while the hypothesis has been very influential, the evidence appears to be inconsistent with this model.[53] Indeed, if we are always in situations that matter to us and our tuning reveals possibilities in our situations, it would seem that events and our mood and behavior could not ever be uncoupled.

Manic and hypomanic symptoms can be precipitated by both positive and negative events, and depression is precipitated by negative events.[54] Three types of events have been studied in mania: negative events, schedule-disrupting events, and goal-attainment events.[55] Events related to personal commitment and efforts predict increases in manic symptoms. This is consistent with ideas that mania is related to reward systems, goals, and attainment. Interestingly, there does not appear to be an elevated rate of other independent, severe negative life events before mania that directly lead to increases in manic symptoms. But negative events predict symptoms (hypomania) in those with depressive cognitive styles or in those already experiencing sub-syndromal symptoms (e.g., hypomania, dysthymia). There is also good evidence that while sleep disruption triggers manic symptoms, events that disrupt a person's schedule do not appear to increase symptoms.

As expected, severe negative life events are similarly related to depression in those who have bipolar disorder, as they are in those who do not have bipolar disorder. Negative life events in bipolar depression have greater impact on females and on those at risk for depression because of negative cognitive styles. But depression in bipolar disorder occurs for reasons not related to life events.

In summary, individual differences as shown in, for example, temperament, genetic influences, in the context of traumatic events related to personal commitment and efforts, create the condition for mania, and for depression in the context of loss of attachment and personal agency.

We next examine how early bipolar disorder appears. First, we consider the emergence of symptoms and then the symptom complex that constitutes bipolar disorder.

Appearance of Symptoms

How early do symptoms of bipolar disorder appear? Symptoms found in bipolar disorder appear early in life. Recall that we suggested in chapters 3 and 8 that the experiences every infant has are conditions that often signal potential danger and potential loss—the conditions for anxiety and sadness. Therefore, everyone is tuned such that particular experiences make both anxiety and depression likely. As we saw earlier, the younger the child, the more difficult it may be to distinguish sadness and anxiety, and the more likely they are to occur together. Here we turn our attention to two groups of children to identify precursors or prodromal symptoms of bipolar disorder. The first approach is to examine characteristics (mood, temperament) of children before they were diagnosed to see if there are particular features that might indicate how the children are tuned.

Symptoms have been identified that often precede the onset of bipolar disorder.[56] Among these are labile mood, depressed mood, and anxiety, as well as symptoms of hypomania or mania. Cognitive symptoms such as poor concentration and difficulty thinking, and motor symptoms, such as agitation, may also precede mania. As noted above, cyclothymia was identified in a number of studies of bipolar youth and was also noted in relatives. Cyclothymic temperament was also identified in depressed children who later developed bipolar disorder.[57]

The second group consists of high-risk children who have a parent or close family member with bipolar disorder. Over 60 percent of the liability to bipolar disorder in adults is attributed to genetic causes, among the highest of psychiatric disorders. With the increased likelihood that a child of a parent with bipolar disorder will develop a bipolar disorder, studying such high-risk offspring is an ideal way to identify mood or behavioral indicators that presage bipolar disorder.

Studies of offspring of adults with bipolar disorder note mood, cognitive, vegetative and motor changes at some point before the onset of frank bipolar disorder.[58] These include anxiety, depression, mood lability, disturbed sleep, and agitation.

Controlled studies show a wide range of psychopathology in preadolescent children of bipolar parents, but they also reveal some interesting common features. In a study comparing offspring of adults with bipolar disorder, children of adults with major depression, and children of adults with orthopedic problems, almost half of the children (average age eleven years) had an anxiety disorder. Almost one in three of the children of adults with bipolar disorder and one in four of those with a parent with major depressive disorder had a depressive disorder or mood disorder. Almost two out of three of the children with two affected parents had a mood disorder.[59] Recurrent depression was also more common in the children of adults with bipolar disorder than in the children of adults with major depression. In contrast, however, to other studies of high-risk offspring, this study did not find elevated rates of disruptive disorders. The differences may be attributable to methodological issues or to greater comorbidity in parents.

Duffy and colleagues followed children of one bipolar parent or two well parents for up to fifteen years. They found that the children of a bipolar parent showed higher rates of early anxiety and sleep disorders, followed by minor mood symptoms and depression before mania emerged. Early anxiety greatly increased the risk of later mania. The earliest symptoms identified in children who later developed bipolar disorder tended to be anxiety and sleep disturbance. Symptoms of depression appeared next, but symptoms of mania or hypomania tended not to emerge until well into adolescence.[60]

A recent study also found that childhood anxiety (and externalizing behavior) predicted mood disorders in the adolescent offspring of adults with bipolar disorder.[61]

SUMMARY

Simply put, bipolar disorder has two poles: mania and depression. Mania is associated with increased positive emotion and may be seen as a state of heightened awareness of positive signals and a heightened drive toward goals, achievement, and reward, even when there are negative consequences to behavior. At the other pole of depression, there is less participation in positive activities, and a loss of interest in pleasurable activities, that may lead to active avoidance of activities associated with positive mood.

The general consensus is that bipolar disorder emerges from abnormalities arising during development in both the structure and function of networks regulating emotional processes, as indicated by decreased connections among ventral prefrontal networks and limbic regions, especially the amygdala. The evidence is also consistent with the idea that bipolar disorder is a disorder of motivational systems and their regulation.

Considerable evidence suggests that genes play a major role in determining the susceptibility to bipolar disorder, possibly with multiple genes each with a small effect. Events are also important. Manic and hypomanic symptoms can be precipitated by both positive and negative events, and depression is precipitated by severe negative events as it is in those who do not have bipolar disorder. Temperament characterized by disinhibition and greater novelty seeking is linked to later bipolar symptoms. Symptoms found in mania appear early in life. Anxiety and sleep disorders, followed by minor mood symptoms and depression before mania emerged. Early anxiety greatly increased the risk of later mania. Symptoms of depression appear next, but symptoms of mania or hypomania tended not to emerge until well into adolescence.

CHAPTER 11

WHEN MOOD IS INDIFFERENT— DISRUPTIVE AND ANTISOCIAL BEHAVIOR

Thomas, a six-year-old, has frequent temper tantrums, both at home and in public. The tantrums can be quite severe, and he often becomes aggressive in an effort to get his way. He is especially defiant with his mother, who reports that Thomas has been this way since birth. She describes him as an irritable, moody child.

Richard, a fourteen-year-old, has been arrested five times for stealing and assault. As a child, he set fires and was known to be cruel to animals. He is manipulative, charming, and cares little for others. He is a poor student and is often truant.

While the disruptive behavior disorders are characterized by defiance of authority, rule breaking, and disregard of the rights of others, the *DSM-5* recognizes that the behavior is the manifestation of problems in regulating emotion and behavior.[1] These disorders are common, highly problematic and are present across the life span. In early childhood disruptive behavior is characterized by defiance of adult authorities, in later childhood and adolescence there is a broader pattern of violation of the basic rights of others or the breaking of age-appropriate societal norms or rules, and in adults there is a pervasive pattern of disregard for, and violation of, the rights of others.[2] Antisocial adults typically first exhibit problem behavior in childhood, and while most children who exhibit disruptive behavior cease to do so over time, a significant subgroup goes on to become antisocial adults.[3] Moreover, stressful life events, a family history of related disorders, and comorbid disorders are commonly observed.

The prevalence of antisocial personality disorder in community settings is 3 percent in males and about 1 percent in females, but the prevalence is much greater in clinical settings and prisons. Conduct disorder (CD) has been found in 1 to 16 percent of boys, and in up 2 to 9 percent of girls; oppositional defiant disorder (ODD) has been reported in 2 to 16 percent of children and is more common in males than in females.[4] The prevalence of CD increases in a linear fashion with age in boys, rising steadily through childhood and adolescence, but in girls the rates are low until adolescence.[5] The kinds of behavior problems also differ by age. Aggressive behavior decreases with age, but status offenses increase with age and are most prevalent in adolescents. Rates of ODD tend to decrease in adolescence, but clinically significant levels of oppositional behavior persist in some and significantly overlap with CD in later childhood and adolescence.

MOOD AND DISRUPTIVE/ANTISOCIAL BEHAVIOR

How can we relate these patterns to mood and tuning? Similar to the disorders we have considered, disruptive and antisocial disorders have mood/emotion (e.g., irritability, anger), cognitive (e.g., perceiving threats and insults), physiological (e.g., changes in heart rate, skin conductance), and action components (e.g., aggression). Disruptive and antisocial individuals appear to be both less sensitive to reward and less sensitive to punishment and aversive signals.[6] They often interpret the behavior of others as intending harm to them and have difficulty constraining their behavior when challenged.[7] They are less able to pick out and process relevant cues, tend to choose an aggressive response over an alternative, and are quicker to act aggressively. This suggests that, like the disorders we have considered so far, disruptive and antisocial behavior can be viewed through the lens of mood and underlying neural circuits, and like the other mood-related disorders the threat appraisal and stress response systems will be involved.

The characteristic moods and emotions in adults with antisocial personality disorder are irritability and anger as well as dysphoria, which includes an inability to tolerate boredom, depressed mood, and complaints of tension.[8] In childhood, irritability and anger are diagnostic features in ODD, and irritability in this context predicts depression in adulthood.[9]

Conduct disorder, however, is an anomaly with regard to mood, and the criteria for CD do not include any indicators of mood or emotion. However, a significant subgroup of youth with CD appear to be indifferent to the feelings and suffering of others, show lack remorse or guilt, and are described as callous and unemotional.[10] They may have grandiose ideas and present with shallow affect and little anxiety. They show persistent problem behavior and are likely to develop antisocial personality disorder as adults, where irritability is a criterion and dysphoria and boredom are common.

The role of mood and disruptive behavior can also be seen in prominent levels of depression and anxiety seen in ODD and CD.[11] Conduct disorder may also increase the risk for later depression by causing stressful life events (peer rejection, expulsion from school), and ODD specifically predicts later depression and anxiety.[12]

CLASSIFICATION OF DISRUPTIVE/ANTISOCIAL BEHAVIOR

How are the disruptive disorders classified? In adults, antisocial personality disorder is defined as a pervasive pattern of disregard for, and violation of, the rights of others.[13] Among the criteria are deceitfulness, impulsivity, reckless disregard for safety of self or others, and irresponsibility. The pattern begins in childhood or early adolescence.

Four symptom dimensions underlie disruptive behavior in youth, and they have different ages of onset.[14] The dimensions are oppositional behavior, aggression, property violations, and status offenses. The range of included behaviors in youth is extensive: being argumentative, angry, resentful, defiant, aggressive, or cruel; destroying property, lying, stealing, running away, truancy, inattentiveness, distractibility, and hyperactivity. Oppositional behavior has the earliest age of onset followed by aggression, property violations, and finally status offenses.

Diagnostically, ODD is defined by irritability and defiance of adult authorities.[15] It is characterized by recurrent defiant, negativistic, disobedient, and hostile behavior. Factor analysis has identified two main factors, one reflecting negative affect and the second reflecting defiance.[16] Others have identified three dimensions, each with specific long-term outcomes.[17] An irritable dimension predicted depression and generalized anxiety disorder, a headstrong dimension predicted ADHD and non-aggressive CD, and a hurtful dimension predicted aggressive CD problems and lack of empathy.

Conduct disorder refers to a persistent and recurrent pattern of behavior whereby the basic rights of others or age-appropriate societal norms or rules are broken.[18] Characteristic behaviors include lying, stealing, fire setting, aggression, property destruction, running away, and truancy. Two ways of sub-typing are the subject of much current research. Moffitt[19] proposed two core forms of disruptive behavior: an early-onset life-course persistent form and an adolescent-onset or limited form. The early-onset form is characterized by disruptive behavior that arises in early childhood, continues through adolescence, and results in antisocial personality disorder in adults. The adolescent-onset form emerged later, and the long-term outcome was less severe. Family dysfunction, including parents with antisocial personality disorder, temperamental risk factors, cognitive deficits, and genetic factors, characterized the early-onset persistent form. Association with delinquent peers and conflict with authority characterized the adolescent-limited form, and the dominant influences are acceptance by peers, social mimicry, and struggles for autonomy. Aggression tends to occur in response to frustration or threat, as opposed to instrumental aggression in the early-onset form.[20]

Antisocial adults and the subgroup of youths with conduct disorder who become antisocial adults tend toward markedly reduced empathy and guilt.[21] The underlying issue seems to be the presence of callous and unemotional (CU) traits. The subgroup of youth showing CU traits is more likely to fit the early-onset persistent form of disruptive behavior. Children who have an early onset of CD and who also have CU traits seem indifferent and tend to show a lack of emotional reactivity to negative stimuli. They are unconcerned by the predicament of others, appearing to lack the ability to experience or attend to the emotion of the other person. These traits make it likely that the child will not develop empathy, guilt, and other aspects of conscience. They prefer novel, exciting, and dangerous activities, and aggression in this group tends to be proactive. Moreover, genetic factors may be more prominent in youth scoring high on both CD and CU traits. In contrast, those who have early onset of CD but do not have CU traits show emotional responses to threat or distress in others but tend to have difficulties regulating emotion, are impulsive, and show reactive aggression.

DISRUPTIVE/ANTISOCIAL BEHAVIOR AND NEURAL CIRCUITS

Although, as with the other disorders, methodological issues including comorbidity and medication status of the subjects may result in disparities in findings regarding brain mechanisms, there is evidence from structural and functional imaging studies in conduct disorder that abnormalities are present in the orbitofrontal cortex (OFC) and ventromedial PFC, including the anterior cingulate, superior temporal lobes, amygdala, and other limbic areas.[22] These findings are consistent with deficits in the regulation of behavior and motivation and the processing of emotions. These regions also regulate the threat response and are involved in reading social cues, e.g., facial expressions or staring, and increases or decreases in the probability of aggression.[23] There is evidence that the structures and circuits specifically involved in identifying and processing fearful expressions may be dysfunctional.[24]

Considerable evidence points to a key role for the amygdala and implicates hyporesponsivity of the amygdala in some. The degree to which CU traits are present may determine the pattern of response shown by the amygdala.[25] When CU traits are not taken into account both hypoactivity and hyperactivity in the amygdala have been reported. Low amygdala activity is found when high CU traits are present when the task involves fearsome faces, but heightened amygdala activity is found when CU traits are less prominent. Reduced amygdala activity could facilitate the development of antisocial behavior, since antisocial individuals appear to be less afraid of the aversive consequences of their behavior. These amygdala findings have been extended recently to include reduced activity in the insula, a region also involved in empathy.[26]

Although the current emphasis is on distinguishing an early-onset and an adolescent-onset type that are thought to differ in underlying mechanisms, reduced amygdala volume has been noted in both age groups, but the adolescent-onset group has also shown reduced right insula volume.[27]

The amygdala response may also be different among those who show reactive as opposed to proactive aggression. In the first group, emotionally evocative stimuli may elicit heightened amygdala activity, suggesting the amygdala is primed to overreact. But in the second group, the amygdala and OFC response is muted, suggesting a different mechanism.[28]

Neurotransmitters are also involved.[29] The serotonin system has been extensively studied because it is linked to sensitivity to punishment and aversive signals, as well as to aggression. Studies show an inverse relationship between serotonin and aggressive behavior in both ODD and CD. There is also evidence of decreased noradrenergic and dopamine function, as shown by altered response to positive emotional stimuli and reward. Further evidence of altered reward processing is shown by consistent reports of low heart rate (associated with reduced sensitivity to rewarding stimuli). Low resting heart rate is specific to conduct disorder, and low resting heart rate predicts later aggressive behavior independent of other factors, e.g., psychosocial and family risk factors.[30] Moreover, low heart rate is heritable, characterizes early onset persistent antisocial individuals, and is found in females as well as males with antisocial behavior. One theory suggests that under-arousal reflects fearlessness in individuals who do not fear the negative consequences of their aggression, and low autonomic system activity may itself be an aversive state that could lead to stimulation seeking to minimize aversive feelings.[31]

STRESS RESPONSE AND
DISRUPTIVE/ANTISOCIAL BEHAVIOR

There is evidence that the stress response is attenuated in disruptive behavior disorders.

The sympathetic nervous system mediates the fast component of the stress response (chapter 6), and the finding of low rate is consistent with reduced response of this component in CD. The classic response to threatening, aversive, or punishing signals is increased cortisol, indicative of an increased hypothalamic-pituitary-adrenal (HPA) response (chapter 6). However, low salivary cortisol is associated with ODD,[32] persistent aggressive behavior,[33] and the presence of CU traits in non-referred adolescents with conduct problems.[34] Low cortisol appears to be particularly associated with the early onset persistently aggressive subtype. These findings suggest that antisocial individuals have a reduced response to stress. Reduced amygdala activity when CU traits are present is also consistent with this, since activation of the amygdala is a key component of the stress response. The combination of the reduced stress response with consequent reduced amygdala activity could facilitate the development of antisocial behavior.

How might the stress system become attenuated? Susman suggests that genetic factors and early-life adversities may predispose some children to show reduced arousal and a lessening of the stress response to novel, unexpected, or threatening situations. The amygdala may be key since stressful events and genetic influences shape the amygdala and its connections to the hypothalamus, hippocampus, and prefrontal cortex (chapters 5 and 6). The amygdala is at the center of the learning of conditioned fear, whereby signals associated with danger become associated with behavioral, autonomic, and endocrine responses. But some youth may be tuned such that they demonstrate fearlessness and stimulus-seeking behavior. They might, for example, seek out dangerous situations to lessen uncomfortable feelings. Susman further suggests that lessening the stress response might be an adaptation to chaotic environments such that a reduced stress response might prevent a constant pattern of activation that could lead to increase in allostatic load.[35]

In summary, evidence suggests that disruptive and antisocial behavior disorders are consistent with deficits in the regulation of behavior and motivation and of processing of emotions. An important subgroup showing CU traits show hypoactivation of the amygdala and an attenuated stress response.

EMERGENCE OF DISRUPTIVE/ANTISOCIAL BEHAVIOR

Multiple theories and models have been advanced to account for disruptive behavior, but no one theory is completely satisfactory.[36] Many risk factors are associated with conduct disorder, ranging from neurocognitive deficits, temperament, personality, and neurochemical and autonomic irregularities, in addition to a wide range of social, family, peer, and community problems. The more risk factors that are present, the more likely CD is to develop. Vulnerabilities for disruptive behavior may include irritability and anger, genetic predispositions, temperament, gender, disturbed attachments, a hostile attributional style, external locus of control, deficient coping strategies, and negative peer influences. To better account for how risk factors might lead to CD, a number of experts are proposing a multiple-developmental-pathways approach wherein a number of different processes may involve distinct combinations of risk factors.

Early health factors may contribute to brain impairment and subsequent antisocial or aggressive behavior.[37] Obstetric factors, e.g., anoxia, forceps delivery, preeclampsia have been implicated. There is substantial evidence linking smoking during pregnancy and subsequent CD and violent behavior. Malnutrition or specific nutritional deficits may also be important. However, obstetric factors are associated with later disruptive behavior only when they are associated with adverse environments, e.g., maternal neglect and unstable family environments. Similarly, minor physical anomalies that may be considered indirect indicators of brain impairment predicted later violent behavior if family environments were unstable. Noradrenergic transmitter functioning may be the mediating link.

Gene-Environment Interactions and Disruptive/Antisocial Behavior

There is growing evidence for genetic contributions, and current research suggests that gene-environment interactions are crucial. A large number of studies have been conducted in twins and in adopted children. Overall, about 40 to 50 percent of the variance is attributed to heritability, and 20 to 30 percent to the shared environment.[38] Studies generally report higher heritability for the early-onset life-course-persistent type in middle childhood, but environmental influences are more dominant for the adolescent-limited form. For example, in a large study of twins examined at age eight to nine years and again at thirteen to fourteen years of age, aggressive, antisocial behavior in childhood was highly heritable with little influence of shared environment, but disruptive behavior without aggression was strongly influenced by both genes and shared environment.[39] In contrast, aggressive and nonaggressive antisocial behaviors in adolescents were influenced by both genes and shared environment. Aggressive behavior appeared to be a more stable heritable trait.

Conduct disorder and ODD are highly correlated with each other and with hyperactivity and inattention. But depression and generalized anxiety are also strongly correlated with CD.[40] Investigators suggest that two genetic influences underlie the correlations of CD with other disorders. One increases the risk for all forms of psychopathology, and one increases the risk for externalizing disorders. They also suggest that non-shared environmental influences differentiate the disorders. In other words, genetic influences set the stage for all disorders, but the environmental influences unique to each individual shape the particular profile of disorder the person develops.

Socioeconomic status and genetic influences also interact.[41] Shared environmental influences were more important in adolescents from lower socioeconomic environments, whereas genetic influences were more important in more advantaged environments. Other studies have examined the interplay of genetic vulnerabilities and physical maltreatment. In a key study, the effect of maltreatment on risk for CD was greatest for children with the highest genetic risk.[42] Environmental influences, e.g., parenting, appeared to be less important in disruptive children who showed CU traits compared to disruptive children who did not show these traits. Furthermore, heritability at age seven was more influential than the environment in predicting disruptive children with callous and unemotional traits.[43]

Specific genes have been examined in a number of studies. The catechol-O-methyltransferase (COMT) gene plays a key role in the prefrontal cortex, where it is important in the breakdown of dopamine, and a variant of the COMT gene is associated with increased CD symptoms.[44] Moreover, there is a significant interaction between the gene variant and low birth weight. Low birth weight is thought to be a good indicator of the quality of the prenatal environment, pointing to a possible gene-environment interaction. A second dopamine-related gene has also been implicated. The seven repeat DRD4 polymorphism, which is linked to lower dopamine receptor function, is associated with disruptive behavior in preschoolers, but only in the presence of maternal insensitivity.[45]

There is an important association between a functional polymorphism in the promoter region of the gene encoding the monoamine oxidase (MAO-A) enzyme and behavior. A deficiency in the MAO-A enzyme can lead to increased levels of dopamine, norepinephrine, and serotonin. Young adults who had been followed as part of a longitudinal study of a community sample of children were studied.[46] Those who carried the low-activity form of the gene had more CD behaviors, but only if they had a childhood history of maltreatment. In another study, low MAO-A activity predicted CD in children and adolescents if they had been exposed to inter-parental violence, parental neglect, and inconsistent discipline.[47] A third study of adults who had histories of documented abuse and neglect before age twelve replicated the finding that early abuse and neglect were associated with later adolescent and adult violent and antisocial behavior.[48] There was no main effect of MAO-A on later behavior, however, there was a significant gene-environment interaction, but only for white subjects. Both male and female subjects who showed the low-activity MAO-A variant showed later violent and antisocial behavior. These studies suggest that low MAO-A activity, if combined with adverse environments, increases the risk for conduct disorder.

Characteristics of the Child

Disruptive behavior may be linked to mood through temperament, and specific temperaments may act as vulnerabilities that predispose a child to disruptive behavior.[49] For example, children who show high rates of negative reactivity, i.e., anger and frustration, and low levels of effortful control may be especially vulnerable. There is evidence that temperament measures that include indicators of negative affect predict both disruptive behavior and anxiety/depressive symptoms at age four years.[50] Irritability, a criterion feature in oppositional defiant disorder, is a key aspect of early temperament and is also linked to later depression. Irritable individuals tend to have a low threshold for frustration, especially when their efforts to reach a goal are interfered with. We can look at irritability as a mood that in the face of challenge becomes the basis of anger and subsequent aggression and temper outbursts.

Disinhibition as a temperamental trait may be another factor. As discussed earlier, youth scoring high on both CD and CU traits prefer novel, exciting, and dangerous activities, and are less distressed by the effects of their behavior toward others.[51]

Relationships and Disruptive/Antisocial Behavior

Parental Psychopathology

Many studies have shown that parental psychopathology is associated with disruptive behavior in both children[52] and adolescents.[53] Maternal depression in particular is a risk factor for child antisocial behavior. Family histories of depression, substance abuse, and/or antisocial personality disorders are important risk factors through their association with parental discord, inconsistent methods of discipline, harsh and abusive practices, neglect, and modeling of inappropriate (e.g., aggressive) behavior.

Parent-Child Conflict

A long-established finding is that in the families of disruptive children, both parents and children engage in coercive cycles of behavior with the result that the parent becomes threatening or harsh while the child remains noncompliant.[54] The child learns to avoid doing what the parent is demanding through a process of negative reinforcement. Coercive cycles ensue that become well-rehearsed sequences almost outside the awareness of the parent and child. Dodge and colleagues have elaborated a biopsychosocial model of chronic conduct problems in adolescents. Central to this model is the notion that the child learns particular patterns of social information processing that become the final pathway through which all influences act.[55] Part of the problem stems from disruptive children often having limited problem-solving ability and difficulty linking events and consequences, leaving them susceptible to negative peer influences.

Attachment and Disruptive/Antisocial Behavior

Mood in disruptive behavior may also be examined in the context of attachment and parent-child relationships. We have already seen how attachment and mood can be linked through the concept of felt security. There is substantial evidence that insecure attachment is linked to externalizing behavior.[56] The association holds across socioeconomic status and time and is stronger in boys than in girls. There may be a direct link in insecurely attached infants and young children who become whiny and defiant in an attempt to maintain proximity to the caretaker, and indirect links may be seen in situations where the parent is uninvolved and unavailable.[57] Compliance with parental requests is hypothesized to result from reciprocity in the relationship that emerges when the parent is responsive and available to meet the child's needs. Furthermore, the child's capacity to regulate their own emotions is thought to result from the degree of security inherent in the parent-child relationship. Thus, a child in an insecure-attachment relationship may be more prone to anger and anxiety.

SUMMARY

While disruptive behavior disorders are characterized by defiance of authority, rule breaking, and disregard of the rights of others, it is becoming clear that the behavior is the manifestation of problems in regulating mood and emotion and behavior. One group, oppositional and defiant children, indeed are often irritable, but others show little emotion. This is a heterogeneous category of children, but two useful groupings are proving influential. One is an early-onset group with persistent behavior problems who often become adolescents with conduct disorder and antisocial adults. The second is an adolescent onset group whose disruptive behavior tends not to persist. The second important issue is the presence of callous and unemotional traits. Antisocial adults and the subgroup of youths with conduct disorder who become antisocial adults tend toward markedly reduced empathy and guilt, reflecting the callous traits. There is evidence from structural and functional imaging studies in conduct disorder that abnormalities are present in circuits consistent with deficits in the regulation of behavior and motivation; processing of emotions and social cues, especially fear expressions; and regulating the threat response. Considerable evidence implicates hyporesponsivity of the amygdala and reduced stress response when

CU traits are present. Temperament characterized by negative affectivity and possibly disinhibition, genetic influences, stress, coercive parenting, and insecure attachment may combine to produce the behavior patterns.

CHAPTER 12

GETTING BACK ON TRACK— PSYCHOLOGICAL AND BEHAVIORAL THERAPY

Typically, when someone goes to see a mental health professional the expectation is that they will be better at the end of treatment. This applies whether a child or adult is involved. The goal of the therapist is to bring about improvement by significantly reducing symptoms or abolishing them. But disorders involving mood tend to be persistent and recurrent. Therefore, while the basic aim of treatment is to relieve acute symptoms, treatment also includes preventing relapse and future episodes. Prevention also extends to targeting asymptomatic individuals who are at risk of developing a disorder (for example, the children of a parent who has a history of depression or bipolar disorder) and those who have symptoms (for example, worries, tantrums) but do not yet show a full disorder;[1] prevention may also target those who have characteristics (e.g., behavioral inhibition) linked to later disorders.[2]

This chapter sketches the core features and procedures of some current approaches, emphasizing those that have empirical support. Before discussing particular approaches we first review the themes of the book, highlighting their relevance to current treatment and prevention approaches. Two additional considerations arise. One is that focusing on mood as tuning opens the door to going beyond symptom remission as the only goal of treatment. The goals of some therapies explicitly do this. For example, psychodynamic therapy aims to foster psychological capacities and resources.[3] Well-Being Therapy attempts to foster resilience, and to provide balance in dimensions that underlie well-being, such as mastery, autonomy, purpose in life and relationships with others.[4] A second consideration is that this approach to mood lends itself to a trans-diagnostic approach, as well as to tailoring interventions to the individual and not focusing on the disorder.

How might our suggested approach to mood as tuning fit with current treatment modalities? The link between mood and what is significant and matters to the child, and the link between mood and the child's possibilities, can be the pathway to getting a better understanding of the child's current situation, how the child got to that place, and what could happen in the future. The narrative of the child's life emerges as developmental influences are explored, especially in terms of the role relationships played in forming the person and the continuing role they play in the person's life. Earlier chapters provided a roadmap showing how environmental events and genetic influences form the neural circuits and systems that underlie mood and shape each person's unique tuning. In particular, we saw that relationships with others and life events, whether positive or negative, profoundly influence tuning over the course of development and the degree to which we are vulnerable or resilient in face of stress. Events that threaten our safety or stability and/or threaten relationships play a key role in the onset and maintenance of disorders involving mood. Since multiple influences (stressful life events, relationships with others, and particular characteristics of individuals, e.g., temperament) contribute to disorder onset, maintenance, and recurrence, treatment and prevention efforts need to be multifaceted, particularly when youth are involved.

This approach has the further advantage of being applicable to everybody, not just the identified patient. Current treatments are often based on the premise that dysfunctional ways of seeing and thinking about events and others leads to mood changes, and it is assumed to be true only of the person with the disorder, making it difficult for others involved (parents, caregivers, partners, spouses, or family members) to see things from the perspective of the affected person. But everybody has mood, and it functions in the same way for all. This perspective provides a way for all to gain a better understanding of what is happening with the distressed child (or adult), and it may also provide a parent or others with a better understanding of why and how they themselves may be having difficulties, and help them see how they may need to change as well as the affected person.

In chapter 2 we saw that mood is intimately involved in revealing our possibilities, paving the way for us to choose our *own* possibilities and become responsible for ourselves and for how we engage with the world. Chapter 2 also suggested that we have little control over our moods. We can neither will nor command our mood to change. However, we have much more control over our emotions and a greater capacity to regulate them. Most of the time we can tell ourselves to stop being angry or discipline ourselves not to get angry when next we meet someone who annoys us. These can be learned or taught as skills. Changing mood seems to require something else, perhaps because mood is more fundamental than emotion, or perhaps because we seek to be in certain moods—at peace or feeling at home and connected to the world. To achieve this may require certain experiences, realizations, and committed action, and the actions may need to be in relation to others. Throughout this book we have seen the many ways relationships influence tuning—both the mood component and the neurobiological underpinnings—and the role they play in the development of disorders. We have also seen that actions are central components of disorders involving mood. This suggests that both relationships and the actions we take need to be addressed to fundamentally change mood.

Classic works such as Viktor Frankl's *Man's Search for Meaning* and the growing literature on resilience support this. Frankl shows the necessity for and the power of choosing one's attitude to find meaning when dealing with difficult or intolerable situations.[5] Rutter suggests that planning, self-reflection, and "active personal agency" be included in efforts to enhance resilience processes in children, arguing that the child needs to feel that he can act to improve his situation rather than feel that all benefits accrue from the actions of the therapist. He suggests providing universal experiences of the kind that foster the development of potentially beneficial attributes.[6] For example, providing experiences of success at school or in some other area of activity may help children take responsibility, exercise a degree of autonomy, and have the opportunity to learn from their own mistakes. This is similar to the ideas linking mood to authenticity (chapter 2).

It may be easier to see how authenticity and meaning are relevant to treatment of adults, but how is it relevant to therapy with children and adolescents? Authenticity and meaning are developmental processes that are continually relevant across the life span. It may seem very abstract, but by nine years of age, children express fears of death. Adolescents often think about mortality and the meaning of life, and suicide and attempted suicide are very significant problems in youth. Medically ill children may face a shortened life span or life-changing circumstances. Abused or neglected children who live in group homes or foster homes may feel unwanted, without value, and like they have no future. But if the child's sense of what is possible can be changed, then mood can be changed, and if a new world of possibilities can be opened up, then more positive, peaceful moods can come to the fore.

There are two additional points. Interventions, whether treatment or prevention, typically adopt a diathesis stress model and address symptoms, vulnerabilities, and the associated risk and protective factors. While specific risk factors associated with each disorder are targeted, prevention also targets general factors (poverty, family dysfunction, abuse) that are associated with increased risk across disorders. Protective factors are equally important. Resilient children (children at risk or exposed to trauma who did not develop a disorder) tend to have certain personal attributes that allow them to take advantage of the presence of other protective factors. Prevention may focus on helping children build relationships and the skills needed to meet age-appropriate developmental tests. Rutter stresses the value of maternal warmth, a positive family atmosphere, and good social relationships as buffers for the child. Good social relationships are necessary and have benefits beyond the provision of coping skills or cognitive strategies. He points out that social relationships are not necessarily skills that are learned, but they are best acquired experientially through guidance.[7] There are benefits to being exposed to and learning to cope successfully with challenges and stressors, all part and parcel of normal development.

The timing of prevention efforts is important.[8] Successful prevention efforts need to occur before the age of onset or the age of peak incidence of a disorder. This means that programs to prevent depression might target late childhood or early adolescence, but prevention of oppositional defiant disorder (ODD) or separation anxiety disorder would need to begin much earlier. One of the benefits of prevention in early and middle childhood is that it may have a steeling or toughening effect so that when major turning points (marriage, work) occur later in life the child is better able to cope with them.[9]

OVERVIEW OF CURRENT THERAPIES

There are many schools of therapy, each with its own theoretical basis, procedures, and techniques. There are three main psychosocial therapies: psychodynamic therapy (PDT), interpersonal psychotherapy (IPT), and cognitive behavioral therapy (CBT). Each has been applied in various ways to prevent and treat anxiety disorders, depression, bipolar disorder, and disruptive behavior. We will discuss each approach as it applies to the different disorders.

In general, interventions focus on the child, the parent or caregiver, the family, and the environmental context. They each have a point of view and procedures that follow from this. Educating children regarding their illness is an important component of many prevention and treatment protocols. With the current emphasis on empirical testing, each has a growing research base. Within each school, there may be distinct variations designed to target specific disorders. Increasingly, therapies are operationalized, and many therapies, especially those based on CBT, are available in manual form with versions focused on a particular disorder and age group. While this is essential for research, the sheer proliferation of manuals presents difficulty in clinical settings.[10] Moreover, this not only reifies the categorical approach and the idea that disorders are discrete, but the person is also in danger of getting lost in the procedures and measurement tools. This has led to the development of trans-diagnostic approaches where, for example, a single treatment model is proposed for all anxiety disorders and unipolar depression.[11]

PSYCHODYNAMIC THERAPY

Modern psychodynamic therapy has a number of distinguishing features[12] and may be more effective in younger children and in those with internalizing disorders and may have more sustained though slower to appear benefits.[13]

Overall, the focus is developmental and is rooted in interpersonal relationships.[14] A basic assumption is that symptoms carry specific psychological meaning, and feelings rather than thoughts and beliefs are emphasized. The therapist helps the person to describe and put words to feelings, including contradictory, troublesome, or unacknowledged feelings. Speaking freely is encouraged, and efforts are directed at behaviors that seek to avoid the exploration and expression of feelings. A second assumption is that early experience with attachment figures influences and may engender recurring themes and patterns in a person's life. The focus is on identifying these recurring themes and patterns. Relationships are explored both in terms of how they are an issue in the present, and how early experiences with attachment figures are influencing the present. In youth, the aim is to put into words the therapist's understanding of what the young person is communicating through play, behavior, and talk. The assumption is that using free play, drawings, or words is the equivalent of free association and reveals feelings and underlying dynamics.

The relationship with the therapist (transference) is a crucial aspect of treatment. The idea is that a particular relationship with the therapist develops in the course of treatment, and the recurrent themes in the person's relationships will express themselves in some way in the relationship with the therapist. This provides a further entry point into better understanding and changing the person's behavior. Similarly, the relationship the child develops with the therapist is at the center of psychodynamic techniques. Here, the transference refers to the relationship the child makes to the therapist that arises from the characteristics of the figures in the child's internal world, not to the real aspects of the therapist's own person and behavior.[15] By observing these elements, the therapist is able to clarify the child's fundamental assumptions about the external world. Conversely, the responses invoked in the therapist by the patient (countertransference) are also important.

Mentalization and reflective functioning are two key concepts in current psychodynamic therapy.[16] Reflective functioning is proposed as the mechanism through which psychodynamic therapy works. Mentalization refers to the ability to understand one's own mind and other people's minds. These concepts are based on the idea of a pre-reflective sense and a reflective sense. The pre-reflective self is the immediate experiencer of life, and the reflective self knows that the self feels, experiences, and reacts. The reflective self is able to reflect on mental experiences whether or not they are conscious, and forms representations of feelings, thoughts, desires, and beliefs. In so doing, the reflective self forms an image of the self as observed by others, of the other as observing, and is capable of reflecting on these observations. For example, a person can have an idea or representation of their being angry distinct from their feeling angry. The caregiver who has the capacity to hold onto complex mental states is better positioned to understand the child's behavior with respect to the child's feelings and intentions. When the caregiver's ability to reflect in this way is adequate, the child is able to develop the ability to self-regulate and to reflect on mental states in themselves. The child's capacity for empathy, intimacy, and insight can grow. Conversely, deficiencies in the caregiver's capacity to mentalize engender problems for the child in these functions.

Anxiety Disorders

Psychodynamic psychotherapy has long been in use as a treatment for anxiety disorders in children and adolescents, but despite an extensive literature, few clinical trials have been carried out.[17] The basic principles behind psychodynamic therapy for anxiety is that much of mental life is unconscious, that genetic and constitutional factors interact with childhood experiences in shaping personality, and that individual symptoms and behaviors serve many functions.[18] Events in life carry meaning, and the psychological meaning may be outside of conscious awareness. The goal of treatment is to reduce anxiety by making these meanings explicit. Typical dynamics concern separation, autonomy, self-esteem, anger, or aggression. Anxiety in youth is similarly seen as a signal of internal distress and conflict that results in internalized, largely unconscious coping strategies, use of defense mechanisms, and compromise formations (see below). Anxiety disorders appear when the signaling system is dysfunctional, and normal behavior and development is disrupted by the anxiety. Anxiety in part results when unacceptable or ambivalent wishes and defense mechanisms evoked in response to those wishes reach a psychological compromise. The unacceptable wishes and fantasies present psychological danger to the individual (child), and unconscious psychological processes referred to as defense mechanisms protect the individual. Should the defenses fail, the child may experience overwhelming anxiety.

Common underlying dynamics relate to attachment figures, and these are typically fear of separation from or fear of loss of attachment figures. A child may have difficulty experiencing or acknowledging anger or ambivalence toward attachment figures. The unacceptable ideas or wishes can be evoked by life events such as the birth of the sibling or the loss of an exclusive hold on a parent. Discord between the parents or abuse are another source of unacceptable ideas or wishes. Perceptual distortions or immature interpretations that result in incorrect meanings of events may be further sources. Preadolescent children may be struggling for mastery over their intellectual and physical skills, and young adolescents may be anxious as they search for an independent identity and increased mastery. In addition, issues related to sexual conflict may emerge in adolescence.

The psychodynamic theory underlying social phobia is that the child has conflicted wishes to be the center of attention, and the normal desire for attention feels unacceptably aggressive to the child. There may be associated guilt and self-punishment. In generalized anxiety disorder normative curiosity and exploration give rise to an inability to relax, hypervigilance, and dread of many normal situations. The assumed underlying conflict is between curiosity and exploration and feeling overwhelmed and out of control. The conflicts in separation anxiety arise from the desire for autonomy and fear of hurting or making a parent angry. The result is feelings of loneliness and fear of rejecting the parent. If conflicted aggression is associated with guilt and negative self-evaluation, then depressive symptoms may arise along with the anxiety symptoms. Physical complaints may also emerge in this situation.

The key components of the psychodynamic treatment of anxiety in children have been summarized in a recent review.[19] A key step is to develop specific psychodynamic formulations of meaning of the anxiety symptoms. Reflective functioning and offering alternative meanings through interpretation of fantasies help the child become reflective and self-observing about the anxiety symptoms. Talk or play allows the therapist to awaken the child's psychological curiosity and reinforce the child's reflective functioning. The "compromise formations" underlying the anxiety are addressed as the child learns to consider other examples of underlying dynamics of her anxiety and to develop new responses.

Working with the child's capacity for mentalization is a further key aspect of treatment. The therapist learns about the child's point of view and helps the child conceptualize what the child can understand might be going on in the mind of another through imagining what the child might feel in a given situation. Psychological defenses presented by the child, e.g., denial, projection, isolation of affect, are interpreted. Unconscious fantasies are explored and connected directly to the anxiety symptoms. The therapist listens carefully to engender in the child a feeling that the child is understood. Exploration of transference and countertransference are further key components.

Depression

Because psychodynamic psychotherapy has been used for a long time to treat depression, there is an extensive clinical literature, but there is a dearth of controlled trials in both adults and youth. However, this situation is changing with the advent of short-term treatments and manualized treatments. But while there is emerging evidence that psychodynamic psychotherapy is effective for depression in adults,[20] some rate it as possibly efficacious for acute treatment and the prevention of recurrence or relapse.[21] There is also some evidence that short-term psychodynamic therapy may be effective in youth.

Psychodynamic psychotherapy for depression is focused on guilt, shame, interpersonal relationships, anxiety, and unacceptable or repressed impulses.[22] The underlying issues and conflicts may derive from difficulties in the relationship between the child and caregivers. A number of elements are commonly found in psychodynamic formulations of depression.[23] The person has an insecure sense of the separate self and a heightened sensitivity to perceived or actual losses and rejections. These lead to a lowering of self-esteem, depressive affects, existential angst, and rage responses. A second element is conflicted anger, where anger, blame, or envy is directed toward others. The result is difficulties in interpersonal relationships with confusion over responsibility and subsequent depressive affects. A third element is guilt and shame. Here feelings and wishes seen as bad or wrong, coupled with doubts over whether the youth's love outweighs aggression, lead to negative views of the self and to self-criticism. There may be idealized and devalued expectations of the self and others that lead to disappointment, anger, and subsequent low self-esteem. The person may defend against these elements by using certain psychological defenses, including denial, projection, passive aggression, and reaction formations where the world is seen as hostile or the self is attacked. The aim of therapy is to address the core elements, leaving the young person better able to manage depressive feelings and aggression, less prone to guilt, more capable of making realistic assessments, more realistic about what he or she is responsible for, with a slightly better-developed sense of agency, and less vulnerable to depression when losses or disappointments occur.

INTERPERSONAL PSYCHOTHERAPY

Interpersonal psychotherapy (IPT) is a psychological treatment that was initially developed for the treatment of depression, but that has been adapted to other disorders. A version for adolescents (IPT-A) has been developed.[24]

As the name of the therapy implies, IPT emphasizes interpersonal and social factors in the understanding and treatment of depressive disorders and focuses on resolving interpersonal difficulties in relationships. But the various biological and developmental influences linked to vulnerability to depression are also recognized. The general format follows two basic principles.[25] One principle is that mood and the person's life situation are related, and the person's task is to resolve the disturbing life events, build social skills, and organize his life. The second is that depression, if the focus, is a medical illness, not the person's fault, and is treatable. Therapy is time limited, typically lasting 12–16 weeks. Because of the emphasis on interpersonal and social factors, the initial assessment requires a detailed history of current and past relationships with significant others, both within and outside the family. Emphasis is placed on the quality and patterning of the interactions, including relationships to authority, dependency and autonomy, intimacy, and trust. There is also an emphasis on cognitions the individual and significant others develop and have about them and each other. Critical components of treatment include identifying triggers of the depression, resolving role disputes, improving social skills, and building more effective social relationships.

Anxiety Disorders

While it is primarily a treatment for depression, IPT has been applied to treat anxiety and trauma-related disorders. For example, IPT has been used in post-traumatic stress disorder (PTSD).[26] Here the IPT approach is used to address the interpersonal consequences of the trauma but without focusing repeatedly on the trauma itself. Feelings and actions that arise in daily life are explored. The person with PTSD is then able to learn to use feelings as the effect of social responses by putting them into words to help renegotiate their interpersonal difficulties. This becomes a way for the person to build social supports.

IPT is helpful in social anxiety disorder, but it may not be better than supportive therapy and is not as effective as CBT.[27] Stangier and colleagues suggest that CBT may be more effective in social anxiety because cognitive approaches more directly address the self-focused attention, recurrent images, memory biases, and safety behaviors that are typical of social anxiety disorder, whereas IPT focuses on interpersonal problems based on the idea that those with social phobias have established negative interpersonal cycles resulting in avoidance and nonassertive social behavior.[28]

Depression

The rationale of IPT is that clinical depression arises in an interpersonal context, and the techniques of IPT encourage mastery of current social roles and adaptation to interpersonal situations. Resolving interpersonal problems is suggested as the mechanism of action.[29]

The protocol for depression calls for the disorder to be defined as a medical illness, and the illness and not the patient is blamed for symptoms. IPT is time limited and is focused on current interpersonal relations of the depressed person. Central issues include losses, such as bereavement separations or divorce; major transitions, perhaps involving changing roles or role disputes; and social issues, including social isolation or social skills deficits. The range of feelings, including moods and emotions, associated with the individual's relationships, are integral to the treatment.

IPT IN YOUTH

IPT-A is a form of IPT adapted for adolescents, where it is an effective treatment for depression,[30] and it is also more effective than usual treatment in depressed adolescents with comorbid anxiety.[31] The goal of IPT-A is to decrease depressive symptoms, educate the adolescent about the link between their symptoms and events in relationships, and help the adolescent develop skills to address interpersonal problems that may be exacerbating or contributing to their depression. IPT-A is also time limited and manualized and is administered once weekly for twelve weeks. Efforts are made to involve parents in all phases of treatment. There are a number of key components to IPT-A. Adolescents and parents are told that the adolescent has a medical illness, that the adolescent's usual activities and performance are being affected by an illness. Parents are instructed and encouraged to have the adolescent participate as much as possible in normal activities. The purpose of this approach is to place the blame for underperformance on the depression, to instill hope, encourage participation in usual activities, and increase involvement in productive behavior. The education phase also includes discussion of the nature of depression, available treatment options, explanation of IPT-A, and the potential for improvement and recovery. A detailed inventory of the adolescent's personal relationships is made. Treatment focuses on current interactions by addressing communication patterns and improving interpersonal problem-solving skills. While IPT-A involves questioning, information gathering, and discussion, treatment can also include role playing and practice in communication. Problem areas that are focused on include grief; interpersonal disputes with peers, teachers, parents, or other family members; typical role transitions experienced by adolescents, including changing schools, puberty, becoming sexually active, parental divorce or illness of a parent; interpersonal deficits, including social isolation and difficulty in beginning and sustaining relationships.

IPT has combined with social rhythm therapy (SRT),[32] and the combined therapy (IPTSRT) has successfully addressed poor compliance with medication, stressful life events, and disturbances in sleep and social routines thought to reflect underlying disturbed circadian rhythms in bipolar disorder. IPTSRT shows promise in adolescents with bipolar disorder.[33] A pilot study in a small group of adolescents suggests that IPTSRT, flexibly applied, can be a helpful addition in treating adolescents in either the manic or depressed phase of their disorder.

Variations on IPTSRT have been incorporated in a family approach to bipolar disorder in youth. Two good examples are (a) multifamily psycho-education groups (MFPG), and (b) RAINBOW Therapy. MFPG focuses on reducing parent-child conflict and disagreement as well as reducing expressed emotion (EE), i.e., critical comments, hostility, and emotional over-involvement, in families.[34] Multiple techniques are used in a structured, curriculum-based format with a group of families. RAINBOW Therapy is a child- and family-focused cognitive behavioral therapy that integrates principles of family-focused therapy with CBT.[35] Each letter of "RAINBOW" refers to a specific compo-nent of the program. The letter R stands for "routine," or having a predictable routine to reduce reactivity. The letter A stands for "affect regulation," and this section includes self-monitoring of mood. Preliminary reports on both MFPG and RAINBOW Therapy are encouraging.

Similar efforts are being directed at prevention, but to date, there have been few studies on preventing bipolar disorder in youth. Efforts are focused on the offspring of adults with at least one bipolar parent, since having an affected parent is the single greatest risk factor for bipolar disorder in youth. Prevention has included pharmacotherapy and psychosocial interventions, especially family-focused therapy (FFT).[36] Family-focused therapy for children at high risk for bipolar disorder include psycho-education sessions, identifying risk and protective factors, developing communication skills including the ability to express positive feelings, problem-solving modules, and review sessions. The objective is to reduce stress, increase resilience and coping, and decrease aversive parent-child interactions. The results suggest that children in targeted programs showed greater improvement in depressive symptoms, decreased hypomanic symptoms, and decreased suicidal ideation over the course of a year than chil-dren who received enhanced care that consisted of a brief psycho-educational treatment that could include their parents.

COGNITIVE BEHAVIORAL THERAPY

Cognitive behavioral therapy (CBT) can be thought of as a family of related interventions that are based on a set of core ideas, procedures, and interventions, but it is not concerned with understanding the origins of the behavior.[37] As the name implies, CBT is based on cognitive theories and operant, classical, and social learning theory. The basic idea is that thoughts cause behavior, and cognitive change is necessary to change behavior. One central idea behind cognitive therapy in youth concerns how children and adolescents think about and interpret their experiences. The idea is that the distressed youth forms inaccurate beliefs about himself and the world and neglects or ignores evidence that would disconfirm the beliefs. The goals of CBT include the reduction of symptoms of anxiety, depression, or intense emotions and their associated cognitions and behaviors, thereby making the person feel better. A further goal is to change self-maintaining maladaptive thoughts and behaviors. A variety of techniques are used to achieve this. They include psycho-education; self-monitoring, including keeping a diary and a record of events and the associated thoughts; cognitive restructuring; and behavioral interventions, including skills building, practice, and exercises.

CBT is designed to be a time-limited focused approach that applies specific techniques to particular disorders. Manuals have been developed that outline the specific procedures. The typical treatment begins with one or two initial sessions focused on educating the child and family about the disorder in question, outlining the rationale of CBT, describing the treatment approach, and emphasizing rapport building and the collaborative nature of the treatment.

Anxiety

The core elements of CBT for anxiety[38] include psycho-education; procedures to develop skills in managing somatic symptoms, for example, relaxation training, diaphragmatic breathing, self-monitoring; exposure to feared stimuli; cognitive restructuring; and developing plans to prevent relapse. Typically the exposure procedures involve four elements: instruction, the development of hierarchies, the exposure procedures, and a focus on generalization and maintenance of improvement. Cognitive restructuring is focused on the connections between maladaptive thinking, anxiety, and anxious behavior. The child is asked to keep a record of distressing situations and her thoughts at the time. The beliefs are challenged by direct discussion or guided discovery. Alternative hypotheses are raised, and experiments may be constructed to test the child's beliefs and to help her develop more accurate ideas. Protocols are available for the treatment of specific anxiety disorders. For example, CBT for specific phobias involves graded exposure to feared situations, as well as modification of unrealistic fears and thinking. In the case of panic disorder, exposure procedures may include addressing somatic symptoms such as shortness of breath or increased heart rate that are typical of panic attacks. To achieve this, the therapist may help the child perform exercises to simulate the symptoms.

There is substantial evidence supporting the efficacy of CBT in treating anxiety disorders in youth.[39] In general, up to two-thirds of children will no longer meet the criteria for an anxiety disorder after twelve to sixteen weeks of CBT. Moreover, treatment gains in some have been maintained for up to nine years. While it is not yet clear what the effective components of CBT are for anxiety disorders in youth, exposure to feared stimuli may be the necessary component of treatment. But whether cognitive restructuring adds anything additional is not known. In adults, it appears that cognitive restructuring does not add benefits beyond those achieved by exposure procedures.[40]

Efforts to prevent anxiety have for the most part adopted a cognitive behavioral approach. They have included universal (all children or adults) as well as targeted (those at risk) approaches. Some have included a parent component. Across all ages, adults and children, CBT prevention efforts have shown small to moderate effects in reducing general anxiety and anxiety disorder symptoms as well as depressive symptoms.[41] The benefits, however, decayed over time. Typical preventive efforts among children are based on a diathesis-stress model of anxiety disorders. The key risk factors taken into account are family history of anxiety disorders, having an inhibited temperament, and overprotective parenting. The idea is that children with a more inhibited temperament and with parents who are stressed, anxious, or depressed and overprotective or harsh in their discipline practices are more likely to develop an anxiety disorder.

Cool Little Kids, a program for preschool children, is a good example of such a CBT effort.[42] The curriculum has a psycho-education component, which addresses parenting strategies to reduce overprotective behavior and the modeling of anxious behavior, as well as components providing graded exposure to uncomfortable situations and opportunities to increase confident behavior. Practice and discussion sessions help reinforce the techniques being learned and facilitate cognitive restructuring of the parents' fears and worries. Results suggest that anxiety is decreased over time. In one study, both the targeted group and the control group became less inhibited over time, and no differences were found in measures of temperament over time. However, in a second study of preschoolers who had both high levels of inhibited temperament and a parent with an anxiety disorder, targeted children became less inhibited over time as well as showing reduced anxiety symptoms.[43]

School-based programs have also shown to be effective both in the short term and long term. One such program is the FRIENDS Program. Here children in the school setting are engaged in groups and individual activities and are taught to identify and understand the complex of anxiety, somatic symptoms, worries, and the dysfunctional behaviors that go with being worried or anxious.[44] Coping and problem-solving skills are taught over a series of sessions during the school day. It was found that feelings of anxiety decreased over the six-month study period.

Depression

CBT was initially developed as a treatment for depression in adults.[45] The basic idea is that inaccurate beliefs and maladaptive information processing play a causal role in depression. Despite earlier findings suggesting that cognitive therapy was effective only in mild or moderate depression, cognitive behavioral therapy is just as effective as medication even for severe depression, and it has a long-term effect protecting against relapse and recurrence.[46] The same authors find that behavioral therapy or behavioral activation (a component of CBT) is also effective in depression.

In recent years, CBT has been widely used in the treatment of depression in youth.[47] The rationale of CBT is that depression is either caused by or is maintained by depressive thought patterns combined with the lack of active and positively reinforcing behavioral patterns. CBT for depressed youth identifies and challenges negative schemas, automatic thoughts, and cognitive distortions as well as developing coping skills, improving interpersonal relationships, social problem solving, and increasing participation in pleasant activities. As in the case of anxiety disorders, manuals have been developed. Adolescents are taught that they can change negative beliefs and feelings surrounding distressing events by questioning, developing hypotheses, and seeking evidence to support or disconfirm beliefs. Their procedures include protocols to develop problem-solving skills that enable the adolescent to generate alternative solutions and identify positive consequences of possible solutions. Additional procedures include techniques to regulate affect by training the adolescent to recognize stimuli that provoke negative emotions and helping them reduce arousal by self-talk and relaxation techniques. There is evidence that CBT either alone or in combination with medication is an effective intervention for depression in adolescents. However, the response rate for CBT was only 43 percent in one major study.[48] When CBT was combined with fluoxetine the response rate was greater than with either fluoxetine or CBT alone. However, when long-term outcome was considered, CBT was as effective as fluoxetine by weeks eighteen to twenty four and was as effective as the combination of fluoxetine and CBT by week thirty-six. This was a rigorous test of CBT, as the study included severely depressed adolescents who were treated across multiple sites, and there was an active pill placebo control, giving credence to this result.[49]

The mechanism of action of CBT is not yet clear in the case of depression, despite the evidence that CBT is an effective treatment for both adults and children. The effective components appear to be procedures targeting changing behavior. Procedures targeting cognitive change, or cognitive restructuring, appear to add little to treatment over and above the behavior change components.[50] Again, this suggests that action is needed to change moods.

There have been a number of successful efforts to prevent depressive symptoms in children and adolescents.[51] Universal prevention as well as targeted prevention have been attempted. Many studies have targeted children at the highest risk, i.e., children with a depressed parent, as well as children and adolescents who have or have had depressive symptoms. In the main, interventions have used cognitive behavioral techniques, and many have included a parent component. Specific and nonspecific risk factors for depression have been addressed. Efforts have focused on improving low self-esteem, improving negative body image, improving social support as well as changing the negative cognitive styles found in depression as well as improving coping skills. Factors that provide protection and are linked to resilience in studies of childhood depression were also addressed. These factors included the presence of supportive adults, strong family relationships, strong peer relationships, good coping skills, and skills in emotion regulation.

Both symptoms of depression and anxiety were reduced in targeted children. Successful interventions helped subjects gain control over negative moods, resolve conflicts that arise at home or with peers, and address dysfunctional thought patterns. Children who are able to focus on relationships, on accomplishing age-appropriate developmental tests, and who better understand their parent's illness tend to be more resilient. There is good evidence that including a family component made a significant difference. The family component educated families about depression to help them recognize and deal with stress and improve parenting skills and coping. Children whose parents were committed to parenting despite their own symptoms, and who had a commitment to relationships, also tended to do well. These characteristics of resilient children and families are consistent with the approach we have taken regarding the role of mood, and they suggest ways to approach prevention. Improvement was also related to the timing of the intervention. The optimal timing appeared to be before full depressive syndromes have developed.

Luby and colleagues initiated treatments for depression in preschoolers that can be applied to prevention.[52] They modified Parent Child Interaction Therapy (PCIT), an intervention successfully used to treat preschool disruptive disorder, by adding a module focusing on emotion development. The module was designed to help children to identify, understand, and label their own emotions. PCIT uses behavioral and play-therapy techniques to improve the quality of the relationship between parents and children, as well as to improve the parents' ability to set effective and nurturing guidelines. By coaching and teaching parents how to optimally interact with their children, Luby and colleagues hope to help preschoolers to more effectively regulate their own emotions.[53] Preliminary results from this approach are very promising and suggest that helping mothers manage their own depression and improve their sense of self-efficacy during pregnancy and their children's early years can prevent depression and anxiety in their children.

Psychosocial Approaches to Mood and Disruptive/Antisocial Behavior

There is considerable evidence that a variety of psychosocial treatments help reduce disruptive behavior,[54] including youth with callous and unemotional (CU) traits. The most effective approach is Parent Management Training. Interventions with children most often focus on problem-solving skills, social skills, the way children think about themselves and their world, and enhancing self-control. Interventions with parents and families most often focus on parenting skills and reducing parent conflict. For young children, there are at least five parent-training programs that have a strong evidence base, and for elementary to high-school-age youth, there are at least six child-training programs with a strong evidence base. However, improvements in behavior do not always last or extend to other settings, e.g., school, neighborhood. As a result, more recent approaches are more comprehensive and include interventions at many levels and in a variety of settings.

Mood elements in disruptive behavior are typically addressed by teaching children how to identify feelings and manage their anger. Treatment often includes problem solving to help defuse anger, often by role playing in situations likely to provoke angry responses. CBT techniques have been adapted to address mood elements in disruptive behavior.[55] The successful programs focus on emotion awareness, perspective taking, and anger management. The idea is to teach children to become more aware of their emotions, particularly the negative ones, so that they better understand the conditions under which they tend to be disruptive. The therapists help to increase emotion awareness by teaching the child to describe and rate the physiological sensations, behaviors, and the typical thoughts that occur in particular situations. Triggers linked to these states are identified. The children are helped to more accurately figure out the intentions of others, and role-playing exercises are typically used to teach perspective taking. The assumption is that if disruptive children have greater emotion awareness and improved perspective taking, they are better able to learn techniques to regulate their anger and will be less likely to be aggressive or otherwise disruptive. Parent-directed components of typical programs teach behavioral techniques and work toward improving family cohesion and the parent-child relationship. They also address how parents' own stress can influence how they react to the child's behavior.

Despite the increase in the number of rigorous manual-driven comprehensive treatments, it is not yet clear what the critical variables are in the treatment of disruptive behavior.[56] However, comorbid depression/anxiety in the child and maternal depression moderate the effects of treatment. Warm and supportive parenting is an important variable. Evidence suggests that parent behavior that is firm but not harsh, consistent, and supportive mitigates the development of CU traits in children and favors the development of empathy and conscience development.[57] A randomized controlled trial providing parent training and support to mothers of children with conduct disorder resulted in improved child behavior and improvement in CU traits. Parent training was aimed at the quality of the mother-child relationship and at helping parents learn how to increase the child's level of pro-social behavior. The program also provided extensive emotional and material support to the mothers. The long-term outcome following such interventions with parent treatment is promising, and treatment gains were maintained at a three-year follow-up, including in children who had CU traits.[58]

Next we consider two approaches whose goals go beyond symptom remission or addressing the person's values or purpose in life.

ACCEPTANCE AND COMMITMENT THERAPY

Acceptance and Commitment Therapy (ACT) is one of a group of acceptance-based therapies related to CBT.[59] The focus is on what the individual values and on how effectively the individual's behavior or thinking supports the values. The goal is to help the person accept difficult internal experiences, whether ideas, images, or emotions, in the service of behavior consistent with their chosen values. ACT grew out of CBT, but differs from it in critical ways. Whereas CBT is based on the idea that thoughts cause behavior and cognitive change is necessary for behavioral change, ACT proposes that psychological events are ongoing and are optimally considered in a situational and historical context. Behaviors can have different functions for a person in different contexts, and behavioral change is achieved through changing the context. ACT focuses on the contexts that regulate or organize thinking or behavior rather than on the content. In other words, there is less interest in what someone worries about than in what the function of the worrying is for that person. A person's learning history and particular ways that language functions result in the meaning context gives to behavior. The ACT model of psychopathology is that while pain, trauma, and loss are part of life, distress and suffering arise through language processes that create unhelpful persistence and strategies that prevent the person from behaving in ways that achieve valued objectives.

The therapist tries to help the individual lead a valued life rather than simply focusing on helping the person to feel less anxious and depressed. Progress is measured by how well the person is living the life he wants to live. The core question asked in ACT is, given the distinction between you and the things you are struggling with trying to change, are you willing to experience those things fully and without defense?

Components of ACT include mindful meditation and processes directed toward commitment and acceptance. There are six core processes in ACT.[60] The first is acceptance or the active and aware embrace of symptoms without making unnecessary attempts to change their form or frequency. For example, somebody with anxiety would be taught to feel the anxiety fully and without defense. The second process attempts to alter the meaning not the content of thoughts by creating contexts that diminish unhelpful functions. Articulating a negative thought, repeating it, and/or other techniques are used to diminish its importance. The third process is "being present." Here the therapist attempts to promote nonjudgmental contact with psychological and environmental mental events and to have patients experience the world more directly, increasing flexibility in their behavior and making actions more consistent with the person's values. The ACT therapist helps the person choose life directions, whether family, career, or spirituality, and encourages patterns of effective action linked to those chosen values.

There is growing evidence that ACT is effective across a broad range of mood and anxiety disorders and is comparable in efficacy to CBT in the short term.[61] However, in a long-term outcome study ACT and CBT were equally effective in treating anxiety in the short-term, but at eighteen months proportionately more in the CBT group continued to report recovery.[62]

Application of ACT among anxious youth is just in the early stages.[63] A small number of studies have targeted anxiety and depression. Case studies suggest that ACT may be used to help with school refusal, obsessive thoughts, and social anxiety. There is also evidence that ACT may be helpful in treating clinically depressed adolescents.

WELL-BEING THERAPY

Well-Being Therapy (WBT) is designed to increase psychological well-being and resilience.[64] Resilience refers to attributes and resources that prevent illness following stressful events in the general population and that prevent relapse after remission of clinical symptoms in the clinical population. Well-being is not defined by the remission or absence of symptoms but rather emphasizes the positive and personal growth that can also result from therapeutic interventions. The primary focus is on helping the individual lead a meaningful and purposeful life as well as having quality ties to others because these are fundamentally connected to overall well-being.

In contrast to CBT, the focus in WBT is on being well and not on psychological distress and negative thinking. The idea is that lack of attention to positive experiences and insufficient capacity to maintain wellness are as important as the detrimental effects of negative automatic thoughts. Therapy sessions are geared toward aspects of psychological well-being. These include establishing mastery over the environment, personal growth, finding a purpose in life, autonomy, self-acceptance, and having positive relations with others. A number of these dimensions address or include mood states. For example, engendering a sense of being able to master the environment addresses feelings people often have about their difficulties in managing their everyday affairs where they feel they are unable to change their context. Addressing personal growth confronts the feeling of being bored and uninterested in life or feeling unable to develop new ways of looking at things or of behaving. Addressing self-acceptance examines how people feel dissatisfied with themselves or feel disappointed about what has gone on in their lives or being troubled about their personal qualities.

They also address certain core notions. One is the importance of interpersonal relationships in the capacity to make and sustain close ties to others. The second is helping to provide a sense of meaning in life, by establishing a sense the person can have goals, aims, and purpose. Finally, autonomy addresses the issue of being over-concerned with the expectations and evaluations of others and feeling that one has to conform to social pressures and the views of others and act in certain ways.

Like CBT, WBT is typically structured with eight to twelve sessions and uses an educational model. Some procedures are very similar to the procedures used in CBT, except the focus is on episodes of well-being. The early phases of WBT focus on paying attention to positive aspects of daily living and emotions. Instances of well-being and instances where the person feels his experience is optimal are targeted. The next phase focuses on any obstacles or triggers that are preventing the person from maintaining moments and feelings of well-being. The third phase targets specific strategies to maintain and enhance well-being. This phase includes scheduling activities to gain mastery, assertiveness training, and problem solving, as well as attempts to modify automatic or irrational thoughts. The approaches taken in phases two and three are similar to CBT procedures, but again the focus is on moments and feelings of well-being as opposed to distress. Translating insights that are gained into action or behavioral terms is what brings about significant improvement.[65]

While as yet there is limited research into the effectiveness of WBT, a number of studies suggest the value of this approach.[66] In a study of generalized anxiety disorder investigators compared a combination of CBT and WBT to CBT alone. Both therapies led to significant reduction in anxiety, but there were great advantages to the combination. In a second, small study of adults with major depression or a number of different anxiety disorders who still had residual symptoms following treatment, WBT was better than CBT in alleviating immediate residual symptoms. Well-Being Therapy has also been helpful in preventing recurrences of depression when used with CBT and in treating cyclothymia. Furthermore, WBT has been used in schools to promote psychological well-being and to reduce distress and somatization, as well as beginning treatment efforts in symptomatic children.[67]

SUMMARY

While the therapies discussed above address many of the principal issues related to mood, they differ in their scope, purpose, underlying rationale, and procedures. The way mood is viewed in this book lends itself to all the approaches, and comports with key elements of each, as can be seen in the following paragraph.

The focus of psychodynamic therapy is developmental and rooted in interpersonal relationships, and feelings rather than thoughts and beliefs are emphasized. Early experience with attachment figures influence and may engender recurring themes and patterns in a person's life, and relationships become a focus of therapy. A core principle of IPT is that mood and the person's life situation are related. IPT also focuses on interpersonal factors in the understanding and treatment of depressive disorders, and on resolving interpersonal difficulties in relationships. The person's task is to resolve disturbing life events, build social skills, and better organize her life. In contrast, CBT is not concerned with understanding the origins of behavior but is based on the idea that dysfunctional thoughts cause changes in mood, and cognitive change is necessary to change behavior. The goals of CBT are to reduce symptoms of anxiety, depression, or intense emotions, and to change the associated dysfunctional cognitions and behaviors as well as the self-maintaining maladaptive thoughts and behaviors. There is a strong action component to CBT where the focus is on behavior change. Well-Being Therapy focuses on resilience, meaning, and purpose in life. ACT focuses on acceptance, helping the person identify what is important to him, increase awareness of other possibilities, and help him take committed action to achieve his goals. The primary focus of WBT is on helping the person lead a meaningful and purposeful life as well as having quality ties to others. The emphasis is on developing the personal attributes and resources that prevent symptoms following stressful events, and this is achieved by focusing on wellness as opposed to distress.

This recap suggests that an optimal approach to resolving mood-related disorders would combine elements of these approaches in a treatment plan that would focus on the individual and not the disorder. Such an individualized approach would take into account the unique characteristics of the individual, the commonalities as well as the differences between disorders, and set the goal of going beyond symptom remission in getting the person back on the track.

Transdiagnostic treatment approaches for anxiety and depression are being considered,[68] motivated in part by the multiplicity of treatment manuals that are in use, as well as the commonalities in cognitive, behavior, and neural dysregulation in these disorders.

CHAPTER 13

GETTING BACK ON TRACK— MEDICATION

While the various therapies address the mood components of tuning, medications target the neurotransmitters that modulate neuro-circuits and events in the synapse. Basically, the idea is that if you change the way the neurotransmitter is acting, you change mood.

The purpose of this chapter is to give the reader an overview of the common medications used to treat mood, to examine their efficacy, and to give some insight into how they may affect neurocircuits involved in tuning. Medications have limited benefits, and so we also explore what, if any, benefits arise from combining medication and therapy. Related to this we will see that increasing research is beginning to show that therapy also affects neurocircuits.

The purpose is not to provide guidance on dosage or specific treatment strategies. The reader interested in more detail is referred to recent comprehensive reviews on depressive disorders,[1] anxiety disorders,[2] and bipolar disorders.[3] Many excellent textbooks are available, and the discussion in the following sections is based largely on *Stahl's Essential Psychopharmacology*.[4] This next section provides background information on the principal classes of medication at issue, antianxiety agents, antidepressants, and a mixed group of medications broadly referred to as mood-stabilizing agents.

ANTIANXIETY AGENTS

The arrival of the benzodiazepines and the tricyclic antidepressants (see below) marked a significant advance in the treatment of anxiety disorders.[5] Benzodiazepines decrease anxiety symptoms by increasing the activity of gamma-aminobutyric acid (GABA), the inhibitory transmitter in the synapse. However, while these medications have a rapid onset and are beneficial under some circumstances, they are associated with adverse effects, dependence, withdrawal symptoms, and rebound effects. As a result, they are not a first-line treatment, and instead, the SSRIs (see below) are preferred.

ANTIDEPRESSANTS

In chapter 4 we outlined the main pathways and the synaptic activity of the key neurotransmitters serotonin, dopamine, and norepinephrine. The basic action of the effective antidepressants is to boost the synaptic action of these monoamines, because the idea was that depression was the result of monoamine deficiency. Antidepressants typically do this by blocking the transporter for the neurotransmitter, thereby raising the level of the neurotransmitter in the synapse. They may also change the expression of genes such that fewer receptors are made. Side effects result because the pathways are widespread and affect multiple areas and functions. A drawback to antidepressants is that they can take a number of weeks to work, if they are going to work at all. Also, suicidality among youth and young adults taking antidepressants has become a significant concern.[6]

There are many classes of antidepressants and a great many individual agents.[7] For many years the major classes of antidepressants were the tricyclic antidepressants (TCAs) and monoamine oxidase inhibitors (MAOIs). MAOIs were the first antidepressants to be developed after it was discovered that depression improved in people with tuberculosis who were treated with medications that blocked monoamine oxidase leading to a deficiency in dopamine. They fell out of favor because of concerns about side effects and drug interactions. The TCAs block the uptake of norepinephrine, and some block both norepinephrine and serotonin. Although there was no evidence that they were more effective as antidepressants than placebo, they were widely used in youth. They also fell out of favor because of troublesome side effects, reports of sudden death in children treated with desipramine (a TCA), and with the arrival of the selective serotonin reuptake inhibitors (SSRIs).

The SSRIs are a major advance on the older medications and have markedly changed the treatment of both depression and anxiety not only in adults but also in youth. They include fluoxetine, sertraline, paroxetine, fluvoxamine, citalopram, and escitalopram. The SSRIs improve symptoms related to negative affect, i.e., guilt, disgust, fear, anxiety, hostility, irritability, and loneliness. But they may have less benefit where there is reduced positive affect. As a result, symptoms such as loss of interest, low energy, and loss of pleasure may persist. This led to the development of medications that not only increase serotonin but also increase the levels of other neurotransmitters, e.g., dopamine.

Serotonin-norepinephrine reuptake inhibitors (SNRIs) comprise a class of medications in which both the serotonin transporter and the norepinephrine transporter are blocked. The result is a boost in serotonin and norepinephrine in the synapse. Dopamine levels in the prefrontal cortex are also increased through an indirect effect. The overall result is potentially increased positive symptoms and decreased negative symptoms. The wider influence of the SNRIs on neurotransmitters, however, means more side effects may arise. The most widely used SNRI is venlafaxine. Other antidepressants selectively block norepinephrine and dopamine reuptake, e.g., bupropion, or they raise serotonin and norepinephrine levels by blocking receptors such as the alpha-2 receptor, e.g., mirtazapine.

MOOD-STABILIZING AGENTS

Mood disorders may result from dysfunction in circuits in which there may be unstable or excessive neurotransmission.[8] In simplified terms, a nerve impulse in neuron A may activate overly sensitive voltage-sensitive sodium channels, leading to excessive release of glutamate (the excitatory transmitter in the synapse) and unpredictable neurotransmission. Postsynaptic NMDA receptors on neuron B receiving this unpredictable neurotransmission from neuron A may then continue the process. The overall result is unstable moods and behaviors. Originally the term *mood stabilizer* referred to drugs to treat mania and prevent recurrence, but it is now clear that no single agent treats all phases of bipolar disorder. Effective agents block voltage-sensitive sodium channels, reduce glutamate release or glutamate effects on NMDA receptors, and reduce dopamine hyperactivity.

Lithium is considered to be the classic mood stabilizer and has been in use for over fifty years. Despite its long history, the mechanism of action of lithium is not well understood, but it may affect signal transduction. Lithium also has extensive side effects and requires monitoring of blood levels. Anticonvulsants are widely used as mood stabilizers. Their use is based on the kindling hypothesis of seizure disorders,[9] but it is not yet known with certainty which specific pharmacological action is linked with which specific clinical action. Valproic acid may inhibit voltage-sensitive sodium channels and enhance the action of GABA, the inhibitory neurotransmitter. Carbamazepine may also work through voltage-sensitive sodium channels.

The so-called second-generation antipsychotics (SGAs) comprise the third class of drugs widely used to treat bipolar disorder. While each of the SGAs has a unique range of pharmacological effects, they tend to reduce psychotic symptoms of mania through dopamine receptor effects and treat the nonpsychotic and depressive symptoms by reducing glutamate hyperactivity through effects on serotonin receptors. The SGAs have significant side effects that may include substantial weight gain and cardio-metabolic complications, insulin resistance, and problems with lipids. In practice, SGAs are often used in combination with lithium or anticonvulsants.

MEDICATION, COMBINED TREATMENT, AND SPECIFIC DISORDERS

Anxiety

Rynn and colleagues provide a comprehensive overview of pharmacotherapy in childhood anxiety, including the use of novel agents.[10] This review and others show substantial evidence that the SSRIs and SNRIs are effective in the treatment of anxiety disorders.[11] They are currently the cornerstones of pharmacotherapy for anxiety disorders in youth. Four SSRIs have been studied—fluvoxamine, fluoxetine, sertraline, and paroxetine—and in general they appear to be equally effective, although head-to-head trials have not been conducted. There is some evidence that extended-release venlafaxine is effective in treating generalized anxiety and social phobia. However, many do not respond to first-line treatment or are refractory, and augmentation or combined therapy may be necessary. The older antidepressants (TCAs) and the benzodiazepines are considered second-line treatments, and benzodiazepines, as noted above, carry considerable risk, while more recently atypical antipsychotics and other agents have been used as adjunctive treatments, but efficacy of these has not been established in youth.

While there have been studies of individual anxiety disorders, comorbidity is so common that much of the research includes children with multiple anxiety disorders. Obsessive-compulsive disorder (OCD), however, has received considerable attention in its own right. The Pediatric Obsessive Compulsive

Disorder Treatment Study (POTS) showed that sertraline or cognitive behavioral therapy (CBT) are more effective than placebo after twelve weeks of treatment.[12] The remission rate was 39 percent for CBT and 21 percent for sertraline, compared to 4 percent remission rate for placebo. However, when sertraline and CBT were combined, the remission rate was 54 percent. As promising as these results are, it is clear that substantial numbers of affected youth will need continued treatment or changes in medication.

The Child/Adolescent Anxiety Multimodal Study (CAMS) compared CBT, sertraline, combined CBT and sertraline, and pill placebo in children and adolescents with moderate to severe separation anxiety disorder, generalized anxiety disorder, or social phobia. Many had more than one disorder. Most subjects were prepubertal. Over twelve weeks of treatment, 60 percent of those receiving CBT and 55 percent of those receiving sertraline were very much or much improved. However, 81 percent of those receiving combination therapy were very much or much improved. Only 4 percent of children responded to placebo.[13]

Depression

While there has been considerable controversy over whether antidepressants are effective in adults in the treatment of depression, current opinion is that antidepressants are indeed superior to placebo, although the advantage is modest.[14] A little over a half of adults with major depression will respond to an antidepressant compared to about a third of patients given placebo. The effect is likely to be stronger for more severely depressed patients. While those studies were conducted in selected patients enrolled in randomized placebo-controlled trials, patients from a range of practice settings were recruited for the STAR*D study (Sequenced Treatment Alternatives to Relieve Depression).[15] The STAR*D study was designed to assess the effectiveness of antidepressants in situations more closely resembling actual practice. In this study patients after an initial trial of medication (citalopram) could switch medications, receive augmentation, or have psychotherapy added. There was no placebo group. Essentially the results showed that 30 percent of patients on the initial medication (citalopram) remitted, and all medications used were equally effective. Moreover, SNRIs showed no advantage over SSRIs.

Numerous studies have been conducted assessing the effects of combining medication and psychotherapy in treating depression. The results suggest there is a small but statistically significant advantage to combined treatment.[16] Combined treatment may lead to longer-lasting improvement and lower rates of relapse. Depressed adults who have a history of childhood trauma or a personality disorder may respond better to combined therapy, and a combined approach may be particularly helpful when depression is chronic.

Prior to 1997, antidepressants were often used to treat depression in children and adolescents, but there was no empirical evidence they were effective. In 1997, the first randomized placebo-controlled trial showed that fluoxetine performed better than placebo in treating depressed children and adolescents.[17] The study was notable in that the trial continued past the usual four or six weeks and went to twelve weeks. This marked the beginning of the era of SSRI use in youth. Early claims were that they were safer, and clearly they had less troublesome side effects than the older TCAs. New medications came on the market and were accompanied by the sharp increase in research studies. New safety concerns also came to light, as will be discussed below. As we saw in the previous chapter there has also been a sharp increase in studies of psychosocial treatments of depression and youth. Although many important findings and recommendations resulted from these studies, key questions remained.

Not all medications are equally effective in treating depression in youth. The most robust evidence favors fluoxetine; there is some evidence favoring sertraline and citalopram; and paroxetine is not effective. Response rates appeared to be of the order of 55 to 60 percent for medication and CBT.[18] This led to key questions: What is the best approach to the 40 percent who do not respond to medication or CBT? What happens if medication and CBT are combined? Two large multisite studies addressing these questions have been published. The first study, Treatment of Adolescents with Depression Study (TADS), compared fluoxetine alone, CBT alone, fluoxetine with CBT, and a pill placebo condition in moderate to severely depressed adolescents. The results were interesting and in some instances unexpected. Over twelve weeks of treatment, the combination of fluoxetine and CBT produced the greatest improvement. Fluoxetine was also found to be effective, but the combination of fluoxetine and CBT was superior. Surprisingly, CBT alone was not better than the placebo condition and not as effective as fluoxetine alone. It is important to note that this was the first study in which CBT was compared against a strong placebo condition.[19] However, in a second report of long-term effectiveness, CBT alone was not as effective as medication alone at eighteen weeks, but at thirty-six weeks there was an 88 percent rate of response for the combined therapy, 81 percent for the fluoxetine alone, and 81 percent for CBT. The overall conclusion was that in the case of moderate to severe depression fluoxetine alone or in combination with CBT is necessary in accelerating improvement.[20]

But what about those who do not respond to the initial course of treatment? In a second large-scale multicenter study, the Treatment of SSRI Resistant Depression in Adolescents (TORDIA), youths who had not improved during an adequate SSRI trial were randomized to an alternative SSRI (paroxetine, citalopram, or fluoxetine), an alternative SSRI and CBT, venlafaxine, or venlafaxine combined with CBT. The combination of CBT and an alternative SSRI showed the highest response rates. The response rates to venlafaxine or the alternative SSRI were the same.[21] In a second report almost 39 percent achieved remission by twenty-four weeks. Those who had shown a clinical response by week twelve were more likely to be in remission at twenty-four weeks, and they also remitted much faster. Overall, about one-third of adolescents who did not respond to the initial course of treatment reached remission with continued treatment, either by switching medication or by combining CBT and an alternative medication.[22]

Bipolar Disorder

As we saw in chapter 10, bipolar disorder is a complex condition with many phases and often has a poor outcome. In adults, there is considerable comorbidity that includes substance use and personality disorders. All this makes the pharmacological treatment a highly complex endeavor. However, current treatment recommendations have been well summarized by Malhi and colleagues.[23]

There is strong evidence that a number of agents are effective in the treatment of acute mania. These include lithium, valproate, or an atypical antipsychotic that may be used alone or in combination depending on the initial presentation. Lithium is effective for euphoric mania, prevents manic episodes and suicide, but is less effective for acute bipolar depression and is not as effective when there is rapid cycling or mixed episodes. Some but not all anticonvulsants are effective in treating mood disorders. Valproic acid is effective in adults in treating acute mania and is commonly used to prevent recurrence. But its prophylactic and antidepressant actions are not well established. SGAs effectively treat mania and prevent the recurrence of mania.

Malhi and colleagues also summarize strategies for managing complex presentations.[24] For example, the treatment of acute bipolar depression is the subject of considerable debate. In particular, support for antidepressants is limited, but there is strong evidence that quetiapine and perhaps olanzapine are effective. Mixed states are common and have highly variable presentations. As a result, combination therapy will be required in most individuals with mixed states. Maintenance treatment is similarly complex because of the high rates of relapse and the recurrent nature of the disorder. A few agents (lamotrigine, olanzapine, and quetiapine) prevent both mania and depression. A variety of other anticonvulsants have been used to treat bipolar disorder but have not been shown to be effective.

In recent years, mood stabilizers have actively been studied in youth and have been widely used in clinical practice. In four open-label trials of lithium the response rate (50 percent reduction in symptoms) for manic symptoms averaged 50 percent (23 to 55 percent).[25] In one of the studies the response rate for lithium used alone was 38 percent. However, in three double-blind studies, lithium was not found to be more effective than placebo. There have been two open-label trials of carbamazepine. The response rates here were 38 percent and 55 percent. In contrast, there have been eight open-label and three double-blind studies of divalproex. Three of the open-label studies were of the agent alone, and the response rate was 43 percent. The anticonvulsants topiramate and oxycarbezapine were not found to be better than placebo in double-blind trials. Overall, there is only some evidence for efficacy of the anticonvulsants after a number of open-label and double-blind trials.

What about SGAs in pediatric bipolar disorder? Here, the data is more promising.[26] The response rates for aripiprazole in open-label studies have been as high as 70 and 79 percent. Double-blind studies showed significantly better response rates than for placebo. Response rates in open-label trials of olanzapine should average response rates of 51 percent. In double-blind studies a response rate of 49 percent was significantly better than that for placebo, which was 22 percent. There is similar data for quetiapine. Quetiapine has been shown to be better than placebo or divalproex, and better than divalproex plus placebo. Risperidone and ziprasidone have both been shown in double-blind studies to be more effective than placebo. One major trial compared lithium, divalproex, and risperidone in medication-naive children and adolescents with a diagnosis of bipolar 1 disorder.[27] Risperidone was the most effective, achieving a 68 percent response rate. Lithium (35 percent) and divalproex (24 percent) were similar. However, response rates differed by site. Moreover, almost all subjects were also diagnosed with attention deficit hyperactivity disorder (ADHD), and severity of ADHD predicted worse outcome.[28] Overall, the evidence favoring SGAs is stronger than the evidence for the anticonvulsants. However, in clinical practice anticonvulsants and SGAs are frequently used in combination.

There have been few studies of pediatric bipolar disorder in which depression was assessed.[29] Response rates in open-label studies of adolescents and older children range from 43 percent to 60 percent. But younger children have also been studied, and the response rate for depressive symptoms was 36 percent among preschoolers.

Pharmacological efforts to prevent bipolar disorder in youth who have a bipolar parent typically include children who already have a mood disorder, ADHD, or at least a moderate level of current symptoms. In open-label studies, mood stabilizers have reduced symptoms in the affected youth, but in one controlled study, the mood-stabilizing agent was no better than placebo, as improvement occurred in both groups of subjects.[30]

MEDICATION, THERAPY, AND NEURAL CIRCUITS

There is evidence that therapies alter the brain functions that underlie the activities they focus on. For example, brief psychodynamic therapy normalizes the hyperactivation of the amygdala and hippocampus and the deactivation of the prefrontal cortex (PFC) seen in panic disorder.[31] Both interpersonal psychotherapy (IPT) and cognitive behavioral therapy (CBT) in depression are associated with normalization of activity in the anterior cingulate cortex (ACC), PFC, and other areas that showed abnormalities before treatment.[32] Enhanced CBT also results in normalization of activity in the circuits (prefrontal-striatum-thalamus) implicated in OCD.[33]

Cognitive therapy and medication may involve similar neural mechanisms in anxiety in that comparison studies suggest they both normalize the circuits involved in fear and negative emotions in anxiety.[34] They may also engage mechanisms distinctive to each in depression.[35] For example, CBT may increase PFC function, whereas antidepressants primarily affect the amygdala. In other words, one may improve top-down regulation, and the other produce bottom-up effects.[36]

Medications also affect the neural circuits and processes that underlie tuning.[37] For example, SSRIs attenuate the amygdala hyperactivity shown in depression, and SSRIs also increase connectivity between the amygdala, the

PFC, and the ACC. SSRIs also increase hippocampal neurogenesis, and lithium blocks the harmful effects of chronic stress on the hippocampus. Hippocampal neurogenesis is hypothesized to be the mechanism of action of antidepressants.

Studies of the effect of medication treatment on neural circuits in youth are just now under way. One interesting recent study found that fluoxetine normalized pretreatment over-activation in response to fearsome faces in the amygdala, orbitofrontal cortex (OFC), and subgenual ACC in depressed youth.[38] Blackford and Pine recently reviewed neural circuit activity and treatment response in childhood anxiety. They note evidence for less clinical improvement to medication or therapy in adolescents with generalized anxiety disorder who showed amygdala activation before treatment. But they also note evidence that successful treatment with CBT or fluoxetine was associated with increased activation to angry faces in the PFC.[39]

Studies in both adults and youth with bipolar disorder show that medications tend to normalize activity in relevant circuits. For example, a consistent finding in the recent literature is that lithium normalizes or increases gray matter volume in the amygdala, hippocampus, and ACC and subgenual cingulate cortex.[40]

The placebo response provides an interesting perspective, showing how circuits change when someone is given a presumed inactive agent.[41] The placebo effect refers to the observation that approximately one-third of patients given an inactive treatment will show benefits. The reasons behind why and how this happens has generated wide interest, and while the final answers are not yet known, active mechanisms appear to be present. Expectation of benefit and attributing the benefit to the placebo are important. Individual differences are also important. Placebo responders tend to be more suggestible, less anxious, and more optimistic, and reward-related circuits and dopamine systems are more readily activated.[42] Circuits involved in assessing and attributing salience or in how distinctive or relevant an event is to the individual are active in pain conditions.[43] These circuits include the ACC, PFC, amygdala, insula, and other areas, and one hypothesis is that they are involved in the placebo effect.

CHAPTER 14

THE CHALLENGE OF MEDICAL ILLNESS

The emergence of a medical illness in a child or adolescent presents many challenges that speak directly to the issues raised in this book. At one end of the spectrum, a major illness may mean that we, or someone close to us, may die in the near future, or that we will need someone to take care of us. At the other end of the spectrum, a minor illness may be no more than uncomfortable and inconvenient, causing us to have to adjust our schedules and take time off work or school. But even minor illness can threaten what is important to us. A seeming insignificant illness or symptom in a child may alarm a parent because of associations the parent has with the symptoms, perhaps because a relative or school friend died as a result of a similar illness. As we saw in chapter 2 the significance of an event does not lie exclusively in the intrinsic properties of the event but in the relation of the event to the person and the person's current concerns. We experience the world, including illness, through the lens of tuning, and our tuning will reveal the possibilities available to us as presented by the illness. But tuning may uncover the possibility of changing ourselves and how we live. What lies behind these claims?

MOOD, INFLAMMATION, AND NEURAL CIRCUITS

First, we examine the link between illness and how we are connected to the world. Earlier chapters sketched how mood is linked to what matters and has significance for us, and how it arises out of the continuous activity of neural circuits and systems that are formed by genetic and environmental influences throughout development to create each person's tuning. The threat and stress response systems can provide a crucial link between illness and mood because they are involved not only in the circuits underlying mood but also in the immune system, the inflammatory response, and the mechanisms of inflammation associated with many chronic illnesses.[1] This holds promise for an integrated view of illness/mood connections, where what happens with illness can be seen as another aspect of how we interact with the world. Viewed in this way, both the illness and any depression or anxiety could result from breakdowns in the underlying mechanisms.

How might this work? The body fights infection by means of an inflammatory response, and the neuroendocrine system plays an important role in regulating the magnitude and duration of this response. When someone is exposed to threats (chapter 6), whether real or imagined, not only is the threat appraisal system activated, but so too is the hypothalamic-pituitary-adrenal (HPA) axis (stress response) and the inflammatory response that is regulated by the HPA axis.[2] For example, threats to social status are associated with changes in autonomic, endocrine, and immune responses that have implications for health.[3]

The response to pathogens begins with the mobilization of pro-inflammatory molecules called cytokines and other inflammatory molecules such as prostaglandins.[4] Concurrent with the pro-inflammatory responses, anti-inflammatory cytokines activate the neuroendocrine system via the hypothalamus to help regulate the inflammatory response. Pro-inflammatory cytokines produce effects, which result in autonomic and behavioral changes that include feelings of depression and irritability, as well as tiredness, sleep disturbance, and impaired memory. This complex is a normal concomitant of viral and bacterial infections and can be elicited during systemic infections, cancer, or autoimmune diseases, and should it continue unchecked, it may lead to depression in vulnerable individuals.[5] Depression, for example, could result from an overactive or protracted stress response or from altered serotonin function due to activation of enzymes that deplete tryptophan, the serotonin precursor. Moreover, there may be specific pathways linking anxiety or negative emotion to inflammatory processes and disease.[6] In addition, exaggerated and sustained threat response activation in anxious persons might lead to chronic inflammation and increased risk of chronic disease because of prolonged activation of the HPA axis, autonomic system response, and inflammatory response.[7]

MOOD, TUNING, AND MEDICAL ILLNESS

The central idea is that mood connects us to the world and reveals the possibilities available to us in our situations, paving the way for choice and action. How a child is tuned, the choices a child makes, and the actions a child takes, determines how likely a child is to be resilient or vulnerable in the face of the new challenges an illness brings. Taking this approach as a framework allows us to look at the characteristics of the child, the family, the social context, the characteristics of the illness, and the ways they interact.

Illness affects the child and family in parallel ways. The degree to which an illness leads to resilience or vulnerability will depend on the same variables we have seen are associated with anxiety and depression. The same is true of the parent. How a parent responds to the illness is a function of the parent's characteristics and life story. We will begin by discussing the characteristics of illness, outlining key features that may differentially affect the child, depending upon his age and developmental issues.

CHALLENGE OF ILLNESS

The range of challenges presented and the possibilities affected by illness is great. For most, many common acute illnesses present no great challenge and have little impact, but for some they represent significant threats. Some illnesses—for example, cystic fibrosis or cancer—carry serious threats in a broad range of domains. Conditions such as asthma, diabetes (type 1, or insulin-dependent diabetes mellitus [IDDM]), and inflammatory bowel disease (IBD) may mean a fluctuating course, hospitalizations, rigorous treatment regimens, and potential significant limits on activities. Such illnesses bring the threat of potential or real loss of possibilities, particularly in relationships, and in some cases the possibility of death or a foreshortened life span. The burden of illness for the child can be quite substantial, e.g., school absence and limitation of activities or significant change in outlook for the future. For families, there can be economic burdens, e.g., time off work and medical expenses. For both, there may significant feelings of loss. It is no surprise that mood may change significantly, not only in the child but also in parents, siblings, and others.

But while symptoms of anxiety and depression are commonly observed in both acute and chronic illness, not all illnesses are necessarily associated with symptoms, at least at the level of diagnosable disorders. Even in childhood cancers[8] and cystic fibrosis[9]—two illnesses where one might expect significant levels of depression and anxiety, given the life-threatening nature and the enormous burden of the illnesses—most children show great resilience.

Who is likely to develop clinical levels of anxiety or depression? Chapters 8–12 outlined the characteristics of at-risk children and the conditions likely to lead to disorders, and can guide discussion in this context. Children who already have an anxiety disorder or depression will likely have experienced the mood and emotion and the cognitive, physiological, and action components of that disorder. Those at risk may show varying degrees of disturbance in these areas. Moreover, affected and at-risk children are likely to have encountered difficult life events and family circumstances and to have a family history of related disorders (very likely an anxious or depressed parent).

Anxiety is concerned with present or future threats of harm, and one can readily see how an illness could be experienced as worrisome, fearful, and a threat to well-being. Not only are there immediate threats (a cause for fear), but there may also be significant threats to future possibilities (a cause for worry). Children who tend to be fearful, anxious, sad, sensitive to punishment, avoidant, and inhibited are more likely to show disorders (chapters 8 and 9). These characteristics, depending on context (anxious or depressed caregiver, quality of caregiving, available supports) and the demands of illness, may lead to sadness, irritability, worry or fear, and avoidant behavior.

Some children show anxiety sensitivity (chapter 8) and believe anxiety symptoms indicate harmful physiological, psychological, or social consequences. They misinterpret bodily sensations, leading to further anxiety or panic.

The information-processing bias toward threat that anxious youth often display (chapter 8) sets the stage for fears of particular situations (medical procedures, blood draws, injections). Anxious children may become fearful of separation from parents, or may fear losing control and as a result may avoid social or performance-related events. The pattern of withdrawal and avoidance consistent with anxiety may lead to poor adherence to treatment and missed appointments. Should an anxious child have an anxious parent, the parent may themselves have similar worries and fears, and the parent's anxiety may complicate the child's response. An anxious parent may have difficulty judging the severity of the child's symptoms, be reluctant to separate from the child, and hinder the child's efforts to manage his or her illness and become autonomous.

Depressive symptoms are linked to situations that reflect loss or threatened loss in relationships that signal attachments, as well as in relationships that reflect agency as expressed in social standing, reputation, and well-being (chapter 9). Here again, an illness may be experienced as threatening in both domains, and the child and family may experience loss, not just of the child's hopes but also of the hopes for the family. Depressed children or those at risk of depression may participate less in positive activities and show less inclination toward positive approach behavior. They may have a selection bias for negative events or stimuli and may tend to make automatic negative appraisals that are difficult to change. These characteristics complicate adaptation to illness, and depressed, sad, or irritable moods may emerge. The child may become discouraged, even hopeless, and lose interest, leading to problems adhering to treatment regimens. And since anxiety arises in situations where well-being is threatened, anxiety will often accompany depression. Disruptive youth often interpret the behavior of others as intending harm to them and act accordingly (chapter 11). Consequently, they may resist and become disruptive when challenged or asked to comply.

Another aspect of the challenge of medical illness is that many medical disorders are familial, and a parent or family member may have the same disorder as the child, or related medical conditions may be found in parents or other family members. For example, a child with inflammatory bowel disease may have a parent or close relative with Crohn's disease, ulcerative colitis, or, perhaps, a history of childhood abdominal pain. In many cases, the parent is coping well, but for others their own experience with illness brings additional anxiety that may complicate how they approach their child's illness. Further difficulties arise if the parent is also depressed or anxious, since parenting styles are linked to children's mood and behavior. Some parents become overprotective, which can cause anxiety in the child. Others may become overcritical or coercive, which can result in depression or noncompliant behavior.

ISSUES IN ASSESSMENT

Deciding what is normal and expected as distinct from pathological can be very challenging in the context of illness. The difficulty arises in part because some degree of distress is normal, and illnesses often have characteristics similar to those of anxiety and depression. Each of the disorders associated with mood have particular mood, emotion, cognitive, physiological, and action components. The features of many illnesses overlap with these components.

Demoralization is a sense of helplessness, futility, and confusion that may be difficult to distinguish from depression.[10] It is found in situations where someone has experienced a series of setbacks and can no longer cope, and it may occur not only in the child but also in caregivers.

Common physiological features of illness that overlap with the features of anxiety and depression include low energy, sleep disturbance, loss of appetite, weight loss, shortness of breath, and increased heart rate. Problems with memory or attention occur in many illnesses or can result from treatment. Changes in motor activity are characteristic of some illnesses.

But sometimes the issue may be a somatoform or somatization disorder (see below). Here the person, whether for cultural or other reasons, is unable or unwilling to recognize and identify the mood components and is focused on the physical symptoms.

DEVELOPMENT, MOOD, AND MEDICAL ILLNESS

The age of the child at the time of illness onset is an important factor in determining the outcome and the burden imposed on the child and family. Characteristics of the illness present different and changing challenges depending on the age and development of the child. For example, some illnesses have a fluctuating course with seemingly unpredictable episodes, while others may be life threatening. Chronic illnesses obviously present the greatest long-term challenges. Illnesses in infancy and during the preschool years can affect the development of attachment and may result in insecure attachment linked to later anxiety and depressive symptoms. Illness at this age may also affect language development, as well as cognitive development associated with increasing exploration of the environment.

Life-threatening situations that can arise in illnesses such as diabetes can lead to significant anxiety in children and parents,[11] especially in younger children who have not yet learned self-care routines. Asthma is another example of an illness[12] where episodic symptoms can lead to significant alterations in routines and to parental reluctance to allow children to engage in activities— all consequences that can foster anxiety among children, as well as less optimal ways of behaving and thinking about themselves and the world.

Difficulties can be amplified in school-aged children as the child's world expands, peers become an increasing part of the child's life, and the demands of school increase. Children's ability to understand and participate in the management of their illness grows during the school years, but they also become aware of how they differ from their peers.

Adolescence brings remarkable change as youths begin to move away from their family and spend more time with peers, as sports become more competitive, and as they enter into romantic relationships. Although there is an increase in the ability to think abstractly over the course of adolescence, early adolescence is a time when the child may rely more on feeling states (chapter 3). In chronic illness, the adolescent, parents, and treatment team may clash as the adolescent seeks autonomy and tries to come to terms with his or her illness. Older adolescents are faced with the transition to early adulthood, the world of work or further school, and the need to plan and come to terms with any limitations imposed by the illness.

Increasing numbers of children are surviving serious illnesses, and this brings new challenges. In addition to the difficulties of returning to school and normal life, perhaps after long absences, the child may have impairments due to treatment or from the illness itself. This is particularly true in the case of childhood cancers,[13] where survivors may have cognitive difficulties as a result of radiation and other treatments.

Surviving a major disease past the teenage years can put stress on relationships, education, career planning and other challenges that face young adults. How they should live becomes an issue. The medically compromised teen may be unsure about and reluctant to commit to relationships because they don't know how long they have to live or whether they can or want to have children. Similar uncertainties may prevent them from going to college or starting a career. For example, children with cystic fibrosis are surviving well into adulthood, but they may have significantly impaired pulmonary function that will affect their health and livelihood.

ANXIETY AND DEPRESSION IN SELECTED ILLNESSES

There is a well-documented increased incidence of anxiety and depression among asthma sufferers. As reviewed by Di Marco and colleagues, from 30 to 43 percent of children with asthma are diagnosed with an anxiety disorder, with generalized anxiety disorder present in 24 percent.[14] Asthma present before age eighteen predicts increased risk for social phobia or panic disorder in early adulthood. There is an increased rate of depression and disruptive behavior, as well as ADHD and learning difficulties. The increased prevalence of anxiety and depression has been found across countries, is stable over time, and is associated with morbidity and often with poor compliance with treatment.

While there has been debate over whether asthma causes the anxiety and depression, or whether anxiety and depression cause asthma, there is growing interest in the possibility that they share an underlying mechanism.[15] The common link may be the stress response and mechanisms underlying inflammation, as discussed above.

Up to 25 percent of youth with inflammatory bowel disease may be depressed, and there is also an increased risk of anxiety disorders.[16] Youth with inactive or mild disease have rates similar to healthy controls, but more severe depression is associated with disease severity. Diabetes is another illness with high rates of depression and anxiety, and studies have been well summarized by Fritsch and colleagues.[17] Disturbed mood is common following diagnosis, and this is not resolved within the first year; diabetic children are at increased risk of later psychological difficulties. Similarly, up to a third of diabetic adolescents may be diagnosed with depression, and suicide and suicide ideation may be significant concerns.

Somatoform disorders are related conditions that also present in the medical setting.[18] In this situation, physical symptoms are the focus of concern, but no diagnosable condition has been found. Sometimes there may be a diagnosed illness, but symptoms are present at a time when there are no objective measures of disease activity. For example, an adolescent with quiescent inflammatory bowel disease may complain of abdominal pain or other gastrointestinal symptoms. Sometimes, isolated symptoms such as fatigue or headache are present but no cause can be found. Studies have shown that children with such medically unexplained symptoms typically have a family member or members with somatic complaints;[19] they show temperamental traits of harm avoidance; behavioral inhibition and worries; and polymorphisms may be present that are associated with anxiety and negative affectivity, for example, the short allele of the serotonin transporter promoter. Evaluating children (or adults) with such presentations can be difficult and frustrating for the medical team. But inquiring into what matters and is significant in such cases can a fruitful way of uncovering the underlying moods and the connections to the child's life, thereby opening the door to understanding the person.

GETTING BACK ON TRACK

Medications

Psychotropic medications are frequently used to treat depression and anxiety in children with chronic illness, but randomized double-blind controlled trials are not available. Most support for their use in youth comes from open-label studies and clinical experience, and a number of such studies are available for anxiety among medically ill youth.[20] The selective serotonin reuptake inhibitors (SSRIs) are the primary medications used, and this applies also to depression. For example, SSRIs have been shown to be well tolerated and to improve both anxiety and depression in youth with cancer. The standard clinical guidelines apply with additional safeguards regarding side effects, adverse effects, and drug interactions.

Psychosocial Interventions

All the psychosocial interventions used to address depression or anxiety (chapter 12) in non-medically ill youth are applicable to those with chronic illness. Education about the illness is a standard part of the care of children with chronic illness and includes parents, caregivers, and often siblings. The educational components focus on increasing knowledge of disease, outcomes, risks, and treatment. Psycho-educational programs to address mood mirror these efforts and can easily be integrated into the overall treatment plan.

In the hospital setting, simple, practical interventions may be needed to combat the helplessness often experienced by families, to restore a sense of autonomy and efficacy, to help ensure rest and sleep, and to ensure appropriate communication with the medical staff.[21]

All the specific psychotherapeutic techniques for depression and anxiety may be adapted in the context of illness. The principles and approaches of psychodynamic therapy, especially the focus on attachment relationships and on the effects of the illness on the child's development and relationships, often inform the approach of hospital and clinic staff. [22] In therapy, the focus is on mentalization or reflective functioning, as described in chapter 12. The idea is that the ability of the parent or caregiver to mentalize may be compromised by the trauma and distress of the child's illness. Recall that reflective functioning refers to the person's capacity to think about what is going on in their own mind as well as someone else's mind in terms of feelings, thoughts, and the interaction of the two minds, and this ability is considered crucial for mutual emotion regulation and self-regulation of emotion. The second important psychodynamic concept relevant to the medically ill child is that of embodied memory traces. The idea here is that experiences can create memory traces that are stored as bodily sensations and gestures[23] and can alter self-representation, leading the child to believe he or she was born that way.

Because of its focus on relationships and life transitions, interpersonal psychotherapy (IPT) (chapter 12) is a promising approach that could benefit youth struggling with chronic illnesses. Illness presents or complicates many of the problem areas that are a central focus of IPT: loss, changing relationships, changing roles, social isolation, changing schools, puberty, becoming sexually active, parental divorce or illness of a parent, difficulty in beginning new relationships. Feelings, including moods and emotions associated with relationships, are integral to IPT, and the techniques encourage mastery of current social roles and adaptation to interpersonal situations, with the goal of resolving interpersonal problems. Particularly relevant in chronic illness are IPT procedures to instruct and encourage the ill youth to participate as much as possible in normal activities and to increase involvement in productive behavior as a means of instilling hope. IPT has been successfully used in among youth with cystic fibrosis,[24] although controlled studies are lacking.

Cognitive behavioral therapy (CBT) has been applied among children suffering from a number of pediatric illnesses and has the most extensive research base.[25] Targets for treatment can include the initial distress experienced by the child at the time of diagnosis, anxiety and pain during procedures or treatment, chronic pain, adherence to medication and other treatments, related psychosocial distress, and helping with the social skills and supports needed to return to school.[26] Techniques such as guided imagery are widely used and are successful in coping with painful or distressing procedures. For example, CBT, distraction, and hypnosis are well established in IDDM for treating needle-related distress.[27]

Well-executed studies of CBT for depression in youth with IBD have been conducted.[28] These studies focused on helping adolescents to determine the appropriate locus of control and to adjust their behavior and thoughts accordingly. Significant improvements that continued over one year were found in those treated with CBT, as compared to treatment as usual. Narrative therapy that emphasized the child's personal story or the narrative of their illness or their family's narrative of the illness has also been shown to be helpful in IBD.[29]

CBT, relaxation therapy, and biofeedback are among the most common therapeutic approaches used among adults with asthma, and they are also are applicable to youth.[30] However, a meta-analysis of interventions to modify health and behavioral outcomes in adults with asthma found that while results were promising, they did not provide firm conclusions as to efficacy.[31] Similarly, a variety of interventions have been used in diabetes. These include CBT in family-based interventions and training in coping skills.[32] However, while these approaches improved psychosocial functioning, there was not always a significant effect on glycemic control. An interesting approach to identifying and effectively treating symptoms in asthma focuses on symptom perception.[33] This approach is based on the observation that most individuals are able to judge their degree of pulmonary function compromise with reasonable accuracy. Some children, however, are very inaccurate and either ignore or underestimate the degree of their impairment, while others overestimate their degree of symptoms.

Acceptance and Commitment Therapy (ACT) and Well-Being Therapy (WBT) are discussed in chapter 12 and are of great interest in relation to chronic illness because their goals go beyond symptom remission. ACT teaches acceptance and mindfulness among other procedures to help the person identify what is important to him, increase awareness of other possibilities, and help him take committed action to achieve his goals.[34] The actions taken are crucial. And in this respect, ACT is relevant because it emphasizes committed action in pursuit of the person's valued goals as a fundamental part of treatment.

So far the research base for ACT is limited to case studies and small-scale trials in anxiety and depression, but to date results are promising (chapter 12). ACT has also been used in cases of chronic pain, where it has been shown to reduce functional impairment and increase quality of life—benefits that were maintained for at least six months.[35] Acceptance has been studied among patients with cystic fibrosis, and adolescents who were better able to accept their disease (adapted to the demands and limitations) reported better psychological functioning.[36]

Well-Being Therapy is designed to increase psychological well-being and resilience.[37]

Many of the issues central to WBT arise in chronic illness. For example, the well adolescent may be struggling with autonomy, finding a direction and focus, feeling unsure of who they are or are becoming, struggling to accept themselves, and encountering difficulties in relationships with family and peers. Chronic illness complicates each of these challenges. The primary focus of WBT is on helping the person lead a meaningful and purposeful life as well as on having quality ties to others, because these are fundamentally connected to overall well-being. The emphasis is on developing the personal attributes and resources that prevent symptoms following stressful events, making the therapy well suited to the challenges of chronic illness. This is in part achieved by techniques that focus on developing the positive, and not just on ameliorating the negative.

CONCLUSION

Each of the approaches just discussed addresses important aspects of the challenges presented by medical illness. Can the ideas in this book add something to understanding and ameliorating distress in the medically ill, and to the wider world of both youth and adults with mood-related disorders? The answer is yes. The link between mood and what is significant and matters, and the link between mood and possibilities, can be the pathway to gaining a better understanding of the person's current situation and how to effect change.

To recap, the core theme of the book is that mood is a central controlling factor that from childhood becomes the basis upon which we choose and act, and sets the stage for the way we are throughout life. Mood reflects the way we are tuned into the world, reveals our possible options in a particular situation, and thereby becomes the basis of action. This connection to the world is built and shaped over the course of development. By considering mood as a phase of the activity of neural circuits and bodily systems that continually process information about the world, we can see that the feelings of mood and the associated bodily systems can provide a mechanism for the connection. Genetic factors and key environmental events interact to shape the development of these circuits and set how they function. Resilience or the capacity to adapt well comes from the connections being able to surmount challenge, and vulnerability and mood-relayed disorders emerge as breakdowns in the connections occur. Throughout the book, we saw repeated evidence that events that threaten our safety or stability, and experiences that in particular threaten our relationships, play a key role not only in the onset and maintenance of mood-related disorders but also in creating the individual characteristics that underlie resilience and vulnerability.

Chapter 2 suggested that we have little control over our moods. We can neither will nor command our mood to change. However, we have much more control over our emotions and a greater capacity to regulate them. Most of the time if someone annoys us, we can tell ourselves to stop being angry, or we can discipline ourselves not to get angry when next we meet that person. These behaviors can be learned or taught as skills. But changing mood seems to require something else, perhaps because mood is more fundamental than emotion. To achieve this may require certain experiences, realizations, and committed actions, and the actions may need to be in relation to others. Throughout this book we have seen the many ways relationships influence tuning—both the mood component and the neurobiological underpinnings, and the role they play in the development of disorders. We have also seen that actions are central components of disorders involving mood. This suggests that both relationships and the actions we take need to be addressed to fundamentally change mood. This approach reveals and connects the crucial issues that need to be addressed and suggests why treatment and prevention efforts need to be multifaceted and tailored to the individual.

Moreover, we are self-constituting, meaning that who we are as agents is manifested by what we do and what we make of ourselves. We saw that mood is intimately involved in revealing our possibilities, paving the way for us to choose our *own* possibilities and become responsible for ourselves and for how we engage with the world. When critical events occur, e.g., serious illness, that bring us face to face with our finite being, anxiety can reveal the fragility and impermanence of the way we live, and we're faced with making choices. But mood, by revealing what is significant for us and what our possibilities are, can enable us to choose our own possibilities and become responsible for ourselves (chapter 2), paving the way for us to choose a way to live that moves toward autonomy and mastery of self and environment. This applies to adults but also to the adolescent and many children, and particularly to parents and caregivers. If the child's sense of what is possible can be changed, then mood can be changed, and if a new world of possibilities can be opened up, then more positive, peaceful moods can come to the fore.

Our approach to mood also supports the idea of a transdiagnostic approach. We noted that (chapter 12) transdiagnostic treatment approaches for anxiety and depression are already underway,[38] motivated in part by the multiplicity of treatment manuals for CBT that are in use, as well as the commonalities in clinical, etiological, and neurobiological features.

A trans-modality and transdiagnostic approach places the person and not the disorder at the center and takes into account the unique characteristics of the individual child, the commonalities as well as the differences between disorders, and goes beyond symptom remission in getting the person back on track.

NOTES

ACKNOWLEDGMENTS

1. Richard Solomon, *No Excuses: Existentialism and the Meaning of Life* (Chantilly VA: Teaching Company, 2000).

CHAPTER 1. OVERVIEW

1. Ralph Waldo Emerson, "Experience," in *Essays and Poems by Ralph Waldo Emerson* (New York: Barnes & Noble Classics, 1967), p. 237.

2. William Butler Yeats, "The Moods," in *The Collected Works of W. B. Yeats*, 14 vols., ed. R. J. Finneran and G. Bornstein (New York: Scribner, 2007), p. 4, "Early Essays," p. 143.

3. Stuart Goldman, "Developmental Epidemiology of Depressive Disorders," *Child and Adolescent Psychiatric Clinics of North America* 21 (2012): 217–35.

4. Ronald M. Rapee, Carolyn A. Schniering, and Jennifer L. Hudson, "Anxiety Disorders during Childhood and Adolescence: Origins and Treatment," *Annual Review of Clinical Psychology* 5 (2009): 311–41.

5. Martin Heidegger, *Being and Time*, trans. J. Macquarrie and E. Robinson (San Francisco: HarperSanFrancisco, 1962), pp. 172–88.

6. Charles B. Guignon, "Authenticity, Moral Values, and Psychotherapy," in *The Cambridge Companion to Heidegger*, ed. Charles B. Guignon (New York: Cambridge University Press, 2006), pp. 284–90.

7. Heidegger, *Being and Time*, pp. 172–88.

8. William Blattner, *Heidegger's Being and Time* (New York: Continuum International, 2007).

9. Heidegger, *Being and Time*, pp. 279–348.

10. Taylor Carman, "Authenticity," in *A Companion to Heidegger*, ed. Hubert L. Dreyfus and Mark A. Wrathall (Malden, MA: Blackwell, 2008), pp. 285–96.

11. Tom Greaves, *Starting with Heidegger* (New York: Continuum International, 2010), pp. 69–72.

12. Eero Castrén, "Is Mood Chemistry?" *Nature Reviews. Neuroscience* 6 (March 2005): 241–46.

13. Paula M. Niedenthal, "Embodying Emotion," *Science* 316 (May 2007): 1002–1005.

14. Matthew Ratcliffe, *Feelings of Being* (New York: Oxford, 2008), pp. 106–37.

15. Castrén, "Is Mood Chemistry?"

16. Erin B. McClure and Daniel S. Pine, "Social Stress, Affect, and Neural Function in Adolescence," in *Adolescent Psychopathology and the Developing Brain*, ed. Daniel Romer and Elaine F. Walker (New York: Oxford University Press, 2007), pp. 219–44.

17. Marian Joëls and Tallie Z. Baram, "The Neuro-Symphony of Stress," *Nature Reviews. Neuroscience* 10 (June 2009): 459–66.

18. McClure and Pine, "Social Stress."

19. Bruce J. Ellis et al., "Differential Susceptibility to the Environment: An Evolutionary-Neurodevelopmental Theory," *Development and Psychopathology* 23, no. 1 (February 2011): 7–28.

CHAPTER 2. WHAT DOES MOOD DO?

1. Martin Heidegger, *Being and Time*, trans. J Macquarrie and E. Robinson (San Francisco: HarperSanFrancisco, 1962).

2. Martin Heidegger, *The Fundamental Concepts of Metaphysics*, trans. William McNeill and Nicholas Walker (Bloomington: Indiana University Press, 1995), pp. 78–167.

3. Matthew Ratcliffe, *Feelings of Being* (New York: Oxford, 2008), pp. 41–57.

4. *Diagnostic and Statistical Manual of Mental Disorders, DSM-IV-TR* (Arlington, VA: American Psychiatric Association, 2000).

5. Gilbert Ryle, *The Concept of Mind* (New York: Barnes & Noble Books, 1949), pp. 83–107.

6. Ibid.

7. Laura Sizer, "What Feelings Can't Do," *Mind & Language* 20, no. 1 (2006): 108–35.

8. Entry for "mood," *Merriam-Webster's Collegiate Dictionary* (Springfield, MA: Merriam-Webster, 2008).

9. *Oxford Companion to Philosophy*, ed. Ted Honderich (New York: Oxford University Press, 2005), p. 619.

10. John R. Searle, *Mind, Language, and Society* (New York: Basic Books, 1998), pp. 76–77.

11. Ryle, *Concept of Mind*, p. 99.

12. Ralph Waldo Emerson, "Experience," in *Essays and Poems by Ralph Waldo Emerson* (New York: Barnes & Noble Classics, 1967), p. 237.

13. Sizer, "What Feelings Can't Do."

14. Searle, *Mind, Language, and Society*, pp. 76–77.

15. Robert C. Solomon, "Emotions and Choice," in *What Is an Emotion?* ed. Robert C. Solomon (New York: Oxford University Press, 2003), pp. 224–35.

16. Ratcliffe, *Feelings of Being*, pp. 1–4.

17. Solomon, "Emotions and Choice," p. 3.

18. *Oxford Companion to Philosophy*, pp. 240–41.

19. Entry for "emotion," *Merriam-Webster's Collegiate Dictionary*.

20. Joseph J. Campos, Carl B. Frankel, and Linda Camras, "On the Nature of Emotion Regulation," *Child Development* 75, no. 2 (2004): 377–94.

21. Sizer, "What Feelings Can't Do."

22. David Watson, *Mood and Temperament* (New York: Guilford Press, 2000), p. 3.

23. Ratcliffe, *Feelings of Being*, pp. 52–57.

24. Heidegger, *Being and Time*, pp. 78–90.

25. Patricia Altenbernd Johnson, *On Heidegger* (Belmont, CA: Wadsworth, 2000), p. 17.

26. Mark Wrathall, *How to Read Heidegger* (New York: W. W. Norton, 2005), p. 37.

27. Heidegger, *Being and Time*, pp. 172–82.

28. William Blattner, *Heidegger's Being and Time* (New York: Continuum International, 2007), pp. 78–90.

29. Wrathall, *How to Read Heidegger*, p. 37.

30. Heidegger, *Fundamental Concepts of Metaphysics*, pp. 66–68.

31. Hubert L. Dreyfus, *Being-in-the-World* (Cambridge, MA: MIT Press, 1991), p. 172.

32. Heidegger, *Being and Time*, pp. 172–79.

33. Ibid., pp. 182–88.

34. René Rosfort and Giovanni Stanghellini, "The Person in Between Moods and Affects," *Philosophy, Psychiatry, & Psychology* 16, no. 3 (2009): 251–66.

35. Ibid.

36. Blattner, *Heidegger's Being and Time*, pp. 76–84.

37. Ratcliffe, *Feelings of Being*, pp. 36–37.

38. Ibid.

39. Heidegger, *Being and Time*, p. 177.

40. Ibid., pp. 228–35.

41. Ibid.

42. Taylor Carman, "Authenticity," in *A Companion to Heidegger*, ed. Hubert L. Dreyfus and Mark A. Wrathall (Malden, MA: Blackwell, 2008) pp. 295–96.

43. Charles B. Guignon, "Authenticity, Moral Values, and Psychotherapy" in *The Cambridge Companion to Heidegger*, ed. Charles G. Guignon (New York: Cambridge University Press, 2006), pp. 284–90.

44. Tom Greaves, *Starting with Heidegger* (New York: Continuum International, 2010), p. 59.

45. Heidegger, *Fundamental Concepts of Metaphysics*, pp. 59–60.

46. Rosfort and Stanghellini, "Person in Between Moods and Affects."

47. Robert C. Solomon, *Living with Nietzsche* (New York: Oxford University Press, 2003), p. 187.

CHAPTER 3. MOOD AND DEVELOPMENT

1. Patrick Burke, "Swallowing and the Organization of Sucking in the Human Newborn," *Child Development* 48 (1977): 523–31.

2. C. K. Crook, "Taste Perception in the Newborn Infant," *Infant Behavior and Development* 1 (1978): 52–69.

3. Jacob E. Steiner et al., "Comparative Expression of Hedonic Impact: Affective Reactions to Taste by Human Infants and Other Primates," *Neuroscience and Biobehavioral Reviews* 25 (2001): 52–74.

4. Robert Siegler, Judy DeLoache, and Nancy Eisenberg, *How Children Develop* (New York: Worth, 2011), pp. 53–58.

5. Ibid.

6. Krista Byers-Heinlein, Tracey C. Burns, and Janet F. Werker, "The Roots of Bilingualism in Newborns," *Psychological Science* 21, no. 3 (2010): 343–48.

7. Matthew Ratcliffe, *Feelings of Being* (New York: Oxford, 2008), pp. 77–101.

8. Philippe Rochat, *The Infants World* (Cambridge, MA: Harvard University Press, 2004), pp. 28–80.

9. Daniel N. Stern, *The Interpersonal World of the Infant* (Lexington, KY: Basic Books, 2000), pp. 53–61.

10. Ed Tronick, *The Neurobehavioral and Social-Emotional Development of Infants and Children* (New York: W. W. Norton, 2007), pp. 348–61.

11. Martin Heidegger, *Fundamental Concepts of Metaphysics*, trans. William McNeill and Nicholas Walker (Bloomington: Indiana University Press, 1995), p. 66.

12. L. Alan Sroufe, *Emotional Development* (Cambridge: Cambridge University Press, 1995), pp. 55–76.

13. Ibid.

14. H. Hill Goldsmith, "Roundtable: What Is Temperament? Four Approaches," *Child Development* 58 (1987): 505–29.

15. Siegler, DeLoache, and Eisenberg, *How Children Develop*, p. 403.

16. Ibid., pp. 404–406.

17. David Watson, *Mood and Temperament* (New York: Guilford Press, 2000), pp. 16–17.

18. Sarah Whittle et al., "The Neurobiological Basis of Temperament: Towards a Better Understanding of Psychopathology," *Neuroscience and Biobehavioral Reviews* 30 (2006): 511–25.

19. Mary K. Rothbart, "Temperament, Development, and Personality," *Current Directions in Psychological Science* 16, no. 4 (2007): 207–12.

20. Dan P. McAdams and Bradley D. Olson, "Personality Development: Continuity and Change Over the Life Course," *Annual Review of Psychology* 61 (2010): 517–42.

21. Kathleen M. Wong and C. Robert Cloninger, "A Person-Centered Approach to Clinical Practice," *Focus* VIII, no. 2 (2010): 199–215.

22. McAdams and Olson, "Personality Development."

23. Avshalom Caspi, Brent W. Roberts, and Rebecca L. Shiner, "Personality Development: Stability and Change," *Annual Review of Psychology* 56 (2005): 453–84.

24. Kathryn A. Degnan, Alisa N. Almas, and Nathan A. Fox, "Temperament and the Environment in the Aetiology of Childhood Anxiety," *Journal of Child Psychology and Psychiatry* 51, no. 4 (2010): 497–517.

25. Carl E. Schwartz et al., "Structural Differences in Adult Orbital and Ventromedial Prefrontal Cortex Predicted by Infant Temperament at 4 Months of Age," *Archives of General Psychiatry* 67, no. 1 (2010): 78–84.

26. Ayelet Lahat et al., "Temperamental Exuberance and Executive Function Predict Propensity for Risk Taking in Childhood," *Development and Psychopathology* 24 (2012): 847–56.

27. Brandi Stupica, Laura J. Sherman, and Jude Cassidy, "Newborn Irritability Moderates the Association between Infant Attachment Security and Toddler Exploration and Sociability," *Child Development* 82, no. 5 (2011): 1381–89.

28. Argyris Stringaris, "Irritability in Children and Adolescents: A Challenge for DSM-5," *European Child & Adolescent Psychiatry* 20 (2011): 61–66.

29. John Bowlby, *Attachment and Loss*, Volume 1, "Attachment" (New York: Basic Books, 1969), pp. 177–209.

30. Alison Gopnik, *The Philosophical Baby* (New York: Picador, 2010), pp. 19–46.

31. Laura E. Brumariu and Kathryn A. Kerns, "Parent-Child Attachment and Internalizing Symptoms in Childhood and Adolescence: A Review of Empirical Findings and Future Directions," *Development and Psychopathology* 22 (2010): 177–203.

32. Jude Cassidy and Lisa J. Berlin, "The Insecure/Ambivalent Pattern of Attachment: Theory and Research," *Child Development* 65 (1994): 971–91.

33. Brumariu and Kerns, "Parent-Child Attachment and Internalizing Symptoms."

34. Grazyna Kochanska and Sanghag Kim, "Toward a New Understanding of Legacy of Early Attachments for Future Antisocial Trajectories: Evidence from Two Longitudinal Studies," *Development and Psychopathology* 24, special issue no. 3 (2012): 783–806.

35. Brian E. Vaughn and Kelly K. Bost, "Attachment and Temperament: Redundant, Independent, or Interacting Influences on Interpersonal Adaptation and Personality Development?" in *Handbook of Attachment*, ed. Jude Cassidy and Philip R. Shaver (New York: Guilford Press, 1999).

36. Stupica, Sherman, and Cassidy, "Newborn Irritability."

37. Bowlby, *Attachment and Loss.*

38. Kenneth S. Kendler et al., "Life Event Dimensions of Loss, Humiliation, Entrapment, and Danger in the Prediction of Onsets of Major Depression and Generalized Anxiety," *Archives of General Psychiatry* 60 (2003): 789–96.

39. David Brent et al., "The Incidence and Course of Depression in Bereaved Youth 21 Months after the Loss of a Parent to Suicide, Accident, or Sudden Natural Death," *American Journal of Psychiatry* 166, no. 7 (2009): 786–94.

40. Siegler, DeLoache, and Eisenberg, *How Children Develop*, p. 386.

41. Carroll E. Izard et al., "The Ontogeny and Significance of Infants' Facial Expressions in the First 9 Months of Life," *Developmental Psychology* 31, no. 6 (1995): 997–1013.

42. Ibid.

43. Tronick, *Neurobehavioral and Social-Emotional Development of Infants and Children*, pp. 362–77.

44. Siegler, DeLoache, and Eisenberg, *How Children Develop*, pp. 385–93.

45. Ibid.

46. Ibid.

47. Jesse J. Prinz, "The Moral Emotions," in *The Oxford Handbook of Philosophy of Emotions*, ed. Peter Goldie (New York: Oxford University Press, 2010), pp. 519–38.

48. Siegler, DeLoache, and Eisenberg, *How Children Develop*, pp. 390–91.

49. Joan Luby et al., "Shame and Guilt in Preschool Depression: Evidence for Elevations in Self-Conscious Emotions in Depression as Early as Age 3," *Journal of Child Psychology and Psychiatry* 50, no. 9 (2009): 1156–66.

50. Peter Muris et al., "Worry in Normal Children," *Journal of the American Academy of Child and Adolescent Psychiatry* 37, no. 7 (1998): 703–10.

51. Peter Muris, Harald Merckelbach, and Ron Collaris, "Common Childhood Fears and Their Origins," *Behavioural Research and Therapy* 35, no. 10 (1997): 929–37.

52. Cynthia G. Last, *Help for Worried Kids* (New York: Guilford Press, 2006), pp. 4–7.

53. Muris, Merckelbach, and Collaris, "Common Childhood Fears."

54. Jukka M. Leppänen and Charles A. Nelson, "Tuning the Developing Brain to Social Signals of Emotions," *Nature Reviews Neuroscience* 10 (2009): 37–47.

55. Siegler, DeLoache, and Eisenberg, *How Children Develop*, pp. 180–81.

56. Leppänen and Nelson, "Tuning the Developing Brain."

57. Tronick, *Neurobehavioral and Social-Emotional Development of Infants and Children*, pp. 362–77.

58. Alice P. Jones et al., "Feeling, Caring, Knowing: Different Types of Empathy Deficit in Boys with Psychopathic Tendencies and Autism Spectrum Disorder," *Journal of Child Psychology and Psychiatry* 51, no. 11 (2010): 1188–97.

59. Siegler, DeLoache, and Eisenberg, *How Children Develop*, pp. 559–62.

60. Prinz, "Moral Emotions," pp. 531–34.

61. Siegler, DeLoache, and Eisenberg, *How Children Develop*, pp. 559–62.

62. Laurence Steinberg, "Cognitive and Affective Development in Adolescence," *Trends in Cognitive Sciences* 9, no. 2 (2005): 69–74.

63. Eric E. Nelson et al., "The Social Re-Orientation of Adolescence: A Neuroscience Perspective on the Process and Its Relation to Psychopathology," *Psychological Medicine* 35 (2005): 163–74.

64. B. J. Casey, Rebecca M. Jones, and Todd A. Hare, "The Adolescent Brain," *Annals of the New York Academy of Sciences* 1124 (2008): 111–26.

65. Laurence Steinberg and Amanda Sheffield Morris, "Adolescent Development," *Annual Review of Psychology* 52 (2001): 83–110.

66. Ibid.

67. Susan Harter et al., "A Model of the Effects of Perceived Parent and Peer Support on Adolescent False Self Behavior," *Child Development* 67 (1996): 360–74.

CHAPTER 4. MOOD AND NEURAL CIRCUITS

1. Matthew Ratcliffe, *Feelings of Being* (New York: Oxford, 2008), pp. 106–37.

2. Eero Castrén, "Is Mood Chemistry?" *Nature Reviews Neuroscience* 6 (2005): 241–46.

3. Luiz Pessoa, "On the Relationship between Emotion and Cognition," *Nature Reviews Neuroscience* 9 (2008): 148–58.

4. Marc D. Lewis, "Bridging Emotion Theory and Neurobiology through Dynamic Systems Modeling," *Behavioral and Brain Sciences* 28 (2005): 169–245.

5. Richard D. Lane et al., "The Rebirth of Neuroscience in Psychosomatic Medicine, Part I: Historical Context, Methods, and Relevant Basic Science," *Psychosomatic Medicine* 71 (2009): 117–34.

6. Tim Dalgleish, Barnaby D. Dunn, and Dean Mobbs, "Affective Neuroscience: Past, Present, and Future," *Emotion Review* 1, no. 4 (2009) 355–68.

7. Joseph LeDoux, *Synaptic Self* (New York: Penguin, 2003), pp. 33–64.

8. Earl K. Miller and Jonathan D. Cohen, "An Integrative Theory of Prefrontal Cortex Function," *Annual Review of Neuroscience* 24 (2001): 167–202.

9. Amy F. T. Arnsten and Katya Rubia, "Neurobiological Circuits Regulating Attention, Cognitive Control, Motivation and Emotion: Disruptions in Neurodevelopmental Psychiatric Disorders," *Journal of the American Academy of Child & Adolescent Psychiatry* 51, no. 4 (2012): 356–67.

10. Pessoa, "On the Relationship between Emotion and Cognition."

11. Amy F. T. Arnsten, "Stress Signaling Pathways That Impair Prefrontal Cortex Structure and Function," *Nature Reviews Neuroscience* 10 (2009): 410–22.

12. Pessoa, "On the Relationship between Emotion and Cognition."

13. Morten L. Kringelbach and Edmund T. Rolls, "The Functional Neuroanatomy of the Human Orbitofrontal Cortex: Evidence from Neuroimaging and Neuropsychology," *Progress in Neurobiology* 72 (2004): 341–72.

14. Kringelbach and Rolls, "Functional Neuroanatomy of the Human Orbitofrontal Cortex."

15. Beatrice de Gelder, "Towards the Neurobiology of Emotional Body Language," *Nature Reviews Neuroscience* 7 (2006): 242–50.

16. Mathieu Roy et al., "Ventromedial Prefrontal-Subcortical Systems and the Generation of Affective Meaning," *Trends in Cognitive Sciences* 16, no. 3 (2012): 147–56.

17. Lane et al., "Rebirth of Neuroscience in Psychosomatic Medicine."

18. Ibid.

19. Alexander J. Shackman et al., "The Integration of Negative Affect, Pain and Cognitive Control in the Cingulate Cortex," *Nature Reviews Neuroscience* 12 (2011): 154–67.

20. Philip Gerard Gasquoine, "Localization of Function in Anterior Cingulate Cortex: From Psychosurgery to Neuroimaging," *Neuroscience and Biobehavioral Reviews* 37 (2013): 340–48.

21. William A. Cunningham and Tobias Brosch, "Motivational Salience: Amygdala Tuning from Traits, Needs, Values, and Goals," *Current Directions in Psychological Science* 21, no. 1 (2012): 54–59.

22. C. Daniel Salzman and Stefano Fusi, "Emotion, Cognition, and Mental State Representation in Amygdala and Prefrontal Cortex," Annual Review of Neuroscience 33 (2010): 173–202.

23. Dalgleish, Dunn, and Mobbs, "Affective Neuroscience."

24. Ralph Adolphs, "What Does the Amygdala Contribute to Social Cognition?" *Annals of the New York Academy of Sciences* 1191 (2010): 42–61.

25. Cunningham and Brosch, "Motivational Salience."

26. Roy et al., "Ventromedial Prefrontal-Subcortical Systems."

27. Joseph LeDoux, "The Emotional Brain, Fear, and the Amygdala," *Cellular and Molecular Neurobiology* 23, no. 4/5 (2003): 727–38.

28. de Gelder, "Towards the Neurobiology of Emotional Body Language."

29. Yvonne M. Ulrich-Lai and James P. Herman, "Neural Regulation of Endocrine and Autonomic Stress Responses," *Nature Reviews Neuroscience* 10 (2009): 397–409.

30. Sarah Whittle et al., "The Neurobiological Basis of Temperament: Towards a Better Understanding of Psychopathology," *Neuroscience and Biobehavioral Reviews* 30 (2006): 511–25.

31. Henk J. Groenewegen, "The Ventral Striatum as an Interface between the Limbic and Motor Systems," *CNS Spectrums* 12, no. 12 (2007): 887–92.

32. A. D. (Bud) Craig, "How Do You Feel—Now? The Anterior Insula and Human Awareness," *Nature Reviews Neuroscience* 10 (2009): 59–70.

33. Elizabeth A. Phelps, "Human Emotion and Memory: Interactions of the Amygdala and Hippocampal Complex," *Current Opinion in Neurobiology* 14 (2004): 198–202.

34. S. B. McHugh et al., "Amygdala and Ventral Hippocampus Contribute Differentially to Mechanisms of Fear and Anxiety," *Behavioral Neuroscience* 118, no. 1 (2004): 63–78.

35. Irving Kupfermann, "Hypothalamus and Limbic System: Peptidergic Neurons, Homeostasis, and Emotional Behavior," in *Principles of Neural Science*, ed. Eric Kandel, James H. Schwartz, and Thomas M. Jessell (East Norwalk, CT: Appleton and Lange, 1991).

36. James P. Kelly and Jane Dodd, "Anatomical Organization of the Nervous System," in *Principles of Neural Science*, ed. Eric Kandel, James H. Schwartz, and Thomas M. Jessell (East Norwalk, CT: Appleton and Lange, 1991).

37. Wayne C. Drevets, "Orbitofrontal Cortex Function and Structure in Depression," *Annals of the New York Academy of Sciences* 1121 (2007): 499–527.

38. Lane et al., "Rebirth of Neuroscience in Psychosomatic Medicine."

39. Susan D. Iversen and Leslie L. Iversen, "Dopamine: 50 Years in Perspective," *Trends in Neurosciences* 30, no. 5 (2007): 188–93.

40. Katherine H. Taber et al., "Neuroanatomy of Dopamine: Reward and Addiction," *Journal of Neuropsychiatry and Clinical Neurosciences* 24, no. 1 (2012): 1–4.

41. R. A. Bressan and J. A. Crippa, "The Role of Dopamine in Reward and Pleasure Behaviour—Review of Data from Preclinical Research," *Acta Psychiatrica Scandinavica* 111, Suppl. 427 (2005): 14–21.

42. Efrain C. Azmitia and Patricia M. Whitaker-Azmitia, "Awakening the Sleeping Giant: Anatomy and Plasticity of the Brain Serotonergic System," *Journal of Clinical Psychiatry* 52, Suppl. 12 (1991): 4–16.

43. Ahmad R. Hariri and Andrew Holmes, "Genetics of Emotional Regulation: The Role of the Serotonin Transporter in Neural Function," *Trends in Cognitive Sciences* 10, no. 4 (2006): 182–91.

44. Susan J. Sara, "The Locus Coeruleus and Noradrenergic Modulation of Cognition," *Nature Reviews Neuroscience* 10 (2009): 211–23.

45. Joseph L. Price and Wayne C. Drevets, "Neural Circuits Underlying the Pathophysiology of Mood Disorders," *Trends in Cognitive Sciences* 16, no. 1 (2012): 61–71.

46. M. L. Phillips, C. D. Ladouceur, and W. C. Drevets, "A Neural Model of Voluntary and Automatic Emotion Regulation: Implications for Understanding the Pathophysiology and Neurodevelopment of Bipolar Disorder," *Molecular Psychiatry* 13 (2008): 833–57.

47. Jennifer Urbano Blackford and Daniel S. Pine, "Neural Substrates of Childhood Anxiety Disorders: A Review of Neuroimaging Findings," *Child and Adolescent Psychiatric Clinics of North America* 21 (2012): 501–25.

48. Christopher G. Davey, Murat Yücel, and Nicholas B. Allen, "The Emergence of Depression in Adolescence: Development of the Prefrontal Cortex and the Representation of Reward," *Neuroscience and Biobehavioral Reviews* 32 (2008): 1–19.

49. Kirsten E. Gilbert, "The Neglected Role of Positive Emotion in Adolescent Psychopathology," *Clinical Psychology Review* 32 (2012): 467–81.

50. Michael H. Rosenbloom, Jeremy D. Schmahmann, and Bruce H. Price, "The Functional Neuroanatomy of Decision-Making," *Journal of Neuropsychiatry and Clinical Neurosciences* 24, no. 3 (2012): 266–77.

51. Whittle et al., "Neurobiological Basis of Temperament: Towards a Better Understanding."

52. Sarah Whittle et al., "Neuroanatomical Correlates of Temperament in Early Adolescents," *Journal of the American Academy of Child and Adolescent Psychiatry* 47, no. 6 (2008): 682–93.

CHAPTER 5. GENES, ENVIRONMENTS, AND NEURAL CIRCUITS

1. Michael Rutter, *Genes and Behavior* (Malden, MA: Blackwell, 2006), pp. 144–53.

2. Ibid., pp. 117–21.

3. Rosemary C. Bagot and Michael J. Meaney, "Epigenetics and the Biological Basis of Gene x Environment Interactions," *Journal of the American Academy of Child & Adolescent Psychiatry* 49, no. 8 (2010): 752–71.

4. Tie-Yuan Zhang and Michael J. Meaney, "Epigenetics and the Environmental Regulation of the Genome and Its Function," *Annual Review of Psychology* 61 (2010): 439–66.

5. Linda Spear, *The Behavioral Neuroscience of Adolescence* (New York: W. W. Norton, 2010), pp. 20–35.

6. Robert Plomin and Kathryn Asbury, "Nature and Nurture: Genetic and Environmental Influences on Behavior," *Annals of the American Academy of Political and Social Science* 600 (2005): 86–98.

7. Yulia Kovas and Robert Plomin, "Learning Abilities and Disabilities," *Current Directions in Psychological Science* 16 (2007): 284–88.

8. Gregory Z. Tau and Bradley S. Peterson, "Normal Development of Brain Circuits," *Neuropsychopharmacology Reviews* 35 (2010): 147–68.

9. Spear, *Behavioral Neuroscience of Adolescence*, pp. 73–90.

10. W. T. Greenough, J. E. Black, and C. S. Wallace, "Experience and Brain Development," *Child Development* 58, no. 3 (1987): 539–59.

11. D. H. Hubel and T. N. Wiesel, "The Period of Susceptibility to the Physiological Effects of Unilateral Eye Closure in Kittens," *Journal of Physiology* 206, no. 2 (1970): 419–36.

12. Christa Payne and Jocelyne Bachevalier, "Neuroanatomy of the Developing Social Brain," in *Handbook of Developmental Social Science*, eds. Michelle De Haan and Megan Gunnar (New York: Guilford, 2009), pp. 38–59.

13. Jukka A. Leppänen and Charles A. Nelson, "Tuning the Developing Brain to Social Signals of Emotions," *Nature Reviews Neuroscience* 10 (2009): 37–47.

14. Michelle De Haan and Anna Matteson, "The Development and Neuronal Bases of Processing Emotion in Faces and Voices," in *Handbook of Developmental Social Science*, eds. Michelle De Haan and Megan Gunnar (New York: Guilford, 2009), pp. 107–121.

15. Payne and Bachevalier, "Neuroanatomy of the Developing Social Brain."

16. Spear, *Behavioral Neuroscience of Adolescence*, pp. 73–90.

17. Tau and Peterson, "Normal Development of Brain Circuits."

18. Sarah Whittle et al., "Neuroanatomical Correlates of Temperament in Early Adolescents," *Journal of the American Academy of Child and Adolescent Psychiatry* 47, no. 6 (2008): 682–93.

19. Payne and Bachevalier, "Neuroanatomy of the Developing Social Brain."

20. B. J. Casey, Rebecca M. Jones, and Todd A. Hare, "The Adolescent Brain," *Annals of the New York Academy of Sciences* 1124 (2008): 111–26.

21. Monique Ernst and Linda Patia Spear, "Reward Systems," in *Handbook of Developmental Social Science*, ed. Michelle De Haan and Megan Gunnar (New York: Guilford, 2009), pp. 324–41.

22. Eric E. Nelson et al., "The Social Re-Orientation of Adolescence: A Neuroscience Perspective on the Process and Its Relation to Psychopathology," *Psychological Medicine* 35 (2005): 163–74.

23. Ibid.

24. Casey, Jones, and Hare, "Adolescent Brain."

25. Christopher G. Davey, Murat Yücel, and Nicholas B. Allen, "The Emergence of Depression in Adolescence: Development of the Prefrontal Cortex and the Representation of Reward," *Neuroscience and Biobehavioral Reviews* 32 (2008): 1–19.

26. Ibid.

27. Carl E. Schwartz et al., "Structural Differences in Adult Orbital and Ventromedial Prefrontal Cortex Predicted by Infant Temperament at 4 Months of Age," *Archives of General Psychiatry* 67, no. 1 (2010): 78–84.

28. Michael Rutter, Terrie E. Moffitt, and Avahalom Caspi, "Gene-Environment Interplay and Psychopathology: Multiple Varieties But Real Effects," *Journal of Child Psychology and Psychiatry* 47, no. 3/4 (2006): 226–61.

29. Patrick M. Fisher, Karen E. Muñoz, and Ahmad R. Hariri, "Identification of Neurogenetic Pathways of Risk for Psychopathology," *American Journal of Medical Genetics Part C (Seminars in Medical Genetics)* 148C (2008): 147–53.

30. Ibid.

31. Turhan Canli and Klaus-Peter Lesch, "Long Story Short: The Serotonin Transporter in Emotion Regulation and Social Cognition," *Nature Neuroscience* 10, no. 9 (2007): 1103–1109.

32. A. Meyer-Lindenberg et al., "Neural Mechanisms of Genetic Risk for Impulsivity and Violence in Humans," *Proceedings of National Science USA* 103, no. 16 (2006): 6269–74.

33. Leppänen and Nelson, "Tuning the Developing Brain to Social Signals of Emotions."

34. Christian Kandler, "Nature and Nurture in Personality Development: The Case of Neuroticism and Extraversion," *Current Directions in Psychological Science* 21, no. 5 (2012): 290–96.

35. Catherine L. Rosenblum, Carolyn J. Dayton, and Maria Muzik, "Infant Social and Emotional Development: Emerging Competence in a Relational Context," in *Handbook of Infant Mental Health*, ed. Charles H. Zeanah (New York: Guilford Press, 2009), pp. 80–203.

36. Robert Siegler, Judy DeLoache, and Nancy Eisenberg, *How Children Develop* (New York: Worth, 2011), pp. 400–407.

CHAPTER 6. WHEN EVENTS THREATEN STABILITY— THE STRESS RESPONSE

1. Marian Joëls and Tallie Z. Baram, "The Neuro-Symphony of Stress," *Nature Reviews Neuroscience* 10 (2009): 459–66.

2. Ibid.

3. Adriana Feder, Eric J. Nestler, and Dennis S. Charney, "Psychobiology and Molecular Genetics of Resilience," *Nature Reviews Neuroscience* 10 (2009): 446–57.

4. Megan Gunnar and Karina Quevedo, "The Neurobiology of Stress and Development," *Annual Review of Psychology* 58 (2007): 145–73.

5. Yvonne M. Ulrich-Lai and James P. Herman, "Neural Regulation of Endocrine and Autonomic Stress Responses," *Nature Reviews Neuroscience* 10 (2009): 397–409.

6. Craig W. Berridge and Barry D. Waterhouse, "The Locus Coeruleus-Noradrenergic System: Modulation of Behavioral State and State-Dependent Cognitive Processes," *Brain Research Reviews* 42 (2003): 33–84.

7. Gunnar and Quevedo, "Neurobiology of Stress and Development."

8. Bruce S. McEwen et al., "Stress and Anxiety: Structural Plasticity and Epigenetic Regulation as a Consequence of Stress," *Neuropharmacology* 62 (2012): 3–12.

9. Gunnar and Quevedo, "Neurobiology of Stress and Development," pp. 145–73.

10. Ibid.

11. Sonia J. Lupien et al., "Effects of Stress throughout the Lifespan on the Brain, Behaviour and Cognition," *Nature Reviews Neuroscience* 10, no. 6 (2009): 434–45.

12. Gunnar and Quevedo, "Neurobiology of Stress and Development," pp. 145–73.

13. Lupien et al., "Effects of Stress throughout the Lifespan on the Brain," pp. 434–45.

14. Ibid.

15. Gunnar and Quevedo, "Neurobiology of Stress and Development," pp. 145–73.

16. Lupien et al., "Effects of Stress throughout the Lifespan on the Brain," pp. 434–45.

17. Tallie Z. Baram et al., "Fragmentation and Unpredictability of Early-Life Experience in Mental Disorders," *American Journal of Psychiatry* 169, no. 9 (2012): 907–15.

18. Christopher Pittenger and Ronald S. Duman, "Stress, Depression, and Neuroplasticity: A Convergence of Mechanisms," *Neuropsychopharmacology Reviews* 33 (208): 88–109.

19. William R. Lovallo et al., "Lifetime Adversity Leads to Blunted Stress Axis Reactivity: Studies from the Oklahoma Family Health Patterns Project," *Biological Psychology* 71 (2012): 344–49.

20. Elisabeth B. Binder and Florian Holsboer, "Low Cortisol and Risk and Resilience to Stress-Related Psychiatric Disorders," *Biological Psychology* 71 (2012): 282–83.

21. Lupien et al., "Effects of Stress throughout the Lifespan on the Brain," pp. 434–45.

22. Udo Dannlowski et al., "Limbic Scars: Long-Term Consequences of Childhood Maltreatment Revealed by Functional and Structural Magnetic Resonance Imaging," *Biological Psychology* 71 (2012): 286–93.

23. N. Tottenham et al., "Elevated Amygdala Response to Faces Following Early Deprivation," *Developmental Science* 14, no. 2 (2011): 190–204.

24. Kerry J. Ressler, "Amygdala Activity, Fear, and Anxiety: Modulation by Stress," *Biological Psychology* 67 (2010): 1117–19.

25. Pittenger and Duman, "Stress, Depression, and Neuroplasticity."

26. Amy F. T. Arnsten, "Stress Signalling Pathways That Impair Prefrontal Cortex Structure and Function," *Nature Reviews Neuroscience* 10 (2009): 410–22.

27. Uma Rao et al., "Hippocampal Changes Associated with Early-Life Adversity and Vulnerability to Depression," *Biological Psychology* 67 (2010): 357–64.

28. Ronald A. Cohen et al., "Early Life Stress and Morphometry of the Adult Anterior Cingulate Cortex and Caudate Nuclei," *Biological Psychology* 59 (2006): 975–82.

29. Lupien et al., "Effects of Stress throughout the Lifespan on the Brain."

30. Cohen et al., "Early Life Stress and Morphometry of the Adult Anterior Cingulate Cortex."

31. Adriana Feder, Eric J. Nestler, and Dennis S. Charney, "Psychobiology and Molecular Genetics of Resilience," *Nature Reviews Neuroscience* 10 (2009): 446–57.

32. Scott M. Monroe and Anne D. Simons, "Diathesis-Stress Theories in the Context of Life Stress Research: Implications for the Depressive Disorders," *Psychological Bulletin* 110, no. 3 (1991): 406–25.

33. Michael Rutter, "Resilience as a Dynamic Concept," *Development and Psychopathology* 24 (2012): 335–44.

34. Michael Rutter, "Annual Research Review: Resilience: Clinical Implications," *Journal of Child Psychology and Psychiatry* 54, no. 4 (2013): 474–87.

35. Rutter, "Resilience as a Dynamic Concept."

36. Carol D. Ryff and Burton Singer, "Interpersonal Flourishing: A Positive Health Agenda for the New Millennium," *Personality and Social Psychology Review* 4, no. 1 (2000): 30–44.

37. Avshaom Caspi et al., "Influence of Life Stress on Depression: Moderation by a Polymorphism in the 5-HTT Gene," *Science* 301 (2003): 386–89.

38. Erin C. Dunn et al., "Research Review: Gene-Environment Interaction Research in Youth Depression—A Systematic Review with Recommendations for Future Research," *Journal of Child Psychology and Psychiatry* 52, no. 12 (2011): 1223–38.

39. Monroe and Simons, "Diathesis-Stress Theories in the Context of Life Stress Research."

40. Jay Belsky and Michael Pluess, "The Nature (and Nurture?) of Plasticity in Early Human Development," *Perspectives on Psychological Science* 4, no. 4 (2009): 345–51.

41. Ibid.

42. Bruce J. Ellis et al., "Differential Susceptibility to the Environment: An Evolutionary-Neurodevelopmental Theory," *Development and Psychopathology* 23, no. 1 (2011): 7–28.

43. Bruce J. Ellis and W. Thomas Boyce, "Differential Susceptibility to the Environment: Toward an Understanding of Sensitivity to Developmental Experiences and Context," *Development and Psychopathology* 23, no. 1 (2011): 1–5.

44. Belsky and Pluess, "Nature (and Nurture?) of Plasticity in Early Human Development."

45. Marilyn J. Essex et al., "Biological Sensitivity to Context Moderates the Effects of the Early Teacher-Child Relationship on the Development of Mental Health by Adolescence," *Development and Psychopathology* 23, no. 1 (2011): 149–61.

46. Rutter, "Annual Research Review."

CHAPTER 7. ISSUES IN PSYCHIATRIC DIAGNOSIS

1. David J. Kupfer, Darrel A. Regier, and Emily A. Kuhl, "On the Road to DSM-V and ICD-11," *European Archives of Psychiatry and Clinical Neuroscience* 258, Suppl. 5 (2008): 2–6.

2. Ibid.

3. Eli Robins and Samuel B. Guze, "Establishment of Diagnostic Validity in Psychiatric Illness: Its Application to Schizophrenia," *American Journal of Psychiatry* 126, no. 7 (1970): 107–11.

4. Diagnostic and Statistical Manual of Mental Disorders, *DSM-IV-TR* (Arlington, VA: American Psychiatric Publishing, 2000).

5. Diagnostic and Statistical Manual of Mental Disorders, *DSM-5* (Arlington, VA: American Psychiatric Publishing, 2013).

6. Robert F. Krueger and Kristian E. Markon, "Understanding Psychopathology: Melding Behavior Genetics, Personality, and Quantitative Psychology to Develop an Empirically Based Model," *Current Directions in Psychological Science* 15 (2006): 113–17.

7. Thomas A. Achenbach and Craig S. Edelbrock, "Psychopathology of Childhood," *Annual Review of Psychology* 35 (1984): 227–56.

8. Robert F. Krueger and Kristian E. Markon, "Reinterpreting Comorbidity: A Model-Based Approach to Understanding and Classifying Psychopathology," *Annual Review of Clinical Psychology* 2 (2006): 111–33.

9. Michael Musalek and Oliver Scheibenbogen, "From Categorical to Dimensional Diagnostics: Deficiency-Oriented Versus Person-Centred Diagnostics," *European Archives of Psychiatry and Clinical Neuroscience* 258, Suppl. 5 (2008): 18–21.

10. Kupfer, Regier, and Kuhl, "On the Road to DSM-V and ICD-11."

CHAPTER 8. WHEN MOODS ARE WORRIED AND FEARFUL— ANXIETY DISORDERS

1. Ronald C. Kessler et al., "Lifetime Prevalence and Age-of-Onset Distributions of DSM-IV Disorders in the National Comorbidity Survey Replication," *Archives of General Psychiatry* 62 (2005): 593–602.

2. Ronald M. Rapee, Carolyn A. Schniering, and Jennifer L. Hudson, "Anxiety Disorders during Childhood and Adolescence: Origins and Treatment," *Annual Review of Clinical Psychology* 5 (2009): 311–41.

3. Ronald C. Kessler et al., "Prevalence, Persistence, and Sociodemographic Correlates of DSM-IV Disorders in the National Comorbidity Survey Replication Adolescent Supplement," *Archives of General Psychiatry* 69, no. 4 (2012): 372–80.

4. Rapee, Schniering, and Hudson, "Anxiety Disorders during Childhood and Adolescence."

5. Ronald C. Kessler et al., "Prevalence, Persistence, and Comorbidity of 12-Month DSM-IV Disorders in the National Comorbidity Survey Replication Adolescent Supplement," *Archives of General Psychiatry* 62 (2005): 617–27.

6. Nicholas B. Allen and Paul B. T. Badcock, "Darwinian Models of Depression: A Review of Evolutionary Accounts of Mood and Mood Disorders," *Progress in Neuro-Psychopharmacology & Biological Psychiatry* 30 (2006): 815–26.

7. Peter Muris et al., "Worry in Normal Children," *Journal of the American Academy of Child and Adolescent Psychiatry* 37, no. 7 (1998): 703–10.

8. Peter Muris, Harald Merckelbach, and Ron Collaris, "Common Childhood Fears and Their Origins," *Behavioural Research and Therapy* 35, no. 10 (1997): 929–37.

9. Michelle G. Craske et al., "What Is an Anxiety Disorder?" *Depression and Anxiety* 26 (2009): 1066–85.

10. Diagnostic and Statistical Manual of Mental Disorders, *DSM-IV-TR* (Arlington, VA: American Psychiatric Publishing, 2000), pp. 429–84.

11. Diagnostic and Statistical Manual of Mental Disorders, *DSM-5* (Arlington, VA: American Psychiatric Publishing, 2013), pp. 189–233.

12. Lisa M. Shin and Israel Liberzon, "The Neurocircuitry of Fear, Stress, and Anxiety Disorders," *Neuropsychopharmacology Reviews* 35 (2010): 169–91.

13. Ibid.

14. Ibid.

15. Jean Kim and Jack Gorman, "The Psychobiology of Anxiety," *Clinical Neuroscience Research* 4 (2005): 335–47.

16. Shin and Liberzon, "Neurocircuitry of Fear, Stress, and Anxiety Disorders."

17. Ibid.

18. Kim and Gorman, "Psychobiology of Anxiety."

19. Katja Beesdo et al., "Common and Distinct Amygdala-Function Perturbations in Depressed vs. Anxious Adolescents," *Archives of General Psychiatry* 66, no. 3 (2009): 275–85.

20. Amy K. Ray et al., "Intrinsic Functional Connectivity of Amygdala-Based Networks in Adolescent Generalized Anxiety Disorder," *Journal of the American Academy of Child & Adolescent Psychiatry* 52, no. 3 (2013): 290–99.

21. B. J. Casey et al., "Transitional and Translational Studies of Risk for Anxiety," *Depression and Anxiety* 28 (2011): 18–28.

22. B. J. Casey, Rebecca M. Jones, and Todd A. Hare, "The Adolescent Brain," *Annals of the New York Academy of Sciences* 1124 (2008): 111–26.

23. Jennifer Urbano Blackford and Daniel S. Pine, "Neural Substrates of Childhood Anxiety Disorders: A Review of Neuroimaging Findings," *Child and Adolescent Psychiatric Clinics of North America* 21 (2012): 501–25.

24. Ibid.

25. Koraly Pérez-Edgar and Nathan A. Fox, "Temperament and Anxiety Disorders," *Child and Adolescent Psychiatric Clinics of North America* 14 (2005): 681–706.

26. Kathleen Ries Merikangas, "Vulnerability Factors for Anxiety Disorders in Children and Adolescents," *Child and Adolescent Psychiatric Clinics of North America* 14 (2005): 649–79.

27. Pérez-Edgar and Fox, "Temperament and Anxiety Disorders."

28. Rapee, Schniering, and Hudson, "Anxiety Disorders during Childhood and Adolescence."

29. Murray B. Stein, Nicholas J. Schork, and Joel Gelernter, "Gene-by-Environment (Serotonin Transporter and Childhood Maltreatment) Interaction for Anxiety Sensitivity, an Intermediate Phenotype for Anxiety Disorders," *Neuropsychopharmacology* 33 (2008): 312–19.

30. Daniel S. Pine, "Research Review: A Neuroscience Framework for Pediatric Anxiety Disorders," *Journal of Child Psychology and Psychiatry* 48, no. 7 (2007): 631–48.

31. Jennifer C. Britton et al., "Development of Anxiety: The Role of Threat Appraisal and Fear Learning," *Depression and Anxiety* 28 (2011): 5–17.

32. Rapee, Schniering, and Hudson, "Anxiety Disorders during Childhood and Adolescence."

33. Carl F. Weems, "Developmental Trajectories of Childhood Anxiety: Identifying Continuity and Change in Anxious Emotion," *Developmental Review* 28 (2008): 488–502.

34. Rapee, Schniering, and Hudson, "Anxiety Disorders during Childhood and Adolescence."

35. Jukka A. Leppänen and Charles A. Nelson, "Tuning the Developing Brain to Social Signals of Emotions," *Nature Reviews Neuroscience* 10 (2009): 37–47.

36. Jennifer Y. F. Lau et al., "Amygdala Function and 5-HTT Gene Variants in Adolescent Anxiety and Major Depressive Disorder," *Biological Psychiatry* 65 (2009): 349–55.

37. Catherine L. Rosenblum, Carolyn J. Dayton, and Maria Muzik, "Infant Social and Emotional Development: Emerging Competence in a Relational Context," in *Handbook of Infant Mental Health*, ed. Charles H. Zeanah (New York: Guilford Press, 2009), pp. 80–203.

38. Stein, Schork, and Gelernter, "Gene-by-Environment Interaction for Anxiety Sensitivity."

39. Rapee, Schniering, and Hudson, "Anxiety Disorders during Childhood and Adolescence."

40. Kenneth S. Kendler et al., "Life Event Dimensions of Loss, Humiliation, Entrapment, and Danger in the Prediction of Onsets of Major Depression and Generalized Anxiety," *Archives of General Psychiatry* 60 (2003): 789–96.

41. Margaret J. Briggs-Gowan et al., "Exposure to Potentially Traumatic Events in Early Childhood: Differential Links to Emergent Psychopathology," *Journal of Child Psychology and Psychiatry* 51, no. 10 (2010): 1132–40.

42. Katja Beesdo et al., "Incidence and Risk Patterns of Anxiety and Depressive Disorders and Categorization of Generalized Anxiety Disorder," *Archives of General Psychiatry* 67, no. 1 (2010): 47–57.

43. Rapee, Schniering, and Hudson, "Anxiety Disorders during Childhood and Adolescence."

44. Laura E. Brumariu and Kathryn A. Kerns, "Parent-Child Attachment and Internalizing Symptoms in Childhood and Adolescence: A Review of Empirical Findings and Future Directions," *Development and Psychopathology* 22 (2010): 177–203.

45. Cristina Colonnesi et al., "The Relation between Insecure Attachment and Child Anxiety: A Meta-Analytic Review," *Journal of Clinical Child & Adolescent Psychiatry* 40, no. 4 (2011): 630–45.

46. Brian E. Vaughn and Kelly K. Bost, "Attachment and Temperament: Redundant, Independent, or Interacting Influences on Interpersonal Adaptation and Personality Development?" in *Handbook of Attachment*, ed. Jude Cassidy and Philip R. Shaver (New York: Guilford Press, 1999).

47. Brumariu and Kerns, "Parent-Child Attachment and Internalizing Symptoms in Childhood and Adolescence."

48. Muris et al., "Worry in Normal Children."

49. Muris, Merckelbach, and Collaris, "Common Childhood Fears and Their Origins."

50. Cynthia G. Last, *Help for Worried Kids* (New York: Guilford Press, 2006), pp. 4–9.

51. Sylvana M. Côté et al., "Depression and Anxiety Symptoms: Onset, Developmental Course and Risk Factors during Early Childhood," *Journal of Child Psychology and Psychiatry* 50, no. 10 (2009): 1201–1208.

52. Nicholas D. Mian et al., "Patterns of Anxiety Symptoms in Toddlers and Preschool-Age Children: Evidence of Early Differentiation," *Journal of Anxiety Disorders* 26 (2012): 102–110.

53. Kendler et al., "Life Event Dimensions of Loss, Humiliation, Entrapment, and Danger."

54. A. R. Matthew et al., "Co-Morbidity between Depressive Disorder and Anxiety Disorders: Shared Etiology or Direct Causation?" *Psychological Medicine* 41, no. 10 (2011): 2023–2034.

55. Douglas E. Williamson et al., "A Genetic Epidemiologic Perspective on Comorbidity of Depression and Anxiety," *Child and Adolescent Psychiatric Clinics of North America* 14 (2005): 707–26.

CHAPTER 9. WHEN MOODS ARE LOW—DEPRESSION

1. David J. Kupfer, Ellen Frank, and Mary L. Phillips, "Major Depressive Disorder: New Clinical, Neurobiological, and Treatment Perspectives," *Lancet* 379 (2012): 1045–1055.

2. Ronald C. Kessler et al., "Lifetime Prevalence and Age-of-Onset Distributions of DSM-IV Disorders in the National Comorbidity Survey Replication," *Archives of General Psychiatry* 62 (2005): 593–602.

3. Stuart Goldman, "Developmental Epidemiology of Depressive Disorders," *Child and Adolescent Psychiatric Clinics of North America* 21 (2012): 217–35.

4. Tracy R. G. Gladstone, William R. Beardslee, and Erin E. O'Connor, "The Prevention of Adolescent Depression," *Psychiatric Clinics of North America* 34 (2011): 35–52.

5. Kessler et al., "Lifetime Prevalence and Age of Onset Distributions of DSM-IV Disorders."

6. Boris Birmaher et al., "Childhood and Adolescent Depression: A Review of the Past 10 Years. Part I," *Journal of the American Academy of Child and Adolescent Psychiatry* 35, no. 11 (1996): 1427–39.

7. Ibid.

8. Maria Kovacs, "Presentation and Course of Major Depressive Disorder during Childhood and Later Years of the Life Span," *Journal of the American Academy of Child and Adolescent Psychiatry* 35, no. 6 (1996): 705–15.

9. Nicholas B. Allen and Paul B. T. Badcock, "Darwinian Models of Depression: A Review of Evolutionary Accounts of Mood and Mood Disorders," *Progress in Neuro-Psychopharmacology & Biological Psychiatry* 30 (2006): 815–26.

10. Diagnostic and Statistical Manual of Mental Disorders, *DSM-IV-TR* (Arlington, VA: American Psychiatric Publishing, 2000), pp. 345–428.

11. Diagnostic and Statistical Manual of Mental Disorders, *DSM-5* (Arlington, VA: American Psychiatric Publishing, 2013), pp. 155–88.

12. P. W. Gold and G. P. Chrousos, "Organization of the Stress System and Its Dysregulation in Melancholic and Atypical Depression: High vs. Low CRN/NE States," *Molecular Psychiatry* 7 (2002): 254–75.

13. Scott C. Matthews and Richard D. Lane, "Neuroimaging of Depression and Other Emotional States," in *Handbook of Behavioral Medicine*, ed. Andrew Steptoe (New York: Springer, 2010), pp. 803–19.

14. Kupfer, Frank, and Phillips, "Major Depressive Disorder."

15. Joseph L. Price and Wayne C. Drevets, "Neural Circuits Underlying the Pathophysiology of Mood Disorders," *Trends in Cognitive Sciences* 16, no. 1 (2012): 61–71.

16. Luke Clark, Samuel R. Chamberlain, and Barbara Sahakian, "Neurocognitive Mechanisms in Depression: Implications for Treatment," *Annual Review of Neuroscience* 32 (2009): 57–74.

17. Katja Beesdo et al., "Common and Distinct Amygdala-Function Perturbations in Depressed vs. Anxious Adolescents," *Archives of General Psychiatry* 66, no. 3 (2009): 275–85.

18. Amy F. T. Arnsten and Katya Rubia, "Neurobiological Circuits Regulating Attention, Cognitive Control, Motivation and Emotion: Disruptions in Neurodevelopmental Psychiatric Disorders," *Journal of the American Academy of Child & Adolescent Psychiatry* 51, no. 4 (2012): 356–67.

19. Michael S. Gaffey et al., "Association between Depression Severity and Amygdala Reactivity during Sad Face Viewing in Depressed Preschoolers: An fMRI Study," *Journal of Affective Disorders* 129 (2011): 364–70.

20. David Pagliaccio et al., "Anomalous Functional Brain Activation Following Negative Mood Induction in Children with Pre-School Onset Major Depression," *Developmental Cognitive Neuroscience* 2 (2012): 256–67.

21. Gold and Chrousos, "Organization of the Stress System."

22. Radu V. Saveanu and Charles B. Nemeroff, "Etiology of Depression: Genetic and Environmental Factors," *Psychiatry Clinics of North America* 35 (2012): 51–71.

23. Eric Nestler and William A. Carlezon Jr., "The Mesolimbic Dopamine Reward Circuit in Depression," *Biological Psychiatry* 59 (2006): 1151–59.

24. Erika E. Forbes, "Where's the Fun in That? Broadening the Focus on Reward Function in Depression," *Biological Psychiatry* 66 (2009): 199–200.

25. Ian H. Gotlib et al., "Neural Processing of Reward and Loss in Girls at Risk for Major Depression," *Archives of General Psychiatry* 67, no. 4 (2010): 380–87.

26. Maria Kovacs and Nestor Lopez-Duran, "Prodromal Symptoms and Atypical Affectivity as Predictors of Major Depression in Juveniles: Implications for Prevention," *Journal of Child Psychology and Psychiatry* 51, no. 4 (2010): 472–96.

27. Sylvana M. Côté et al., "Depression and Anxiety Symptoms: Onset, Developmental Course and Risk Factors during Early Childhood," *Journal of Child Psychology and Psychiatry* 50, no. 10 (2009): 1201–1208.

28. R. H. Belmaker and Galila Agam, "Major Depressive Disorder," *New England Journal of Medicine* 358, no. 1 (2008): 55–68.

29. Saveanu and Nemeroff, "Etiology of Depression."

30. Côté et al., "Depression and Anxiety Symptoms."

31. Argyris Stringaris et al., "Adult Outcomes of Youth Irritability: A 20-Year Prospective Community-Based Study," *American Journal of Psychiatry* 166 (2009): 1048–1054.

32. Erin C. Dunn et al., "Research Review: Gene-Environment Interaction Research in Youth Depression—A Systematic Review with Recommendations for Future Research," *Journal of Child Psychology and Psychiatry* 52, no. 12 (2011): 1223–38.

33. Saveanu and Nemeroff, "Etiology of Depression."

34. John M. Weir, Arthurine Zakama, and Uma Rao, "Developmental Risk I: Depression and the Developing Brain," *Child and Adolescent Psychiatric Clinics of North America* 21 (2012): 237–59.

35. Ian M. Goodyer et al., "Polymorphisms in BDNF (Val66Met) and 5-HTTLPR, Morning Cortisol and Subsequent Depression in At-Risk Adolescents," *British Journal of Psychiatry* 197 (2010): 365–71.

36. Jennifer Y. F. Lau et al., "Amygdala Function and 5-HTT Gene Variants in Adolescent Anxiety and Major Depressive Disorder," *Biological Psychiatry* 65 (2009): 349–55.

37. Stephan Collishaw et al., "Resilience to Adult Psychopathology Following Childhood Maltreatment: Evidence from a Community Sample," *Child Abuse & Neglect* 31 (2007): 211–29.

38. William R. Beardslee, Tracy R. G. Gladstone, and Erin E. O'Connor, "Developmental Risk of Depression: Experience Matters," *Child and Adolescent Psychiatric Clinics of North America* 21 (2012): 261–78.

39. Scott M. Monroe and Mark W. Reid, "Life Stress and Major Depression," *Current Directions in Psychological Science* 18, no. 2 (2009): 68–72.

40. Kenneth S. Kendler et al., "Life Event Dimensions of Loss, Humiliation, Entrapment, and Danger in the Prediction of Onsets of Major Depression and Generalized Anxiety," *Archives of General Psychiatry* 60 (2003): 789–96.

41. Constance Hammen, "Adolescent Depression: Stressful Interpersonal Contexts and Risk for Recurrence," *Current Directions in Psychological Science* 18, no. 4 (2009): 200–204.

42. Ibid.

43. Joan L. Luby et al., "The Clinical Significance and Preschool Depression: Impairment in Functioning and Clinical Markers of the Disorder," *Journal of Affective Disorders* 112 (2009): 111–19.

44. Margaret J. Briggs-Gowan et al., "Exposure to Potentially Traumatic Events in Early Childhood: Differential Links to Emergent Psychopathology," *Journal of Child Psychology and Psychiatry* 51, no. 10 (2010): 1132–40.

45. Beardslee, Gladstone, and O'Connor, "Developmental Risk of Depression."

46. Ibid.

47. Monroe and Reid, "Life Stress and Major Depression."

48. Kovacs and Lopez-Duran, "Prodromal Symptoms and Atypical Affectivity."

49. Côté et al., "Depression and Anxiety Symptoms."

50. Ed Tronick, *The Neurobehavioral and Social-Emotional Development of Infants and Children* (New York: W. W. Norton, 2007), pp. 274–92.

51. Laura E. Brumariu and Kathryn A. Kerns, "Parent-Child Attachment and Internalizing Symptoms in Childhood and Adolescence: A Review of Empirical Findings and Future Directions," *Development and Psychopathology* 22 (2010): 177–203.

52. Ashley M. Groh et al., "The Significance of Insecure and Disorganized Attachment for Children's Internalizing Symptoms: A Meta-Analytic Study," *Child Development* 83, no. 2 (2012): 591–610.

53. Brumariu and Kerns, "Parent-Child Attachment."

54. Kovacs and Lopez-Duran, "Prodromal Symptoms and Atypical Affectivity."

55. Côté et al., "Depression and Anxiety Symptoms."

56. Joan L. Luby, "Preschool Depression: The Importance of Identification of Depression Early in Development," *Current Directions in Psychological Science* 19, no. 2 (2010): 91–95.

57. Luby et al., "Clinical Significance and Preschool Depression."

58. Joan L. Luby et al., "Preschool Depression: Homotypic Continuity and Course Over 24 Months," *Archives of General Psychiatry* 66, no. 8 (2009): 897–905.

CHAPTER 10. WHEN MOODS ARE HIGH AND LOW— BIPOLAR DISORDER

1. G. S. Malhi et al., "Balanced Efficacy, Safety, and Tolerability Recommendations for the Clinical Management of Bipolar Disorder," *Bipolar Disorders* 14, Suppl. 2 (2012): 1–21.

2. Jules Angst and Andreas Marneros, "Bipolarity from Ancient to Modern Times: Conception, Birth and Rebirth," *Journal of Affective Disorders* 67 (2001): 3–19.

3. Kathleen R. Merikangas et al., "Lifetime and 12-Month Prevalence of Bipolar Spectrum Disorder in the National Comorbidity Survey Replication," *Archives of General Psychiatry* 64 (2007): 543–52.

4. John I. Nurnberger Jr., "Genetics of Bipolar Disorder: Where We Are and Where We Are Going," *Depression and Anxiety* 29 (2012): 991–93.

5. Robert M. Post et al., "Incidence of Childhood-Onset Bipolar Illness in the USA and Europe," *British Journal of Psychiatry* 192 (2008): 150–51.

6. Carmen Moreno et al., "National Trends in the Outpatient Diagnosis and Treatment Bipolar Disorder in Youth," *Archives of General Psychiatry* 64, no. 9 (2007): 1032–1039.

7. Joseph C. Blader and Gabrielle A. Carlson, "Increased Rates of Bipolar Disorder Diagnoses among U.S. Child, Adolescent, and Adult Inpatients, 1996–2004," *Biological Psychiatry* 62, no. 2 (2007): 107–14.

8. Ann R. Van Meter, Ana Lúcia R. Moreira, and Eric A. Youngstrom, "Meta-Analysis of Epidemiologic Studies of Pediatric Bipolar Disorder," *Journal of Clinical Psychiatry* 72, no. 9 (2011): 1250–56.

9. Boris Birmaher et al., "Clinical Course of Children and Adolescents with Bipolar Spectrum Disorders," *Archives of General Psychiatry* 63 (2006): 175–83.

10. Barbara Geller et al., "Child Bipolar I Disorder," *Archives of General Psychiatry* 65, no. 10 (2008): 1125–33.

11. Merikangas et al., "Lifetime and 12-Month Prevalence of Bipolar Spectrum Disorder."

12. Birmaher et al., "Clinical Course of Children and Adolescents with Bipolar Spectrum Disorders."

13. Julie Linke et al., "Increased Medial Orbitofrontal and Amygdala Activation: Evidence for a Systems-Level Endophenotype of Bipolar I Disorder," *American Journal of Psychiatry* 169 (2012): 316–25.

14. Nicholas B. Allen and Paul B. T. Badcock, "Darwinian Models of Depression: A Review of Evolutionary Accounts of Mood and Mood Disorders," *Progress in Neuro-Psychopharmacology & Biological Psychiatry* 30 (2006): 815–26.

15. John Gruber et al., "Risk for Mania and Positive Emotional Responding: Too Much of a Good Thing?" *Emotion* 8, no. 1 (2008): 23–33.

16. Warren Mansell and Rebecca Pedley, "The Ascent into Mania: A Review of Psychological Processes Associated with the Development of Manic Symptoms," *Clinical Psychology Review* 28 (2008): 494–520.

17. Claudia Lex, Martin Hautzinger, and Thomas D. Meyer, "Cognitive Styles in Hypomanic Episodes of Bipolar I Disorder," *Bipolar Disorders* 13 (2011): 355–64.

18. Diagnostic and Statistical Manual of Mental Disorders, *DSM-IV-TR* (Arlington, VA: American Psychiatric Publishing, 2000), pp. 345–428.

19. Richard Harrington and Tessa Myatt, "Pediatric Bipolar Disorder," *Biological Psychiatry* 53, no. 11 (2003): 961–69.

20. Diagnostic and Statistical Manual of Mental Disorders, *DSM-5* (Arlington, VA: American Psychiatric Publishing, 2013), pp. 123–54.

21. Anna R. Van Meter, Eric A. Youngstrom, and Robert L. Findling, "Cyclothymic Disorder: A Critical Review," *Clinical Psychology Review* 32 (2012): 229–43.

22. Eric A. Youngstrom, Boris Birmaher, and Robert L. Findling, "Pediatric Bipolar Disorder: Validity, Phenomenology, and Recommendations for Diagnosis," *Bipolar Disorders* 10 (2008): 194–214.

23. Ellen Leibenluft, "Severe Mood Dysregulation, Irritability, and the Diagnostic Boundaries of Bipolar Disorder in Youths," *American Journal of Psychiatry* 168 (2011): 129–42.

24. Ibid.

25. Argyris Stringaris et al., "Adult Outcomes of Youth Irritability: A 20-Year Prospective Community-Based Study," *American Journal of Psychiatry* 166 (2009): 1048–54.

26. David Axelson et al., "Examining the Proposed Disruptive Mood Dysregulation Disorder Diagnosis in Children in the Longitudinal Assessment of Manic Symptoms Study," *Journal of Clinical Psychiatry* 73, no. 10 (2012): 1342–50.

27. Stephen M. Strakowski et al., "The Functional Neuroanatomy of Bipolar Disorder: A Consensus Model," *Bipolar Disorders* 14 (2012): 313–25.

28. Ahmad R. Hariri, "The Highs and Lows of Amygdala Reactivity in Bipolar Disorders," *American Journal of Psychiatry* 169, no. 8 (2012): 780–83.

29. Jennifer Townsend and Lori L. Altshuler, "Emotion Processing and Regulation in Bipolar Disorder: A Review," *Bipolar Disorders* 14 (2012): 326–39.

30. Ibid.

31. Linke et al., "Increased Medial Orbitofrontal and Amygdala Activation."

32. Leslie A. Hulvershorn et al., "Neural Activation during Facial Emotion Processing in Unmedicated Bipolar Depression, Euthymia, and Mania," *Biological Psychiatry* 17 (2012): 603–10.

33. Cynthia M. Schumann, Melissa D. Bauman, and David G. Amaral, "Abnormal Structure or Function of the Amygdala Is a Common Component of Neurodevelopmental Disorders," *Neuropsychologia* 49 (2011): 745–59.

34. Pilyoung Kim et al., "Differing Amygdala Responses to Facial Expressions in Children and Adults with Bipolar Disorder," *American Journal of Psychiatry* 169 (2012): 642–49.

35. Stewart A. Shankman et al., "Deficits in Emotion Recognition in Pediatric Bipolar Disorder: The Mediating Effects of Irritability," *Journal of Affective Disorders* 144 (2013): 134–40.

36. Brendan A. Rich et al., "Different Neural Pathways to Negative Affect in Youth with Pediatric Bipolar Disorder and Severe Mood Dysregulation," *Journal of Psychiatric Research* 45 (2011): 1283–94.

37. C. Daban et al., "Hypothalamic-Pituitary-Adrenal Axis and Bipolar Disorder," *Psychiatric Clinics of North America* 28 (2005): 469–80.

38. Anne Duffy et al., "Biological Indicators of Illness Risk in Offspring of Bipolar Parents: Targeting the Hypothalamic-Pituitary-Adrenal Axis and Immune System," *Early Intervention in Psychiatry* 6 (2012): 128–37.

39. C. S. Ostiguy et al., "Sensitivity to Stress among the Offspring of Parents with Bipolar Disorder: A Study of Daytime Cortisol Levels," *Psychological Medicine* 41 (2011): 2447–57.

40. Mark A. Ellenbogen et al., "High Cortisol Levels in the Offspring of Parents with Bipolar Disorder during Two Weeks of Daily Sampling," *Bipolar Disorders* 12 (2010): 77–86.

41. Angst and Marneros, "Bipolarity from Ancient to Modern Times."

42. O. D. Howes et al., "A Comprehensive Review and Model of Putative Prodromal Features of Bipolar Affective Disorder," *Psychological Medicine* 41 (2011): 1567–77.

43. F. J. Kochman et al., "Cyclothymic Temperament as a Prospective Predictor of Bipolarity and Suicidality in Children and Adolescents with Major Depressive Disorder," *Journal of Affective Disorders* 85 (2005): 181–89.

44. Rene L. Olvera et al., "Assessment of Personality Dimensions in Children and Adolescents with Bipolar Disorder Using the Junior Temperament and Character Inventory," *Journal of Child and Adolescent Psychopharmacology* 19, no. 1 (2009): 13–21.

45. D. R. Hirshfeld-Becker et al., "Behavioral Inhibition in Preschool Children at Risk Is a Specific Predictor of Middle Childhood Society Anxiety: A Five-Year Follow-Up," *Journal of Developmental and Behavioral Pediatrics* 28, no. 3 (2007): 225–33.

46. Lauren B. Alloy and Lyn Y. Abramson, "The Role of the Behavioral Approach System (BAS) in Bipolar Spectrum Disorders," *Current Directions in Psychological Science* 19, no. 3 (2010): 189–94.

47. Jeffrey A. Gray, "Brain Systems That Mediate Both Emotion and Cognition," *Cognition & Emotion* 4, no. 3 (1990): 269–88.

48. Alloy and Abramson, "Role of the Behavioral Approach System."

49. Rachel E. Bender and Lauren B. Alloy, "Life Stress and Kindling in Bipolar Disorder: Review of the Evidence and Integration with Emerging Biopsychosocial Theories," *Clinical Psychology Review* 31 (2011): 383–98.

50. Nurnberger Jr., "Genetics of Bipolar Disorder."

51. Sheri L. Johnson, "Life Events in Bipolar Disorder: Towards More Specific Models," *Clinical Psychology Review* 25 (2005): 1008–1027.

52. Robert M. Post, "Kindling and Sensitization as Models for Affective Episode Recurrence, Cyclicity, and Tolerance Phenomena," *Neuroscience and Biobehavioral Reviews* 31 (2007): 858–73.

53. Bender and Alloy, "Life Stress and Kindling in Bipolar Disorder."

54. Alloy and Abramson, "Role of the Behavioral Approach System."

55. Johnson, "Life Events in Bipolar Disorder."

56. Howes et al., "Comprehensive Review and Model of Putative Prodromal Features of Bipolar Affective Disorder."

57. Kochman et al., "Cyclothymic Temperature as a Prospective Predictor of Bipolarity."

58. Joan L. Luby and Neha Navsaria, "Pediatric Bipolar Disorder: Evidence for Prodromal States and Early Markers," *Journal of Child Psychology and Psychiatry* 51, no. 4 (2010): 459–71.

59. Caroline Vandeleur et al., "Mental Disorders in Offspring of Parents with Bipolar and Major Depressive Disorders," *Bipolar Disorders* 14 (2012): 641–53.

60. Anne Duffy et al., "Early Stages in the Development of Bipolar Disorder," *Journal of Affective Disorders* 121 (2010): 127–35.

61. John I. Nurnberger Jr. et al., "A High-Risk Study of Bipolar Disorder: Childhood Clinical Phenotypes as Precursors of Major Mood Disorders" *Archives of General Psychiatry* 68, no. 10 (2011): 1012–20.

CHAPTER 11. WHEN MOOD IS INDIFFERENT— DISRUPTIVE AND ANTISOCIAL BEHAVIOR

1. Diagnostic and Statistical Manual of Mental Disorders, *DSM-5* (Arlington, VA: American Psychiatric Publishing, 2013).

2. Rolf Loeber et al., "Development and Etiology of Disruptive and Delinquent Behavior," *Annual Review of Clinical Psychology* 5 (2009): 291–310.

3. Terrie E. Moffitt, "Adolescence-Limited and Life-Course-Persistent Antisocial Behavior: A Developmental Taxonomy," *Psychological Review* 100, no. 4 (1993): 674–701.

4. Rolf Loeber, Jeffrey Burke, and Dustin A. Pardini, "Perspectives on Oppositional Defiant Disorder, Conduct Disorder, and Psychopathic Features," *Journal of Child Psychology and Psychiatry* 50 (2009): 133–42.

5. Barbara Maughan et al., "Conduct Disorder and Oppositional Defiant Disorder in a National Sample: Developmental Epidemiology," *Journal of Child Psychology and Psychiatry* 45, no. 3 (2004): 609–21.

6. Walt Matthys, Louk J. M. J. Vanderschuren, and Dennis J. L. G. Schutter, "The

Neurobiology of Oppositional Defiant Disorder and Conduct Disorder: Altered Functioning in Three Mental Domains," *Developmental and Psychopathology* 25, no. 1 (2012): 193–207.

7. Kenneth A. Dodge et al., "Peer Rejection and Social Information-Processing Factors in the Development of Aggressive Behavior Problems in Children," *Child Development* 74, no. 2 (2003): 374–93.

8. Diagnostic and Statistical Manual of Mental Disorders, *DSM-IV-TR* (Arlington, VA: American Psychiatric Publishing, 2000).

9. Argyris Stringaris, "Irritability in Children and Adolescents: A Challenge for DSM-5," *European Child and Adolescent Psychiatry* 20 (2011): 61–66.

10. R. J. R. Blair et al., "The Development of Psychopathy," *Journal of Child Psychology and Psychiatry* 47, no. 3/4 (2006): 262–75.

11. Khrista Boylan et al., "Comorbidity of Internalizing Disorders in Children with Oppositional Defiant Disorder," *European Child & Adolescent Psychiatry* 16, no. 8 (2007): 484–94.

12. Benjamin B. Lahey and Irwin D. Waldman, "Annual Research Review: Phenotypic and Causal Structure of Conduct Disorder in the Broader Context of Prevalent Forms of Psychopathology," *Journal of Child Psychology and Psychiatry* 53, no. 5 (2012): 536–57.

13. Diagnostic and Statistical Manual of Mental Disorders, *DSM-IV-TR.*

14. Lahey and Waldman, "Annual Research Review."

15. Ibid.

16. Loeber et al., "Development and Etiology of Disruptive and Delinquent Behavior."

17. Stringaris, "Irritability in Children and Adolescents."

18. Lahey and Waldman, "Annual Research Review."

19. Moffitt, "Adolescence-Limited and Life-Course-Persistent Antisocial Behavior."

20. Blair et al., "Development of Psychopathy."

21. Ibid.

22. Katya Rubia, "'Cool' Inferior Frontostriatal Dysfunction in Attention-Deficit/Hyperactivity Disorder Versus 'Hot' Ventromedial Orbitofrontal-Limbic Dysfunction in Conduct Disorder: A Review," *Biological Psychiatry* 69 (2011): e69–e87.

23. Blair et al., "Development of Psychopathy."

24. Abigail A. Marsh and R. J. R. Blair, "Deficits in Facial Affect Recognition among Antisocial Populations: A Meta-Analysis," *Neuroscience and Biobehavioral Reviews* 32, no. 3 (2008): 454–65.

25. Essi Viding et al., "Amygdala Response to Preattentive Masked Fear in Children with Conduct Problems: The Role of Callous-Unemotional Traits," *American Journal of Psychiatry* 169 (2012): 1109–16.

26. Catherine L. Sebastian et al., "Neural Responses to Affective and Cognitive Theory of Mind in Children with Conduct Problems and Varying Levels of Callous-Unemotional Traits," *Archives of General Psychiatry* 69, no. 8 (2012): 814–22.

27. Graeme Fairchild et al., "Brain Structure Abnormalities in Early-Onset and Adolescent-Onset Conduct Disorder," *American Journal of Psychiatry* 168 (2011): 624–33.

28. R. J. R. Blair, "Neuroimaging of Psychopathy and Antisocial Behavior: A Targeted Review," *Current Psychiatry Reports* 12 (2010): 76–82.

29. Matthys, Vanderschuren, and Schutter, "Neurobiology of Oppositional Defiant Disorder."

30. Jame Ortiz and Adrian Raine, "Heart Rate Level and Antisocial Behavior in Children and Adolescents: A Meta-Analysis," *Journal of American Academy of Child and Adolescent Psychiatry* 43, no. 2 (2004): 154–62.

31. Stephanie H. M. van Goozen et al., "The Evidence for a Neurobiological Model of Childhood Antisocial Behavior," *Psychological Bulletin* 133, no. 1 (2007): 149–82.

32. Ibid.

33. Keith McBurnett et al., "Mood and Hormone Responses to Psychological Challenge in Adolescent Males with Conduct Problems," *Biological Psychiatry* 57 (2005): 1109–16.

34. Bryan R. Loney et al., "The Relation between Salivary Cortisol, Callous-Unemotional Traits, and Conduct Problems in an Adolescent Non-Referred Sample," *Journal of Child Psychology and Psychiatry* 47, no. 1 (2006): 30–36.

35. Elizabeth J. Susman, "Psychobiology of Persistent Antisocial Behavior: Stress, Early Vulnerabilities and the Attenuation Hypothesis," *Neuroscience and Biobehavioral Reviews* 30 (2006): 376–89.

36. Isabela Granic and Gerald R. Patterson, "Toward a Comprehensive Model of Antisocial Development: A Dynamic Systems Approach," *Psychological Review* 113, no. 1 (2006): 101–31.

37. Adrian Raine, "Annotation: The Role of Prefrontal Deficits, Low Autonomic Arousal, and Early Health Factors in the Development of Antisocial and Aggressive Behavior in Children," *Journal of Child Psychology and Psychiatry* 43, no. 4 (2002): 417–34.

38. Terrie E. Moffitt, "The New Look of Behavioral Genetics in Developmental Psychopathology: Gene-Environment Interplay in Antisocial Behaviors," *Psychological Bulletin* 131, no. 4 (2005): 533–54.

39. Thalia C. Eley, Paul Lichtenstein, and Terrie E. Moffitt, "A Longitudinal Behavioral Genetic Analysis of the Etiology of Aggressive and Nonaggressive Antisocial Behavior," *Development and Psychopathology* 15 (2003): 383–402.

40. Lahey and Waldman, "Annual Research Review."

41. Catherine Tuvblad, Martin Grann, and Paul Lichtenstein, "Heritability for Adolescent Antisocial Behavior Differs with Socioeconomic Status: Gene-Environment Interaction," *Journal of Child Psychology and Psychiatry* 47, no. 7 (2006): 734–43.

42. Sara R. Jaffee et al., "Nature x Nurture: Genetic Vulnerabilities Interact with Physical Maltreatment to Promote Conduct Problems," *Development and Psychopathology* 17 (2005): 67–84.

43. Essi Viding et al., "Evidence for Substantial Genetic Risk for Psychopathy in 7-Year-Olds," *Journal of Child Psychology and Psychiatry* 46, no. 6 (2005): 592–97.

44. Anita Thapar et al., "Catechol O-Methyltransferase Gene Variant and Birth Weight Predict Early-Onset Antisocial Behavior in Children with Attention-Deficit/Hyperactivity Disorder," *Archives of General Psychiatry* 62 (2005): 1275–78.

45. Marian J. Bakermans-Kranenburg and Marinus H. van Ijzendoorn, "Gene-Environment Interaction of the Dopamine D4 Receptor (DRD4) and Observed Maternal Insensitivity Predicting Externalizing Behavior in Preschoolers," *Developmental Psychobiology* 48 (2006): 406–409.

46. Avshalom Caspi et al., "Role of Genotype in the Cycle of Violence in Maltreated Children," *Science* 297 (2002): 851–54.

47. Debra L. Foley et al., "Childhood Adversity, Monoamine Oxidase A Genotype, and Risk for Conduct Disorder," *Archives of General Psychiatry* 61 (2004): 738–44.

48. Valentina Nikulina, Cathy Spatz Widom, and Linda M. Brzustowicz, "Child Abuse and Neglect, MAOA, and Mental Health Outcomes: A Prospective Examination," *Biological Psychiatry* 71 (2012): 350–57.

49. Paul J. Frick and Amanda Sheffield Morris, "Temperament and Developmental Pathways to Conduct Problems," *Journal of Clinical Child and Adolescent Psychology* 33, no. 1 (2004): 54–68.

50. Loeber et al., "Developmental and Etiology of Disruptive and Delinquent Behavior."

51. Paul J. Frick, "Developmental Pathways to Conduct Disorder," *Child and Adolescent Psychiatric Clinics of North America* 15 (2006): 311–31.

52. Julia Kim-Cohen et al., "Maternal Depression and Children's Antisocial Behavior," *Archives of General Psychiatry* 62 (2005): 173–81.

53. Mark F. Feinberg et al., "Parenting and Adolescent Antisocial Behavior and Depression: Evidence of Genotype x Parenting Environment Interaction," *Archives of General Psychiatry* 64 (2007): 457–65.

54. Gerald R. Patterson, John B. Reid, and Thomas J. Dishion, *Antisocial Boys* (Eugene, OR: Castalia, 1992).

55. Dodge et al., "Peer Rejection and Social Information-Processing Factors."

56. R. Pasco Fearon et al., "The Significance of Insecure Attachment and Disorganization in the Development of Children's Externalizing Behavior: A Meta-Analytic Study," *Child Development* 81, no. 2 (2010): 435–56.

57. Sarit Guttmann-Steinmetz and Judith A. Crowell, "Attachment and Externalizing Disorders: A Developmental Psychopathology Perspective," *Journal of American Academy of Child and Adolescent Psychiatry* 45, no. 4 (2006): 440–51.

CHAPTER 12. GETTING BACK ON TRACK— PSYCHOLOGICAL AND BEHAVIORAL THERAPY

1. Tracy R. G. Gladstone, William R. Beardslee, and Erin E. O'Connor, "The Prevention of Adolescent Depression," *Psychiatric Clinics of North America* 34 (2011): 35–52.

2. Jordana K. Bayer et al., "Translational Research to Prevent Internalizing Problems Early in Childhood," *Depression and Anxiety* 28 (2011): 50–57.

3. Jonathan Shedler, "The Efficacy of Psychodynamic Psychotherapy," *American Psychologist* 65, no. 2 (2010): 98–109.

4. Chiara Ruini and Giovanni A. Fava, "Role of Well-Being Therapy in Achieving a Balanced and Individualized Path to Optimal Functioning," *Clinical Psychology and Psychotherapy* 19 (2012): 291–304.

5. Viktor E. Frankl, *Man's Search for Meaning* (Boston: Beacon Press, 2006), pp. 65–80.

6. Michael Rutter, "Annual Research Review: Resilience: Clinical Implications," *Journal of Child Psychology and Psychiatry* 54, no. 4 (2013): 474–87.

7. Ibid.

8. Gladstone, Beardslee, and O'Connor, "Prevention of Adolescent Depression."

9. Rutter, "Annual Research Review."

10. Michelle G. Craske, "Transdiagnostic Treatment for Anxiety and Depression," *Depresion and Anxiety* 29 (2012): 749–53.

11. Ibid.

12. Shedler, "Efficacy of Psychodynamic Psychotherapy."

13. Nick Midgley and Eilis Kennedy, "Psychodynamic Psychotherapy for Children and Adolescents: A Critical Review of the Evidence Base," *Journal of Child Psychotherapy* 37, no. 3 (2011): 232–60.

14. Norka T. Malberg and Linda C. Mayes, "The Contemporary Psychodynamic Developmental Perspective," *Child and Adolescent Psychiatric Clinics of North America* 22 (2013): 33–49.

15. Nick Midgley et al., "Psychodynamic Psychotherapy as Treatment for Depression in Adolescence," *Child and Adolescent Psychiatric Clinics of North America* 22 (2013): 67–82.

16. Peter Fonagy et al., "The Capacity for Understanding Mental States: The Reflective Self in Parent and Child and Its Significance for Security of Attachment," *Infant Mental Health Journal* 12, no. 3 (1991): 201–18.

17. AACAP Official Action, "Practice Parameter for the Assessment and Treatment of Children and Adolescents with Anxiety Disorders," *Journal of the American Academy of Child and Adolescent Psychiatric* 46, no. 2 (2007): 267–83.

18. American Psychiatric Association (APA), *Practice Guidelines for the Treatment of Patients with Panic Disorder*, 2nd ed. (Washington, DC: American Psychiatric Association [APA], 2009).

19. Gabrielle Silver, Theodore Shapiro, and Barbara Milrod, "Treatment of Anxiety in Children and Adolescents: Using Child and Adolescent Anxiety Psychodynamic Psychotherapy," *Child and Adolescent Psychiatric Clinics of North America* 22 (2013): 83–96.

20. Shedler, "Efficacy of Psychodynamic Psychotherapy."

21. Steven D. Hollon and Kathryn Ponniah, "A Review of Empirically Supported Psychological Therapies for Mood Disorders in Adults," *Depression and Anxiety* 27 (2010): 891–932.

22. Work Group on Major Depressive Disorder, "Practice Guideline for the Treatment of Patients with Major Depression Disorder," *American Journal of Psychiatry* 16, no. 10 (2010): 1–118.

23. Midgley et al., "Psychodynamic Psychotherapy as Treatment for Depression in Adolescence."

24. Anat Brunstein Klomek and Laura Mufson, "Interpersonal Psychotherapy for Depressed Adolescents," *Child and Adolescent Psychiatric Clinics of North America* 15 (2006): 959–75.

25. John C. Markowitz and Myrna M. Weissman, "Interpersonal Psychotherapy: Principles and Applications," *World Psychiatry* 3, no. 3 (2004): 136–39.

26. John C. Markowitz, "IPT and PTSD," *Depression and Anxiety* 27 (2010): 879–81.

27. Ulrich Stangier et al., "Cognitive Therapy vs. Interpersonal Psychotherapy in Social Anxiety Disorder: A Randomized Controlled Trial," *Archives of General Psychiatry* 68, no. 7 (2011): 692–700.

28. Ibid.

29. Markowitz and Weissman, "Interpersonal Psychotherapy: Principles and Applications."

30. Klomek and Mufson, "Interpersonal Psychotherapy for Depressed Adolescents."

31. Hami F. Young, Laura Mufson, and Mark Davies, "Impact of Comorbid Anxiety in an Effectiveness Study of Interpersonal Psychotherapy for Depressed Adolescents," *Journal of the American Academy of Child and Adolescent Psychiatry* 45, no. 8 (2006): 904–12.

32. Ellen Frank et al., "Two-Year Outcomes for Interpersonal and Social Rhythm Therapy in Individuals with Bipolar I Disorder," *Archives of General Psychiatry* 62 (2005): 996–1004.

33. Stefanie A. Hlastala et al., "Interpersonal and Social Rhythm Therapy for Adolescents with Bipolar Disorder: Treatment Development and Results from an Open Trial," *Depression and Anxiety* 27 (2010): 457–64.

34. Mary A. Fristad et al., "Impact of Multifamily Psychoeducational Psychotherapy in Treating Children Aged 8 to 12 Years with Mood Disorders," *Archives of General Psychiatry* 66, no. 9 (2009): 1013–21.

35. M. N. Pavuluri et al., "Child- and Family-Focused Cognitive-Behavioral Therapy for Pediatric Bipolar Disorder: Development and Preliminary Results," *Journal of the American Academy of Child and Adolescent Psychiatry* 43, no. 5 (2004): 528–37.

36. David J. Miklowitz and Kiki D. Chang, "Prevention of Bipolar Disorder in At-Risk Children: Theoretical Assumptions and Empirical Foundations," *Development and Psychopathology* 20 (2008): 881–97.

37. Robert D. Friedberg and Gina M. Brelsford, "Core Principles in Cognitive Therapy with Youth," *Child and Adolescent Psychiatric Clinics of North America* 20 (2011): 369–78.

38. Laura D. Seligman and Thomas H. Ollendick, "Cognitive-Behavioral Therapy for Anxiety Disorders in Youth," *Child and Adolescent Psychiatric Clinics of North America* 20 (2011): 217–38.

39. Ibid.

40. Lisa W. Coyne, Louise McHugh, and Evan R. Martinez, "Acceptance and Commitment Therapy (ACT): Advances and Applications with Children, Adolescents, and Families," *Child and Adolescent Psychiatric Clinics of North America* 20 (2011): 379–99.

41. Alyson K. Zalta, "A Meta-Analysis of Anxiety Symptom Prevention with Cognitive-Behavioral Interventions," *Journal of Anxiety Disorders* 25 (2011): 749–60.

42. Bayer et al., "Translational Research to Prevent Internalizing Problems Early in Childhood."

43. Susan J. Kennedy, Ronald M. Rapee, and Susan L. Edwards, "A Selective Intervention Program for Inhibited Preschool-Aged Children of Parents with an Anxiety Disorder: Effects on Current Anxiety Disorders and Temperament," *Journal of the American Academy of Child and Adolescent Psychiatry* 48, no. 6 (2009): 602–609.

44. Paula M. Barrett et al., "Long-Term Outcomes of an Australian Universal Prevention Trial of Anxiety and Depression Symptoms in Children and Youth: An Evaluation of the Friends Program," *Journal of Clinical Child and Adolescent Psychology* 35, no. 3 (2006): 403–11.

45. Donna M. Sudak, "Cognitive Behavioral Therapy for Depression," *Psychiatric Clinics of North America* 35 (2012): 99–110.

46. Hollon and Ponniah, "Review of Empirically Supported Psychological Therapies for Mood Disorders in Adults."

47. Anthony Spirito et al., "Cognitive-Behavioral Therapy for Adolescent Depression and Suicidality," *Child and Adolescent Psychiatric Clinics of North America* 20 (2011): 191–204.

48. The TADS Team, "The Treatment for Adolescents with Depression Study (TADS): Long-Term Effectiveness and Safety Outcomes," *Archives of General Psychiatry* 64, no. 10 (2007): 1132–44.

49. Carolyn A. McCarty and John R. Weisz, "Effects of Psychotherapy for Depression in Children and Adolescents: What We Can (and Can't) Learn from Meta-Analysis and Component Profiling," *Journal of the American Academy of Child and Adolescent Psychiatry* 46, no. 7 (2007): 879–86.

50. Coyne, McHugh, and Martinez, "Acceptance and Commitment Therapy."

51. Gladstone, Beardslee, and O'Connor, "Prevention of Adolescent Depression."

52. Joan L. Luby, "Treatment of Anxiety and Depression in the Preschool Period," *Journal of the American Academy of Child and Adolescent Psychiatry* 52, no. 4 (2013): 346–58.

53. Shannon N. Lenze, Jennifer Pautsch, and John Luby, "Parent-Child Interaction Therapy Emotion Development: A Novel Treatment for Depression in Preschool Children," *Depression and Anxiety* 28 (2011): 153–59.

54. Sheila M. Eyberg, Melanie M. Nelson, and Stephen R. Boggs, "Evidence-Based Psychosocial Treatments for Children and Adolescents with Disruptive Behavior," *Journal of Clinical Child and Adolescent Psychology* 37, no. 1 (2008): 215–37.

55. John E. Lochman et al., "Cognitive Behavioral Therapy for Externalizing Disorders in Children and Adolescents," *Child and Adolescent Psychiatric Clinics of North America* 20 (2011): 305–18.

56. Eyberg, Nelson, and Boggs, "Evidence-Based Psychosocial Treatments for Children and Adolescents with Disruptive Behavior."

57. Renee McDonald et al., "Effects of a Parenting Intervention on Features of Psychopathy in Children," *Journal of Abnormal Child Psychology* 39 (2011): 1013–23.

58. David J. Kolko et al., "Community vs. Clinic-Based Modular Treatment in Children with Early-Onset ODD or CD: A Clinical Trial with 3-Year Follow-Up," *Journal of Abnormal Child Psychology* 37 (2009): 591–609.

59. Steven C. Hayes et al., "Acceptance and Commitment Therapy: Model, Processes and Outcomes," *Behaviour Research and Therapy* 44 (2006): 1–25.

60. Ibid.

61. Ibid.

62. Evan M. Forman et al., "Long-Term Follow-Up of a Randomized Controlled Trial Comparing Acceptance and Commitment Therapy and Standard Cognitive Behavior Therapy for Anxiety and Depression," *Behavior Therapy* 43 (2012): 801–11.

63. Coyne, McHugh, and Martinez, "Acceptance and Commitment Therapy."

64. Ruini and Fava, "Role of Well-Being Therapy."

65. Giovanni A. Fava and Elena Tomba, "Increasing Psychological Well-Being and Resilience by Psychotherapeutic Methods," *Journal of Personality* 77, no. 6 (2009): 1903–34.

66. Ruini and Fava, "Role of Well-Being Therapy."

67. Elena Tomba et al., "Differential Effects of Well-Being Promoting and Anxiety-Management Strategies in a Non-Clinical School Setting," *Journal of Anxiety Disorders* 24 (2010): 326–33.

68. Craske, "Transdiagnostic Treatment for Anxiety and Depression."

CHAPTER 13. GETTING BACK ON TRACK—MEDICATION

1. Dara Sakolsky and Boris Birmaher, "Developmentally Informed Pharmacotherapy for Child and Adolescent Depressive Disorders," *Child and Adolescent Psychiatric Clinics of North America* 21 (2012): 313–25.

2. Moira Rynn et al., "Advances in Pharmacotherapy for Pediatric Anxiety Disorders," *Depression and Anxiety* 28 (2011): 76–87.

3. G. S. Malhi et al., "Balanced Efficacy, Safety, and Tolerability Recommendations for the Clinical Management of Bipolar Disorder," *Bipolar Disorders* 14, Suppl. 2 (2012): 1–21.

4. Stephen M. Stahl, *Stahl's Essential Psychopharmacology* (New York: Cambridge University Press, 2008).

5. Ibid., pp. 721–71.

6. Sakolsky and Birmaher, "Developmentally Informed Pharmacotherapy."

7. Stahl, *Stahl's Essential Psychopharmacology*, pp. 511–666.

8. Ibid., pp. 665–719.

9. Ibid.

10. Rynn et al., "Advances in Pharmacotherapy for Pediatric Anxiety Disorders."

11. Katharina Manassis, Kelly Russell, and Amanda S. Newton, "The Cochrane Library and the Treatment of Childhood and Adolescent Anxiety Disorders: An Overview of Reviews," *Evidence-Based Child Health: A Cochrane Review Journal* 5 (2010): 541–54.

12. Pediatric OCD Treatment Study (POTS) Team, "Cognitive-Behavior Therapy, Sertraline, and Their Combination for Children and Adolescents with Obsessive-Compulsive Disorder: The Pediatric OCD Treatment Study (POTS) Randomized Controlled Trial," *Journal of the American Medical Association* 292, no. 16 (2004): 1969–76.

13. John T. Walkup, "Cognitive Behavioral Therapy, Sertraline, or a Combination in Childhood Anxiety," *New England Journal of Medicine* 359, no. 26 (2008): 2753–66.

14. Daniel Carlat, "Evidence-Based Somatic Treatment of Depression in Adults," *Psychiatric Clinics of North America* 35 (2012): 131–42.

15. B. N. Gaynes et al., "The STAR*D Study: Treating Depression in the Real World," *Cleveland Clinic Journal of Medicine* 75, no. 1 (2008): 57–66.

16. Fredric N. Busch and Larry S. Sandberg, "Combined Treatment of Depression," *Psychiatric Clinics of North America* 35 (2012): 165–79.

17. Graham J. Emslie et al., "Fluoxetine in Child and Adolescent Depression: Acute and Maintenance Treatment," *Depression and Anxiety* 7 (1998): 32–39.

18. Fadi T. Maalouf and David A. Brent, "Child and Adolescent Depression Intervention Overview: What Works, for Whom and How Well?" *Child and Adolescent Psychiatric Clinics of North America* 21 (2012): 299–312.

19. Treatment for Adolescents with Depression Study (TADS) Team, "Fluoxetine, Cognitive-Behavioral Therapy, and Their Combination for Adolescents with Depression: Treatment for Adolescents with Depression Study (TADS) Randomized Controlled Trial," *Journal of the American Medical Association* 292 (2004): 807–20.

20. The TADS Team, "The Treatment for Adolescents with Depression Study (TADS): Long-Term Effectiveness and Safety Outcomes," *Archives of General Psychiatry* 64, no. 10 (2007): 1132–44.

21. David Brent et al., "Switching to Another SSRI or to Venlafaxine with or without Cognitive Behavioral Therapy for Adolescents with SSRI-Resistant Depression: The TORDIA Randomized Controlled Trial," *Journal of the American Medical Association* 299, no. 8 (2008): 901–13.

22. Graham J. Emslie et al., "Treatment of Resistant Depression in Adolescents (TORDIA): Week 24 Outcomes," *American Journal of Psychiatry* 167 (2010): 782–91.

23. Malhi et al., "Balanced Efficacy, Safety, and Tolerability Recommendations for the Clinical Management of Bipolar Disorder."

24. G. S. Malhi et al., "The Clinical Management of Bipolar Disorder Complexity Using a Stratified Model," *Bipolar Disorders* 14, Suppl. 2 (2012): 66–89.

25. Howard Y. Liu et al., "Pharmacologic Treatments for Pediatric Bipolar Disorder: A Review and Meta-Analysis," *Journal of the American Academy of Child and Adolescent Psychiatry* 50, no. 8 (2011): 749–62.

26. Ibid.

27. Barbara Geller et al., "A Randomized Controlled Trial of Risperidone, Lithium, or Divalproex Sodium for Initial Treatment of Bipolar I Disorder, Manic or Mixed Phase, in Children and Adolescents," *Archives of General Psychiatry* 69, no. 5 (2012): 515–28.

28. Benedetto Vitiello et al., "Treatment Moderators and Predictors of Outcome in the Treatment of Early Age Mania (TEAM) Study," *Journal of the American Academy of Child and Adolescent Psychiatry* 51, no. 9 (2012): 867–78.

29. Liu et al., "Pharmacologic Treatments for Pediatric Bipolar Disorder."

30. David J. Miklowitz and Kiki D. Chang, "Prevention of Bipolar Disorder in At-Risk Children: Theoretical Assumptions and Empirical Foundations," *Development and Psychopathology* 20 (2008): 881–97.

31. Manfred E. Beutel et al., "Changes of Brain Activation Pre- Post Short-Term Psychodynamic Inpatient Psychotherapy: An fMRI Study of Panic Disorder Patients," *Psychiatry Research: Neuroimaging* 184 (2010): 96–104.

32. Mario Beauregard, "Mind Does Really Matter: Evidence from Neuroimaging Studies of Emotional Self-Regulation, Psychotherapy, and Placebo Effect," *Progress in Neurobiology* 81 (2007): 218–36.

33. Ibid.

34. Patricia Ribeiro Porto et al., "Does Cognitive Behavioral Therapy Change the Brain? A Systematic Review of Neuroimaging in Anxiety Disorders," *Journal of Neuropsychiatry and Clinical Neurosciences* 21 (2009): 114–25.

35. K. Goldapple et al., "Modulation of Cortical-Limbic Pathways in Major Depression: Treatment-Specific Effects of Cognitive Behavior Therapy," *Archives of General Psychiatry* 61, no. 1 (2004): 34–41.

36. Robert DeRubeis, Greg J. Siegle, and Steven D. Hollon, "Cognitive Therapy versus Medication for Depression: Treatment Outcomes and Neural Mechanisms," *Nature Reviews Neuroscience* 9 (2008): 788–96.

37. Goldapple et al., "Modulation of Cortical-Limbic Pathways in Major Depression."

38. R. Tao et al., "Brain Activity in Adolescent Major Depressive Disorder before and after Fluoxetine Treatment," *American Journal of Psychiatry* 169 (2012): 381–88.

39. Jennifer Urbano Blackford and Daniel S. Pine, "Neural Substrates of Childhood Anxiety Disorders: A Review of Neuroimaging Findings," *Child and Adolescent Psychiatric Clinics of North America* 21 (2012): 501–25.

40. Danella M. Hafeman et al., "Effects of Medication on Neuroimaging Findings in Bipolar Disorder: An Updated Review," *Bipolar Disorders* 14 (2012): 375–410.

41. Beauregard, "Mind Does Really Matter."

42. Lauren Y. Atlas and Tor D. Wager, "How Expectations Shape Pain," *Neuroscience Letters* 520, no. 2 (2012): 140–48.

43. David Borsook et al., "Pain and Analgesia: The Value of Salience Circuits," *Progress in Neurobiology* 104 (2013): 93–105.

CHAPTER 14. THE CHALLENGE OF MEDICAL ILLNESS

1. Margaret E. Kemeny and Manfred Schedlowski, "Understanding the Interaction between Psychosocial Stress and Immune-Related Diseases: A Stepwise Progression," *Brain, Behavior, and Immunity* 21 (2007): 1009–18.

2. Aoife O'Donovan et al., "Exaggerated Neurobiological Sensitivity to Threat as a Mechanism Linking Anxiety with Increased Risk for Diseases of Aging," *Neuroscience and Biobehavioral Reviews* 37 (2013): 96–108.

3. Margaret E. Kemeny, "Psychobiological Responses to Social Threat: Evolution of a Psychological Model in Psychoneuroimmunology," *Brain, Behavior, and Immunity* 23 (2009): 1–9.

4. Quentin J. Pittman, "A Neuro-Endocrine-Immune Symphony," *Journal of Neuroendocrinology* 23 (2011): 1296–97.

5. Robert Dantzer et al., "From Inflammation to Sickness and Depression: When the Immune System Subjugates the Brain," *Nature Review Neuroscience* 9 (2008): 46–57.

6. Aoife O'Donovan et al., "Clinical Anxiety, Cortisol and Interleukin-6: Evidence for Specificity in Emotion-Biology Relationships," *Brain, Behavior, and Immunity* 24 (2010): 1074–77.

7. O'Donovan et al., "Exaggerated Neurobiological Sensitivity to Threat."

8. Brian P. Kurtz and Annah N. Abrams, "Psychiatric Aspects of Pediatric Cancer," *Child and Adolescent Psychiatric Clinics of North America* 19 (2010): 401–421.

9. Michelle M. Ernst, Mark C. Johnson, and Lori J. Stark, "Developmental and Psychosocial Issues in Cystic Fibrosis," *Child and Adolescent Psychiatric Clinics of North America* 19 (2010): 263–83.

10. James L. Griffith and Lynne Gaby, "Brief Psychotherapy at the Bedside: Countering Demoralization from Medical Illness," *Psychosomatics* 46, no. 2 (2005): 109–16.

11. Sandra L. Fritsch, Mark W. Overton, and Douglas R. Robbins, "The Interface of Child

Mental Health and Juvenile Diabetes Mellitus," *Child and Adolescent Psychiatric Clinics of North America* 19 (2010): 335–52.

12. Todd E. Peters and Gregory K. Fritz, "Psychological Considerations of the Child with Asthma," *Child and Adolescent Psychiatric Clinics of North America* 19 (2010): 319–33.

13. Kurtz and Abrams, "Psychiatric Aspects of Pediatric Cancer."

14. Fabiano Di Marco, Pierachille Santus, and Stefano Centanni, "Anxiety and Depression in Asthma," *Current Opinion in Pulmonary Medicine* 17 (2011): 39–44.

15. Ibid.

16. Eva Szigethy, Laura McLafferty, and Alka Goyal, "Inflammatory Bowel Disease," *Child and Adolescent Psychiatric Clinics of North America* 19 (2010): 301–18.

17. Fritsch, Overton, and Robbins, "Interface of Child Mental Health and Juvenile Diabetes Mellitus."

18. Mary Lynn Dell and John V. Campo, "Somatoform Disorders in Children and Adolescents," *Psychiatric Clinics of North America* 34 (2011): 643–60.

19. Ibid.

20. Maryland Pao and Abigail Bosk, "Anxiety in Medically Ill Children/Adolescents," *Depression and Anxiety* 28 (2011): 40–49.

21. Griffith and Gaby, "Brief Psychotherapy at the Bedside."

22. Ariane Schwab, Sandra Rusconi-Serpa, and Daniel S. Schechter, "Psychodynamic Approaches to Medically Ill Children and Their Traumatically Stressed Parents," *Child and Adolescent Psychiatric Clinics of North America* 22 (2013): 119–39.

23. Ibid.

24. Ernst, Johnson, and Stark, "Developmental and Psychosocial Issues in Cystic Fibrosis."

25. Rachel D. Thompson, Patty Delaney, and Inti Flores, "Cognitive-Behavioral Therapy for Children with Comorbid Physical Illness," *Child and Adolescent Psychiatric Clinics of North America* 20 (2011): 329–48.

26. Pao and Bosk, "Anxiety in Medically Ill Children/Adolescents."

27. Fritsch, Overton, and Robbins, "Interface of Child Mental Health and Juvenile Diabetes Mellitus."

28. Szigethy, McLafferty, and Goyal, "Inflammatory Bowel Disease."

29. Ibid.

30. Peters and Fritz, "Psychological Considerations of the Child with Asthma."

31. Janelle Yorke, Sharon L. Fleming, and Caroline Shuldham, "Psychological Interventions for Adults with Asthma: A Systematic Review," *Respiratory Medicine* 101 (2007): 1–14.

32. Fritsch, Overton, and Robbins, "Interface of Child Mental Health and Juvenile Diabetes Mellitus."

33. Thompson, Delaney, and Flores, "Cognitive-Behavioral Therapy for Children with Comorbid Physical Illness."

34. Lisa W. Coyne, Louise McHugh, and Evan R. Martinez, "Acceptance and Commitment

Therapy (ACT): Advances and Applications with Children, Adolescents, and Families," *Child and Adolescent Psychiatric Clinics of North America* 20 (2011): 379–99.

35. Ibid.

36. Annabelle Casier et al., "Acceptance and Well-Being in Adolescents and Young Adults with Cystic Fibrosis: A Prospective Study," *Journal of Pediatric Psychology* 36, no. 4 (2011): 476–87.

37. Chiara Ruini and Giovanni A. Fava, "Role of Well-Being Therapy in Achieving a Balanced and Individualized Path to Optimal Functioning," *Clinical Psychology and Psychotherapy* 19 (2012): 291–304.

38. Michelle G. Craske, "Transdiagnostic Treatment for Anxiety and Depression," *Depression and Anxiety* 29 (2012): 749–53.

INDEX

abuse and neglect of children, 26, 38, 55, 75, 77, 147–48, 151
   and anxiety disorders, 92, 97
   and conduct disorder, 141
   and depression, 108, 110, 111
ACC. *See* anterior cingulate cortex (ACC)
Acceptance and Commitment Therapy (ACT), 163–64, 166, 189
ACTH. *See* adrenocorticotropic hormone (ACTH)
"active personal agency," 147
actor, person as (behaving), 34
acute stress, 55, 72, 74, 92
   acute stress disorder, 91. *See also* post-traumatic stress disorder (PTSD)
adenine, 59
ADHD. *See* attention deficit hyperactivity disorder (ADHD)
adolescence
   adolescent development and issues during, 26, 29, 34, 42–43, 90, 147, 151, 157, 185, 189, 191
   and anxiety disorders, 38, 57, 88, 93–95, 97, 98, 101, 107, 150, 178
      frequency of, 87, 88
   and behavior problems, 133, 134, 135–36, 137, 138, 140, 141, 142, 143. *See also* antisocial behavior; callous and unemotional traits

(CU); conduct disorder (CD); disruptive behavior; oppositional defiant disorder
   and bipolar disorder, 17, 118, 121, 122–23, 124–25, 130, 131, 176–77
   brain and neural network development during, 63–64, 73, 75, 76, 97, 107, 108, 124, 125
      pruning of synapses, 62, 63
   and depression, 38, 75, 108, 110, 111, 114, 148, 159–60, 164, 174–75
      frequency of, 103–104
   and illnesses, 179, 185, 186, 188, 189
   impact of adversity on, 76
   IPT-A therapy for adolescents, 153, 155–56
   and mood, 42–43
   negative affectivity, 58, 75
   and panic disorder, 89
   and social phobias, 100
   and suicide, 147
   therapies for, 147, 150, 173, 174–75, 176–77, 178
      Child/Adolescent Anxiety Multimodal Study (CAMS), 173
      IPT-A therapy, 153
   See also child development

229